Entry Into the Inconceivable

Entry Into
the Inconceivable

An Introduction to Hua-yen Buddhism

THOMAS CLEARY

University of Hawaii Press • *Honolulu*

Library of Congress Cataloging in Publication Data

Cleary, Thomas F., 1949–
   Entry into the inconceivable.

   Includes bibliographical references.
   1. Hua-yen Buddhism—Doctrines.   I. Title.
BQ8218.3.C55   1983   294.3'92   83–3613
ISBN 0–8248–0824–X

Contents

Preface

BUDDHISM, systematized some two and a half thousand years ago, is one of the oldest religions on earth. Subsequently spreading over Asia through numerous cultural spheres, it became, more than a philosophy, a body of many philosophical systems embracing a wide variety of beliefs and practices. Generally speaking, however, it may be said that all forms of Buddhism comprise three spheres of learning: ethics, concentration methods, and analytic insight. These three spheres of learning support, enhance, and complete one another, and it is through their mutual interaction and development that Buddhism aims to realize human potential. Corresponding to these three spheres of learning, Buddhist literature includes three general types of material: precepts, scriptures, and philosophical treatises. Because of the interweaving of the three fields of learning, scriptures and treatises include ethical material as well as meditational and analytic principles. Scriptures are presented as the teaching emerging from the meditations of the Buddha. Although there are a great many scriptures, the major schools of Buddhism which arose in China and spread throughout East Asia usually concentrated on one or more as basic texts. Among the principal schools of Buddhism in China was the school known as Hua-yen—Garland or Flower Ornament. Based on a vast scripture by that name, the Hua-yen teaching is one of the crowns of Buddhism. This volume is an introduction to the philosophy, meditation, and ethics of Hua-yen Buddhism as set forth in the works of its great expositors in the golden age of Chinese Buddhism.

Introduction

IN RECENT YEARS there has developed in the West considerable inter-
est in the philosophy of Hua-yen Buddhism, a holistic, unitarian
approach to Buddhism which has enriched the intellectual life of
East Asia for well over a thousand years. The basic scripture of
Hua-yen Buddhism, known as the Garland (Sanskrit *Avataṃsaka*)
or Flower Ornament (Chinese *Hua-yen*) scripture, contains all the
Buddhist teachings in a harmonious, multifaceted array; one of the
most highly valued of all Buddhist scriptures in Asia, it presents a
highly advanced metaphysic and an elaborate body of developmen-
tal material aimed at the completion of the human being.

The projection of the Hua-yen teaching in Asia was aided by
the expository work of several great doctors of the teaching in T'ang
dynasty China (A.D. 618–907) when that civilization was at the
zenith of intellectual and cultural influence. These masters of Hua-
yen teachings produced extensive commentaries and analyses relating to the principles and practices dealt with in the enormous Hua-
yen scripture, and they codified the essential principles in a number
of compact treatises. These commentaries and treatises clarify the
integral relation between what is unique in the Hua-yen perspective
and what is generally shared in common with other Buddhist for-
mats.

Hua-yen Buddhism is famed for its intriguing philosophy, but
it is perhaps most useful to consider Hua-yen metaphysics primarily
in terms of instrumental value. That is to say, the philosophy may be
considered not so much the establishment of a system of thought for
its own sake or as an object of belief or ground of contention but

rather as a set of practical exercises in perspective—new ways of looking at things from different points of view, of discovering harmony and complementarity underlying apparent disparity and contradiction. The value of this exercise is in the development of a round, holistic perspective which, while discovering unity, does not ignore diversity but overcomes mental barriers that create fragmentation and bias.

The Hua-yen doctrine shows the entire cosmos as one single nexus of conditions in which everything simultaneously depends on, and is depended on by, everything else. Seen in this light, then, everything affects and is affected by, more or less immediately or remotely, everything else; just as this is true of every system of relationships, so is it true of the totality of existence. In seeking to understand individuals and groups, therefore, Hua-yen thought considers the manifold as an integral part of the unit and the unit as an integral part of the manifold; one individual is considered in terms of relationships to other individuals as well as to the whole nexus, while the whole nexus is considered in terms of its relation to each individual as well as to all individuals. The accord of this view with the experience of modern science is obvious, and it seems to be an appropriate basis upon which the question of the relation of science and bioethics—an issue of contemporary concern—may be resolved.

The ethic of the Hua-yen teaching is based on this fundamental theme of universal interdependence; while the so-called bodhisattva, the person devoted to enlightenment, constantly nourishes aspiration and will going beyond the world, nevertheless the striving for completion and perfection, the development of ever greater awareness, knowledge, freedom, and capability, is continually reinvested, as it were, in the world, dedicated to the liberation and enlightenment of all beings. The awakening and unfolding of the complete human potential leads to realms beyond that of conventional experience, and indeed to ultimate transcendence of all conditional experience, yet the bodhisattva never maligns the ordinary and does not forsake it, instead translating appropriate aspects of higher knowledge into insights and actions conducive to the common weal.

It is generally characteristic of Mahāyāna or universalistic

Buddhism that the mundane welfare of beings is considered a legitimate, if not ultimate, aim of bodhisattva activity, and many aspects of the ethical and practical life of bodhisattvas may be seen in this light. While psychological and physical well-being is not considered the ultimate goal, it might appropriately be thought of as an elementary stage in the realization of humanity, a removal of conflicts and anxieties to free more energy for higher development. It is axiomatic, based on the world view of Buddhism, that since all people and indeed all creatures share in each other's existence, there is no true benefit for one group alone that is won at the cost of another. It is said to be characteristic of Buddhas, enlightened people, that they look upon all creatures as equal in essence (though not the same in terms of characteristics); although the needs of individuals may differ in detail, they are all equal insofar as they are dependent beings interrelated to one another. Bodhisattvas therefore strive to benefit all equally, without losing sight of the diversity and complexity of the means necessary to accomplish this end.

THE HUA-YEN SCRIPTURE

To appreciate fully the comprehensive scope and detail of the Hua-yen teaching, it is necessary of course to delve into the scripture itself. Portions of this immense scripture were among the first Buddhist literature to be introduced to China, and translation of Hua-yen material went on in that country for centuries. Fragmentary translation seems to have begun in the second century; during the next two centuries at least a dozen separate translations from five books of the Hua-yen appeared, one book being translated no less than four times. The famous "Ten Stages" book, often treated as an individual scripture, was first translated in the third century.

In the early fifth century a much better translation of the "Ten Stages" was made, to be shortly followed by a comprehensive translation of the whole known Hua-yen scripture. This latter work remained the standard text for nearly three hundred years, until it was supplanted in the late seventh century by a monumental translation of a newly imported text. In the eighth century yet another translation of the "Ten Stages" book was made, and the final and longest book, which, like the "Ten Stages," survives in Sanskrit as a separate scripture, was also retranslated. Because of the amount of material involved, a review of the contents of each book of the Hua-yen scripture will be deferred to an appendix to this volume; at this point we can get a glimpse of the structure, content, and atmosphere of the scripture by reviewing some of the highlights of the final, most grandiose book: "Entering the Realm of Reality."

This final assembly of the scripture begins with the Buddha in a pavilion in a grove in India, surrounded by five hundred great bodhisattvas, five hundred lesser saints, and innumerable nature spirits. Reflecting on the difficulty of comprehending the perspective, knowledge, power, concentration, and other qualities of Buddhas, the assembly wish that the Buddha would reveal to them the course of his development, explaining it in accord with their various states and capacities of understanding. The Buddha, divining their thoughts, "fills the universe with great compassion" and enters concentration—whereupon all worlds become beautified and pure. Suddenly the pavilion and grove become boundlessly vast and magnificently arrayed; at the same time, the same vision is seen taking place in every world in the universe. Then, from inconceivably distant worlds in the ten directions, come bodhisattvas bringing all sorts of mystical clouds; the bodhisattvas from the zenith display, in every part of their bodies and accoutrements, the practices of all Buddhas of all times. Describing these bodhisattvas of the ten directions, the scripture says:

> All were born from the practices and vows of Samantabhadra Bodhisattva; with the eye of pure knowledge they saw the Buddhas of all times and listened to the cycles of teachings set in motion by all the Buddhas; they had already reached the Other Shore of freedom; in each moment of thought they manifested great psychic transformations and approached all the Buddhas, with one body filling the assemblies of all Buddhas in all worlds; in a single atom they showed all objects in all worlds, to teach and mature all sentient beings, never missing the right time; from a single pore they emitted the sounds of the teaching of all Buddhas; they knew that all living beings are like illusions; they knew that all Buddhas are like reflections; they knew that all births in all realms of being are like

dreams; they knew that all consequences of actions are like reflections in a mirror; they knew that all originations are like mirages; they knew that all worlds are like magical productions; they had accomplished the powers and fearlessness of enlightened ones; brave and independent, they were capable of the "lion roar" [refuting all concepts]; they entered deeply into the inexhaustible sea of intelligence and attained knowledge of the rules of the languages of all creatures; they traveled unhindered through the realm of space; they knew all things, without any impediment; they have purified all the realms of psychic powers of bodhisattvas; with bold energy they crushed the armies of demons; they always comprehended past, present, and future by means of wisdom; they knew that all things are like space and were free from contention and grasping; though they strove diligently, yet they knew that omniscience ultimately comes from nowhere; though they observed objects, they knew that all existents are ungraspable; by means of knowledge of expedients they entered all realms; by means of knowledge of equality they entered all lands. . . .

The scripture goes on to say that the lesser saints, however, did not even perceive this vista of the Buddha and bodhisattvas—they lacked the past mental development to do so and dwelt in one-sided emptiness, ultimate quiescence, and personal liberation. The scripture likens this situation to someone in a crowd having a glorious dream which is not known to others because they are not having the same dream, or to someone entering various states of concentration unknown to others who are not in those states.

Then the ten leading bodhisattvas each utter verses of praise of the Buddha, trying to broaden the perspective of the saints. Next Samantabhadra expounds the "lionstretch concentration," and the Buddha radiates light to induce the bodhisattvas into this concentration, revealing all Buddha-lands in the universe, each containing an equal number of Buddha-lands in each atom. The bodhisattvas then witness the deeds of the Buddhas in all those lands and attain myriad profound concentrations whence issue myriad kinds of knowledge and power; then the bodhisattvas emanate light from every pore, showing all kinds of teachings and practices of bodhisattvas. Finally the bodhisattva representing wisdom, Mañjuśrī, comes forth with a great host, makes offerings to the Buddha, then goes south and dwells among humans. Eventually Mañjuśrī comes to a city where five hundred laymen, five hundred laywomen, five hundred boys, and five hundred girls gather. The boys are led by a youth named Sudhana; Mañjuśrī, looking into Sudhana's past development, expounds the teaching to him and sends him on a pilgrimage to visit teachers to learn all the various facets of bodhisattvahood. The bulk of the book then recounts Sudhana's journey, through which he attains the stages of bodhisattvahood hitherto described in the scripture. These teachers include Buddhist monks and nuns, male and female lay Buddhists, non-Buddhists, wizards, night spirits, and so on, who tell him of what they have realized, expounding wide-ranging, often very abstract teachings, recapitulating everything in the scripture; after imparting his or her knowledge to Sudhana, each bodhisattva assures Sudhana that his or her own attainments are no match for those of all the bodhisattvas and sends Sudhana to another teacher for further development.

Toward the end of his journey Sudhana is directed to Maitreya, the Buddha-to-be, personification of loving-kindness. Sudhana comes to a great tower, the "tower of the treasury of adornments of the illuminator [Vairocana]," which represents the cosmos as seen by bodhisattvas. He reflects that this tower is the abode of bodhisattvas who understand the emptiness, signlessness, and wishlessness of all things, the abode of those whose intent it is to benefit all beings, of those who have already left all worlds but who appear in the world to edify people, of those who observe emptiness yet do not form the view of emptiness, of those who course in formlessness yet always enlighten those who cling to forms, of those who practice wishlessness yet do not give up the will for enlightening practice, and so on; in this vein Sudhana extols the qualities of bodhisattvas. Then Maitreya appears. He praises Sudhana before a great assembly and then extensively praises the determination for enlightenment. Finally Maitreya has Sudhana enter the tower, which is then seen to be boundlessly vast, as extensive as space, and magnificently adorned with all manner of embellishments. Sudhana also sees that inside the tower are innumerable similarly adorned towers, each as extensive as space, yet not interfering with each other.

This image symbolizes a central Hua-yen theme represented time and again throughout the scripture—all things, being interdependent, therefore imply in their individual being the simultaneous being of all other things. Thus it is said that the existence of each element of the universe includes the existence of the whole universe and hence is as extensive as the universe itself. This point, a basic premise of the whole Hua-yen teaching, is dealt with in more detail in the treatises translated in this volume.

At this point Sudhana enters unimpeded liberation and perceives all kinds of inconceivable realms in the features of the towers, including the career and deeds of Maitreya Bodhisattva as well as all manner of worlds and beings and all things in the universe. Then Maitreya enters the tower, bids Sudhana rise from his trance, and explains to him, "The nature of things is thus: these are appearances manifested by the assemblage of causes and conditions of bodhisattvas' knowledge of things; thus their intrinsic nature is like phantasms, like dreams, like shadows, like reflections. . . ." Subsequently Maitreya further instructs Sudhana, telling him of bodhisattvas' ten kinds of birthplace: "The determination for enlightenment is the birthplace of bodhisattvas, as they are born in the house of Buddhahood; faith is the birthplace of bodhisattvas, as they are born in the house of wise teachers; the stages of enlightenment are the birthplace of bodhisattvas, as they are born in the house of transcendent practices; great vows are the birthplace of bodhisattvas, as they are born in the house of sublime actions; great compassion is the birthplace of bodhisattvas, as they are born in the house of charity, kind words, altruism, and cooperation; contemplation and observation according to truth are the birthplace of bodhisattvas, as they are born in the house of transcendent knowledge; the great vehicle of universal enlightenment is the birthplace of bodhisattvas, as they are born in the house of skill in means of liberation; edifying sentient beings is the birthplace of bodhisattvas, as they are born in the house of Buddhahood; knowledge, wisdom, and skill in means is the birthplace of bodhisattvas, as they are born in the house of acceptance of the nonorigination of things; acting on all truths is the birthplace of bodhisattvas, as they are born in the house of all enlightened ones of past, present, and future."

Maitreya then continues: "Bodhisattvas have transcendent

knowledge for their mother and skill in expedient means for their father; transcendent generosity is their wet nurse, transcendent morality is their nurse; transcendent tolerance is their adornment, transcendent effort is what nourishes and raises them; transcendent meditation is what bathes and washes them; good friends are their teachers, all the factors of enlightenment are their companions; all virtuous ways are their retinue, all bodhisattvas are their siblings; the determination for enlightenment is their house, practicing in accord with truth is the rule of the house; the stages of enlightenment are the location of the house, the acceptances are the family; great vows are the policy of the house; fulfilling enlightening practices is following the rule of the house; encouraging the progress of the great vehicle is succession to the family business."

Maitreya goes on to say that once they are born in this house, "because they know that all things are like reflected images, they do not despise any world; because they know that all things are like magical productions, they have no attachment to any realm of being; because they know that all things have no self, they teach beings indefatigably; because their essential nature is great kindness and compassion, they embrace all sentient beings without feeling strain; because they realize that birth and death are like dreams, they live through all ages—becoming, subsistence, decay, annihilation—without fear; because they know that sense faculties, sense consciousnesses, and sense data are the same as the elemental cosmos, they do not destroy objects; because they know that all conceptions are like mirages, they enter all realms of being without giving rise to delusion or confusion; because they know that all things are like illusions, they enter realms of demons without becoming affected or attached; because they know the body of reality, no afflictions can fool them; because they are free, they can pass through any realm without hindrance."

Finally Maitreya sends Sudhana to see Mañjuśrī again. Passing through more than a hundred and ten cities, Sudhana comes to a city called Sumana and stands before the gate thinking of Mañjuśrī and seeking him. Then Mañjuśrī extends his right hand over a hundred and ten leagues, pats Sudhana on the head, and teaches him and enables him to accomplish innumerable teachings and to be imbued with the infinite light of great knowledge, empowering him to attain the boundless memory power, vows, concentrations, psychic powers, and knowledge of bodhisattvas, thus introducing Sudhana to the site of the practice of Samantabhadra, and also placing Sudhana in Mañjuśrī's own abode—symbolizing Sudhana's actualization of both knowledge (the realm of Mañjuśrī) and action (the realm of Samantabhadra). Then Mañjuśrī disappears, and Sudhana wishes to see Mañjuśrī as well as all teachers, "numerous as atoms in the cosmos," to associate with them, serve them, and learn all knowledge from them. Then, wishing to see Samantabhadra, Sudhana develops "a great mind vast as space, an unhindered mind relinquishing all worlds and free from attachments, an unobstructed mind everywhere carrying out all obstruction-nullifying practices, an unimpeded mind entering into all oceans of spaces, a pure mind entering into all realms of knowledge, a clearly aware mind perceiving the adornments of the site of enlightenment, a vast broad mind entering into the ocean of all enlightening teachings, an all-pervasive mind edifying all sentient beings, an immeasurable mind purifying all lands, an inexhaustible mind living through all ages, an ultimate mind directed toward the ten powers of enlightenment"—whereupon he perceives ten auspicious signs and ten kinds of light and then Samantabhadra sitting in the Buddha's assembly. Observing Samantabhadra, he sees in every pore every feature of the mundane and spiritual worlds, and finally he sees himself in Samantabhadra's being, traversing infinite realms, coursing in a sphere of endless, inexhaustible knowledge, ultimately becoming equal to Samantabhadra and the Buddha, filling the cosmos. The scripture ends with a lengthy eulogy of Buddhahood. This concludes what many have considered the most grandiose, the most comprehensive, and the most beautifully arrayed of the Buddhist scriptures.

HUA-YEN STUDIES IN CHINA

The T'ang dynasty (618–907), during which the Hua-yen school of Buddhism emerged and was fully articulated, was a period of remarkable activity in Chinese Buddhism as a whole. At least thirty-nine Indian and Central Asian monks provided Chinese translations of hundreds of Buddhist texts, while over fifty Chinese monks traveled to India and other parts of Asia in search of Buddhist learning and lore. Eight compilations of the Buddhist canon were made by imperial order, and several major schools of Buddhism became firmly established during this era.

The most creative and definitive period in the history of the Hua-yen school—the era of the first three founders or "patriarchs," spanning roughly the seventh century—followed directly upon or coincided with the consolidation of the other major schools of Chinese Buddhism. It was the correlation of the Hua-yen teachings with the specific formulations of these other schools that then formed one of the main thrusts of the work of the fourth and fifth patriarchs of Hua-yen Buddhism.

Historically speaking, it is often said that there are four major schools of Chinese Buddhism—the T'ien-t'ai, Hua-yen, Ch'an, and Ching-t'u schools. The former two are usually noted for their philosophy while the latter two are noted for their meditational practices; both philosophy and practice are, however, included in all four schools with varying degrees of emphasis and complexity. In addition to these four major schools, the San-lun and Fa-hsiang schools are also worthy of mention, as the metaphysical and psychological doctrines of these schools were largely incorporated into the four major schools while remaining fields of specialist study in themselves as well.

The T'ien-t'ai school, one of the great pillars of Far Eastern Buddhism, was fully articulated by the illustrious Chih-i (531–597), whose work was then faithfully handed down and further clarified by subsequent T'ien-t'ai masters in a coherent succession. The Hua-yen scripture was included by Chih-i in the pan-Buddhist scheme of T'ien-t'ai studies, considered the very first of the Buddha's revelations and containing a wide range of teachings from elementary to advanced. At this time specialist studies in the Hua-yen were still focused mainly on the Indian Buddhist philosopher Vasubandhu's famous commentary on the "Ten Stages" book of the Hua-yen.

The San-lun or "Three Treatises" school, which is also called the Middle Way school and the Emptiness school, may be traced back to the school of the great translator Kumarajiva in the early fifth century, whose translations included a rendition of the "Ten Stages" book of the Hua-yen as well as many other works which became standard in the San-lun and T'ien-t'ai schools. The San-lun school became renowned in the seventh century at the hands of the dynamic Chi-tsang (547–621), one of China's great dialecticians. The twin-truth hermeneutical scheme clarified by Chi-tsang, through which all the Buddha's teachings are understood in terms of two truths or two levels of reality—the absolute, referring to emptiness of inherent nature, and the conventional, referring to conditionality or relativity—is very much in evidence in Hua-yen interpretation and is essential to proper understanding of the scripture.

The Fa-hsiang or Characteristics of Phenomena school, also called the Wei-shih or Consciousness Only school, left an indelible mark on Buddhism in the Far East. The influence of this trend was greatly enhanced by the work of the translator Hsuan-tsang (602–664), whose lifetime corresponds to that of the second patriarch of Hua-yen Buddhism. The third and most renowned of Hua-yen patriarchs himself was chosen as a member of Hsuan-tsang's translation team in his youth, but finally left because of disagreement with Hsuan-tsang's views. The devices of the Consciousness Only school are often used particularly by the third and fourth Hua-yen patriarchs in elucidating points of the scripture as well as in doctrinal treatises.

The Ch'an and Pure Land schools, two of the most powerful and durable of Chinese Buddhist movements, were also firmly established during the seventh century. The Pure Land school was popularized by Tao-ch'o (d. 629) and Shan-tao (d. 681); elements of its teaching and practice are to be found in the Hua-yen scripture and were incorporated into the T'ien-t'ai and Ch'an schools as well. The independent Ch'an school came to public light with the work of the fourth patriarch Tao-hsin (d. 650), flourished greatly in the next two generations, and continued to make an enormous impact on China for hundreds of years thereafter. As we shall presently see, not only did the later Hua-yen patriarchs also study Ch'an but Ch'an teachers themselves often made extensive use of the Hua-yen teachings.

The Hua-yen teachings were originally projected in the Chinese field largely through the work of five eminent monks who are known as the founders or patriarchs of the Hua-yen school: Tu Shun

(557–640), Chih-yen (600–668), Fa-tsang (643–712), Cheng-kuan (738–839 or 760–820), and Tsung-mi (780–841). These masters produced commentaries on the Hua-yen scripture as well as doctrinal codices to concentrate and crystallize the ideas of the Hua-yen scripture for transmission in the Chinese cultural sphere.

Tu Shun, popularly regarded as an embodiment of the spirit of wisdom, passed on the teachings contained in the works known as *Fa-chieh kuan*, "Contemplation of the Realm of Reality" (or *Hua-yen fa-chieh hsuan*, "Mysteries of the Realm of Reality of the Hua-yen"), *Hua-yen wu chiao chih-kuan*, "Cessation and Contemplation in the Five Teachings of the Hua-yen," and *Hua-yen i-ch'eng shih hsuan men*, "Ten Mysterious Gates of the Unitary Vehicle of the Hua-yen." The "Contemplation of the Realm of Reality" is essentially concerned with the resolution of emptiness and existence and the interrelation of all things in the universe; it introduces the concepts of noumenon *(li)* and phenomena *(shih)* and their interpenetration, which became basic terms of subsequent expositions of Hua-yen philosophy.

The "Cessation and Contemplation in the Five Teachings of the Hua-yen" is a systematic description of successive stages of mental stabilization and analytic contemplation. This treatise summarizes main points of Buddhist teaching, and its scheme was later developed as part of the doctrinal classification system of the Hua-yen school established by Fa-tsang. Each step represents a phase in the development of Buddhism, culminating in the "all in one, one in all" perspective of the Hua-yen doctrine.

The "Ten Mysterious Gates" explores ten subtle perspectives, based on interdependent origination, illustrating the harmonious interrelation and intercommunion of all things; the elements of this analytic framework appear in the "Contemplation of the Realm of Reality," were subsequently presented as "Ten Mysterious Gates" by Tu Shun's disciple Chih-yen based on the former's explanation, and then were modified somewhat by the third Hua-yen patriarch, Fa-tsang.

Chih-yen, known as the second patriarch of Hua-yen Buddhism, studied with Tu Shun and transmitted teachings which were to become fundamental instruments of Hua-yen exposition. Chih-yen also wrote a commentary on the Hua-yen scripture, called *Hua-*

yen ching sou hsuan chi, "Record of Searches into the Mysteries of the Hua-yen Scripture," based on the sixty-scroll translation of Buddhabhadra, as well as a compendium of articles on topics found in the Hua-yen scripture, called *Hua-yen ching nei chang men teng tsa k'ung mu chang*. He also wrote *Hua-yen wu shih yao wen-ta*, "Fifty Essential Questions and Answers on the Hua-yen," dealing with problematic issues. Aside from these works on the Hua-yen, Chih-yen also composed two commentaries on the *Vajraccedika-prajñā-pāramitā* scripture. Although all these works are extant, it is said that Chih-yen wrote others which are now lost.

Fa-tsang, the third patriarch, was a prolific writer who further elaborated and systematized the efforts of his predecessors. His work firmly established the philosophy of the Hua-yen school, and he is sometimes considered the school's true founder; indeed, the school is in fact often called by Fa-tsang's honorific name Hsien-shou, bestowed on him by the T'ang dynasty empress Wu Tse-t'ien, who appointed him a "National Teacher" *(kuo-shih)*. Fa-tsang was a member of the board of scholars assisting in the new translation of the Hua-yen scripture done by Śīksānanda under the patronage of Empress Wu Tse-t'ien. He also personally expounded the philosophy of the Hua-yen to the empress, from which effort came his famous "Treatise on the Golden Lion," summarizing the main points of Hua-yen metaphysics.

Like Chih-yen, Fa-tsang too produced a commentary on the earlier sixty-scroll translation of the Hua-yen scripture: *Hua-yen ching t'an hsuan chi*, "Record of Investigation into the Mysteries of the Hua-yen Scripture." He also made two brief commentaries called *Hua-yen ching chih kuei*, "The Gist of the Hua-yen Scripture," and *Hua-yen ching wen i kang mu*, "Outline of the Text and Doctrine of the Hua-yen Scripture." His *Hua-yen ts'e lin*, "Forest of Topics in the Hua-yen," is another brief treatment of important ideas presented in the scripture.

Perhaps the most famous, if not the most accessible, of Fa-tsang's doctrinal works is his *Hua-yen i ch'eng chiao i fen ch'i chang*, "Treatise on the Divisions of Doctrine in the Unitary Vehicle of the Hua-yen." Also known by the briefer title *Wu chiao chang*, "Treatise on the Five Teachings," this work contains Fa-tsang's taxonomy of the Buddhist teachings, presenting the classificatory schemes of other teachers and expounding the doctrines and comprehensive perspective of the Hua-yen. His *Hua-yen yu hsin fachieh chi,* "Record of Musings on the Realm of the Teaching of the Hua-yen," contains an elaboration of Tu-shun's "Cessation and Contemplation in the Five Teachings of the Hua-yen" and also presents a scheme of doctrinal classification showing the progression from one phase to the next.

Fa-tsang's other works on the Hua-yen include *Hua-yen ching kuan-mai i chi,* "Record of Doctrines Forming the Pulse of the Hua-yen Scripture," using the elements of the structure and doctrines of the scripture to illustrate each other; *Hua-yen fa p'u-t'i-hsin chang,* "Treatise on Development of the Will for Enlightenment According to the Hua-yen," dealing with approaches to the teachings and presenting detailed outlines of Hua-yen dialectics and contemplative exercises. He also wrote *Hua-yen wen-ta,* "Questions and Answers on the Hua-yen," *Hua-yen ching ming fa p'in nei li san pao chang,* "Treatise on the Three Treasures Established in the Book on Clarification of Method in the Hua-yen Scripture," and *Hua-yen ching i-hai pai men,* "A Hundred Gates of the Ocean of Meanings in the Hua-yen Scripture," all dealing with various aspects of the teachings. His *Hua-yen ching p'u-hsien kuan-hsing fa-men,* "Teaching of the Contemplative Practice of Samantabhadra in the Hua-yen Scripture," is a brief exposition of the approach to meditational practice; his *Hsiu hua-yen ao chih wang chin huan yuan kuan,* "Cultivation of Contemplation of the Inner Meaning of the Hua-yen: The Ending of Delusion and Return to the Source," written in his old age, is a concise summary of the philosophical and practical bases of Hua-yen meditation. Besides these doctrinal tracts on Hua-yen philosophy, Fa-tsang also wrote a history of the transmission of the Hua-yen scripture to China and made several commentaries on other scriptures and treatises. /

Cheng-kuan, the fourth patriarch, is famed for his extensive commentary and subcommentary on the new eighty-scroll translation of the Hua-yen scripture; he also wrote a commentary on the new forty-scroll translation of the Gaṇḍavyūha made by Prajñā. In addition, he wrote two short works on the scripture, *Hua-yen ching ju fa-chieh p'in shih pa wenta,* "Eighteen Questions and Answers on the 'Entry into the Realm of Reality' Book of the Hua-yen Scripture," dealing with the Gaṇḍavyūha, and *Hua-yen ching chi ch'u chiu hui sung shih chang*, "Explanations of Verses on the Seven Locations and Nine Assemblies of the Hua-yen Scripture," presenting mnemonic verses indicating the teachings presented in each division of the scripture along with explanations of the verses. Cheng-kuan also wrote a detailed commentary on Tu Shun's seminal "Contemplation of the Realm of Reality" and composed several treatises of his own: *Wu yun kuan*, "Contemplation of the Five Clusters," dealing with meditation on the absence of self in persons; *San sheng yuan-jung kuan*, "Contemplation of the Merging of the Three Sages," a treatise on the noumenal and phenomenal aspects of complete enlightenment symbolized by Vairocana Buddha and the bodhisattvas Samantabhadra and Mañjuśrī; and *Hua-yen hsin-yao famen*, "Teaching of the Mind Essentials of the Hua-yen," presented as an answer to the query of Emperor Shun-tsung (r. 805), giving Cheng-kuan's Ch'an teaching.

The fifth patriarch of the Hua-yen school, Tsung-mi, was, like Cheng-kuan, versed in the teachings of Ch'an Buddhism as well. His famous *Ch'an yuan chu ch'uan chi tou hsu*, "Comprehensive Introduction to a Collection of Expositions of the Sources of Ch'an," analyzes various trends in Ch'an Buddhist teachings in terms reminiscent of the work of Tu Shun and also relates the Hua-yen, T'ien-t'ai, and Ch'an teachings to each other. Other works of Tsung-mi include a commentary on Cheng-kuan's commentary on the new translation of the Gaṇḍavyūha, a commentary on Tu Shun's "Contemplation of the Realm of Reality," and a commentary and subcommentary on the *Yuan-chiao ching*, "Scripture on Complete Enlightenment," a perennial favorite among meditators in China. He also wrote a short treatise called *Yuan jen lun*, "Study of the Basis of Man," in which he outlines a scheme of human spiritual development, including a succession of teachings, Taoist and Confucian as well as Buddhist.

While these five masters are traditionally considered the founders of the Hua-yen school, one might mention another figure who made a significant contribution to Hua-yen studies during this era: the layman Li T'ung-hsuan. An eccentric recluse of the eighth century, Li made a profound study of the Hua-yen scripture and wrote a commentary called *Hua-yen lun*, "Discourse on the Hua-yen," which became famous and was especially esteemed by Ch'an Buddhists. He also wrote *Hua-yen ching chueh i lun*, "Treatise on Resolution of Doubts on the Hua-yen Scripture," *Hua-yen ching ta i*, "Overall Idea of the Hua-yen Scripture," and *Chieh mi hsien chih ch'en pei shih ming lun*, "Treatise on Ten Clarifications Dissolving Confusion, Uncovering Knowledge, and Developing Compassion." Ch'an histories contain records of people having enlightenment experiences from reading the works of Li T'ung-hsuan, and it is said that Ch'an Buddhists generally favored his commentary on the scripture over that of Cheng-kuan.

The imperial persecution of Buddhism and purge of Buddhist establishments carried out in China in the mid-840s dealt a telling blow to formal Buddhist studies in China, a stroke which only the Ch'an and Pure Land schools survived with vigor. The codification of the Hua-yen teachings may be said to have been completed by the five founders of the school; although Hua-yen studies continued after this point in China, they were not necessarily confined within what we might think of as a school or sect. After the passing of Tsung-mi, the most outstanding exponent of the Hua-yen philosophy over the following centuries is said to be Tzu-jui (n.d.) of the eleventh century. Usually known as Ch'ang-shui, Tzu-jui had a spiritual awakening during his study of the *Śūraṅgama* scripture and later became a recognized successor of the famed Ch'an master Lang-ya Hui-chiao (n.d.). He eventually had more than a thousand students and expounded the *Śūraṅgama* scripture and the *Mahāyāna-śraddhotpāda-śāstra* according to the principles of the Hua-yen school formulated by Fa-tsang. Tzu-jui's disciple Ching-yuan (1011–1088) studied the Hua-yen and other scriptures and treatises under several teachers, including Tzu-jui. He composed a commentary on Cheng-kuan's commentary on the Hua-yen scripture, as well as commentaries on Fa-tsang's "Treatise on the Golden Lion," Fa-tsang's "Return to the Source," and Tsung-mi's "Study of the Basis of Man."

Although study of the Buddhist scriptures never died out entirely in China, it was the masters of the Ch'an school who wielded the most influence after the persecution of 845–847. As centuries passed, various trends in Chinese Buddhism tended to reamalgamate as specialists in particular branches of Buddhist philosophy or practice endeavored to communicate their teachings in harmony with and even through the media of other specialist branches. The Hua-yen scripture long had a considerable influence beyond the confines of the Hua-yen school proper, and the philosophy of the Hua-yen teachings is particularly apparent in the works of many of the great Ch'an masters.

Two of the most important masters in the Ch'an tradition, from whom all the major sects were descended, were Shih-t'ou Hsi-ch'ien (700–790) and Ma-tsu Tao-i (709–788). The former, in his esteemed tract *Ts'an-t'ung-ch'i,* "Communion of Difference and Sameness," uses the Hua-yen theme of relativity and the terms "noumenon" and "phenomena" with extraordinarily clever metaphors to illustrate the essential unity and subtle distinction of matter and emptiness. Ma-tsu, for his part, used the Hua-yen idea of the absolute unity of being, the all-inclusiveness of the "nature of things," and the practice of the "oceanic reflection concentration" or holistic awareness which is the basis of the Hua-yen experience. Ma-tsu's illustrious successor Pai-chang Huai-hai (720–814) used Hua-yen themes even more extensively, and allusions to motifs from the scripture as well as treatises of the Hua-yen masters can be found throughout his sayings.

Hua-yen philosophy can also be found in the teachings of all the founders of the five major schools of Ch'an. We can see reflections of Hua-yen dialectic in the "four propositions" device of Lin-chi I-hsuan (d. 867), founder of the Lin-chi school; in the substance-function symbology of Kuei-shan Ling-yu (770–853) and Yang-shan Hui-chi (813–890), founders of the Kuei-Yang school; in the "five positions of absolute and relative" scheme of Tung-shan Liang-chieh (806–869) and Ts'ao-shan Pen-chi (840–901), founders of the Ts'ao-Tung school; and in the talks, poetry, and meditation topics of Yun-men Wen-yen (d. 949) and Fa-yen Wen-i (885–958), founders of the Yun-men and Fa-yen schools. Fa-yen even went so far as to cite the Hua-yen scripture as a paragon of religious literature in his criticism of the trend toward careless and arbitrary Ch'an writing.

Among later Chan masters who used Hua-yen Buddhism in their teachings one may cite as outstanding examples T'ou-tzu I-ch'ing (eleventh century), who revived the Ts'ao-Tung school of Ch'an and was nicknamed Hua-yen Ch'ing because of his deep study of this scripture; Ta-hui Tsung-kao (1086–1163), one of the most outstanding Ch'an masters of the Sung dynasty, who often quoted the Hua-yen scripture in his lectures; Hung-chih Cheng-chiao (1091–1153), among the greatest of literary figures in Ch'an, who included extracts from the Hua-yen scripture among his meditation themes for Ch'an students; Chen-hsieh Ch'ing-liao (twelfth century), who used Hua-yen philosophy in his presentation of Pure Land Buddhist teaching; and Han-shan Te-ch'ing (1546–1623), who made an edition of Cheng-kuan's great commentary to promote Hua-yen studies in his time.

EMPTINESS AND RELATIVITY

To delve into the philosophy of Hua-yen Buddhism, it is necessary to deal with the doctrine of emptiness, which is central to Buddhism. Classical Buddhist literature indicates plainly that this has always been one of the most alarming and easily misunderstood aspects of Buddhism. Proper understanding of this doctrine is considered essential, however, and three basic principles deemed crucial to true appreciation of emptiness are set forth: emptiness does not mean absence or nonexistence; emptiness is not apart from existents; and emptiness is not itself an entity. Perhaps the most straightforward way to understand emptiness intellectually is in terms of relativity, interdependence, and impermanence—the nonabsoluteness of existence. In this review of the Hua-yen scripture we have seen these themes set forth repeatedly.

In Buddhist literature we find statements that appear to say "X is not X" or "there is no X," and by literalist interpretation these are all too easily misconstrued as paradoxical, illogical, or simply nonsensical. Sometimes they are considered a kind of shock treatment; though this may be one of their functions, they are not so limited, provided further thought is applied. What these statements present, besides a challenge to fixed conceptions, is a shift in perspective. A statement which appears to say "X is not X" may mean "the conventionally agreed upon idea of a phenomenon labeled X is not the ultimate essence or reality of X," or "the temporary phenomenon called X is not an enduring self-subsistent X," or "the concept conventionally associated with the name X is not itself an objectively

real phenomenon of which the name X is an inherent property."
Similarly, "there is no X" may mean "there is no permanent, objective reality which ineluctibly corresponds to the idea associated
with the name X," or simply "there is no permanent X" or "there is
no self-defined X," or "names do not correspond to realities," or
"things are not what we think they are." Why do the scriptures not
simply come right out and specify just what they mean? We must
remember that scriptures in Buddhism are not intended to present
doctrines to be accepted or rejected as dogma but have as an important function the provocation of thought and reflection.

To discover how bare statements of the "X is not X" variety
can yield coherent meanings through appropriate interpretation,
we may turn to a commentary on the popular "Diamond (Cutter)"
scripture, which is famous for such remarks. For example, the scripture says, "The minds spoken of by the Buddha are not minds; this
is called mind." The commentary attributed to the sixth patriarch
of Ch'an Buddhism (Hui-neng; 638–713) says, "Each sentient being
has various different states of mind; though these states of mind be
many, they are all called false mind. If you recognize that the false
mind [mental states] is not the mind itself, this is called mind—this
'mind' is the real mind, the constant mind. . . ."[1] Here "mind is not
mind" means that passing states of mind are not the real mind.
Another passage of the scripture says, "What are called virtues the
Buddha says are not virtues—this is called virtue." The same commentary says, "Cultivating all kinds of virtues in hopes of reward is
not virtue. Practicing the various means of transcendence and religious practices without looking for reward is called virtue."[2]

A very simple and useful way to glimpse emptiness—usually
defined in the Hua-yen scripture as emptiness of intrinsic nature or
own being—is by considering things from different points of view.
What for one form of life is a waste product is for another form of
life an essential nutrient; what is a predator for one species is prey
to another. In this sense it can be seen that things do not have fixed,
self-defined nature of their own; what they "are" depends upon the
relationships in terms of which they are considered. Even if we say
that something is the sum total of its possibilities, still we cannot
point to a unique, intrinsic, self-defined nature that characterizes
the thing in its very essence.

The same argument can be applied to space and time. In terms of our everyday perceptions, an atom is small; but in terms of the space between subatomic particles relative to the size of the particles, we can say the atom is indeed enormous. In ordinary human terms, a day is short; but from the point of view of an insect that lives only a day it is as seventy years to a human or centuries to a tree. This perception of the relativity or nonabsoluteness of measurements of time and space is frequently represented in the Huayen scripture and is a key to unlocking the message of its "inconceivable" metaphors.

The point of all this is not, of course, confined to abstract philosophy. The obvious drawback to considering things to be just what we conceive them to be is that it can easily blind us to possibilities we have never thought of; moreover, it can foster prejudices in dealings with the world, leading to unhealthy conditions due to failure to consider things in a broad perspective.

We can therefore say that what a thing "is," being dependent on the context which defines it, may be considered to have as many aspects as there are things in the universe, since something "exists" in a certain way vis-à-vis every other thing. What a thing "is" in terms of the practical, everyday world of an individual or group, therefore, depends upon, or exists in terms of, an assigned definition which focuses on the possibilities considered relevant to the needs or interests or conditioning of the individual or group—thus narrowing down a virtually infinite range into a manageable, thinkable set. When Buddhist teaching says that things are empty or do not exist as such, what is often meant by "things" or "phenomena" in such statements is things *as they are conceived of*—the point is then that a name or definition does not encompass or capture a thing, either in its essence or in the totality of possibilities of its conditional existence.

To pursue the matter more deeply, when we consider the idea of the world as conceptions based on perceptions based on sensations, we can see that we have no further direct evidence for anything phenomenal beyond sense. If we seek corroboration of sense by sense, we find that we cannot reach beyond sense, so to speak, except by inference. We cannot therefore directly "apprehend" the objective world; we can only reflect impressions. This "emptiness of ungraspability" is among the major avenues of contemplation leading to authentic appreciation of emptiness.

THE THREE NATURES

We may develop our understanding of emptiness in the Buddhistic sense with greater precision by reference to the doctrine of the "three natures." This scheme, usually associated with the Consciousness Only school of Buddhism, was also incorporated by Fa-tsang into his overall presentation of Hua-yen teaching and used by Cheng-kuan to clarify certain statements made in the Hua-yen scripture. According to this explanation, the three natures of all phenomena are the nature of pure imagination or mental construction (called in Chinese "that which is clung to by total conceptualization"), relative nature, and true or absolute nature.

Let us take, for the sake of illustration, the example of a chair. It may be something to sit on and rest, something to stand on to reach a higher place, something to hang clothes on or put books on; it may be pieces of wood and cloth; it may be kindling for a fire, food for termites, even a weapon or tool of destruction. What it "is," therefore, depends on the definition and use to which it is put. The chair as a thing in itself is thus but a definition or mental construction; the chair as a conditional existence, being dependent upon its materials and construction as well as factors which define it functionally as a chair, is the relative nature of a chair. The nonexistence of a self-existent, self-defined "chair," then, is the real or absolute nature of a chair.

It should be pointed out that this example is not quite in accord with traditional illustration, which usually presents the imaginary or conceptual nature as being akin to misapprehending a piece of rope as a snake or a tree stump as a ghost in the dark. The relative nature in this case is that the rope is a rope and not a snake. The real nature is that the rope is not a rope but a collection of fibers. I have departed from this pattern because I wish to show that the ultimately arbitrary nature of definitions can be observed by broadening one's perspective and considering different points of view, yet without destroying the relative validity or usefulness of a particular definition in a given context.

These three natures may be easily understood in terms of the relationship of sense faculties, consciousness, and sense data. The nature of mental construction is the conceptual order (including perceptual order) which we learn to accept as "the world." The relative nature is the conditional existence of the world of experience as a relationship of sense faculties, sense consciousnesses, and sense data. Thus we can see that the order is a mental projection or construction rather than an inherently fixed property of an objective world as conceived. The real nature is the lack of independent existence of senses, consciousnesses, and data—existing only in relation to each other, as such they have no absolute existence.

In his "Treatise on the Five Teachings," Fa-tsang explains that each of the three natures has two senses. The true or real nature has the sense of not changing and the sense of going along with conditions: the sense of not changing refers to the emptiness or nonabsoluteness of that which is conditional; the sense of going along with conditions refers to conditional existence, outside of which there is no emptiness. The relative nature has the sense of seeming to exist and the sense of having no essential nature—that is, conditions have apparent existence, relative to one another, but they have no absolute existence independent of each other. The nature of conceptual clinging has the sense of mentally existing and the sense of really not existing—that is, definitions exist in the mind but not in objective reality.

Fa-tsang explains that in terms of the true nature's sense of not changing, the relative nature's sense of having no essential nature, and the conceptual nature's sense of not really existing, the three natures are identical. It is in this sense, he points out, that scripture says, "Sentient beings are of themselves nirvanic and are not further extinguished." Fa-tsang goes on to say that in terms of the true nature's sense of going along with conditions, the relative nature's sense of seeming to exist, and the conceptual nature's sense of mentally existing, the three natures are not different; it is in this sense, he says, that the Hua-yen scripture states, "The reality-body revolving in mundane existence is called sentient beings."

Fa-tsang explains that because attachment (conceptualization) clings to the seeming and takes it for real, there is no different phenomenon—that is to say, the mental existence of attachment of conceptualization is none other than the seeming existence of the relative; apart from the attachment the seeming does not arise, so the seeming existence of the relative nature is equal to the mental existence of the conceptual nature. The same is true of the true nature's going along with conditions, because if there were no attachment, there would be no going along with conditions.

Pursuing this reasoning, Fa-tsang goes on to expound the essential nondifference of the two senses of the three natures. For example, though the real nature, going along with conditions, becomes defiled or pure, it never loses its inherent purity—that is indeed why it can become defiled or pure according to conditions. This purity is likened to a clear mirror reflecting the defiled and pure while never losing the clarity of the mirror—indeed it is precisely because the mirror does not lose its clarity that it can reflect defiled and pure forms. By the reflection of defiled and pure forms, in fact, we can know that the mirror itself is clear. So it is, Fa-tsang explains, with the principle of true thusness: it not only becomes defiled and pure without affecting its inherent purity but by its becoming defiled or pure its inherent purity is revealed. Not only does it reveal its inherent purity without obliterating defilement and purity; it is precisely because of its inherent purity that it can become defiled and pure. Here "inherent purity" means emptiness of inherently fixed nature whereas relative "defilement" and "purity" depend on action and the experiencing mind. All mundane and holy states are manifestations of "thusness," yet the essential nature of thusness—which is naturelessness—is not affected.

This brings us to the relative nature. Fa-tsang says that although it is through causes and conditions that seeming existence appears, yet this seeming existence cannot have inherent nature or essential reality because whatever is born of conditions has no essence or nature of its own. If it is not essenceless, then it does not depend on conditions; and if it does not depend on conditions, then it is not seeming existence. Since the establishment of seeming existence must proceed from a set of conditions, it has no inherent reality of its own. Therefore, Fa-tsang continues, the *Ta-chih-tu lun* says: "Observe that all things are born from causes and conditions, and so have no individual reality, and hence are ultimately empty. Ultimate emptiness is called transcendent wisdom."[3] By conditional

origination, Fa-tsang points out, absence of inherent nature is revealed; when the *Chung lun* says "because there is the truth of emptiness, all things can be established,"[4] this is showing conditional
production by means of absence of inherent nature. Fa-tsang then
quotes the *Nirvāṇa* scripture, saying, "[Phenomena] exist because of
causality and are void because of essencelessness,"[5] concluding that
absence of inherent nature and causality are identical. Thus are the
real nature and the relative nature harmonized and seen to be different views of the same truth.

Turning to the nature of conceptual clinging, Fa-tsang goes on
to say that although existence appears according to attachments in
the mind, in truth it is ultimately nonexistent, because what is nonexistent is fancied to be existent. He likens this notion to imagining a
tree stump to be a ghost whereas there is no ghost in the stump.
Because it is imaginary, it is in reality nonexistent; and because of its
nonexistence there can be the imagination. Thus the imaginary or
conceptual nature is reconciled with the real nature, inasmuch as
the real or true nature is the true nature of the imaginary, being the
lack of objective reality in conception. In his "Hundred Gates of the
Ocean of Meanings," Fa-tsang says that "data are not themselves
objects—they must depend on the mind; mind is not of itself mind—
it must depend on an object. Because they are interdependent, there
is no definite origination in the objective realm."[6]

THE FOUR REALMS OF REALITY

The dialect of Hua-yen philosophy is consummated in the doctrine of the four realms of reality, comprehending both conventional and absolute reality. The four realms are the realm of phenomena, the realm of noumenon (which means the principle of
emptiness), the realm of noninterference between noumenon and
phenomena, and the realm of noninterference among phenomena.

The reality-realm of the mutual noninterference of noumenon
and phenomena in essence refers to the identity of existence and
emptiness, a teaching fundamental to all the universalist (Mahāyāna) schools of Buddhism. Realization of this realm occupies the
third of the five stages of development outlined in Tu Shun's "Cessation and Contemplation in the Five Teachings of the Hua-yen" and

is considered in detail, from ten points of view, in Tu Shun's "Contemplation of the Reality-Realm."

In terms of the relativity or interdependence of things, the noninterference of noumenon and phenomena simply means that the relative or conditional existence of things is not opposed to their absolute emptiness (or emptiness of their absoluteness); indeed, relative existence and absolute emptiness are, to use a popular Ch'an metaphor, "two faces of the same die." Things which exist interdependently have no inherent nature or identity of their own—it is precisely this nonindependence, this nonabsoluteness, in Buddhist metaphysics called "emptiness," which allows things to exist relatively and interdependently.

This noninterference of noumenon and phenomena can be viewed perhaps more easily from another angle—that of impermanence. The principle of impermanence corresponds to the noumenal or empty side of things; the mutual interpenetration of impermanence and temporal existence is a matter of daily experience and need not be argued. The Buddhist approach in this regard is not to try in vain to resist impermanence or to ignore it, but to clarify awareness of impermanence and use that awareness for a specific purpose.

As is made clear in Tu Shun's treatise on cessation and contemplation, focus on emptiness or noumenon is used for the purpose of detachment from the world, resulting not only in serenity and dispassion, but also in awareness which is not bound to the world or hindered by views of the world. On the other hand, focus on existence or phenomena is used for the purposes of transcending detachment itself and developing compassion and practical knowledge. Contemplation of the mutual effacement of noumenon and phenomena as existing in themselves is used for the purpose of developing the ability to dwell neither on the world nor on the transcendental plane of dispassion. Contemplation of the interdependence and coexistence of emptiness and existence, noumenon and phenomena, is used as a basis for being in the world but not of the world, transcending the world while in its very midst.

Tu Shun's "Contemplation of the Reality-Realm" explores ten aspects of the noninterference of noumenon and phenomena. The first aspect presented is that of noumenon pervading phenomena.

This means that emptiness, the conditional, dependent nature of things, is wholly present in all things; in terms of impermanence, it means that transience is inherent in all things.

Second is the aspect of phenomena pervading noumenon. This means that the noumenon in any particular phenomenon is the same as the noumenon in all other phenomena; therefore the noumenal nature of a phenomenon is coextensive with all noumenon, which is coextensive with the whole universe, since the noumenon is in everything. This is like saying that the impermanence in one thing is the same impermanence that is in all things or that the space in one atom, seen from the standpoint of space itself and not the boundaries of phenomena, is one with the whole of space.

Third is the aspect of the formation of phenomena based on noumenon. This means that since phenomena are conditional their existence depends on their relativity—they can only exist because of their very lack of inherent identity. As that which is absolute and self-existent cannot by definition relate to anything else, things, the practical existence of which is dependent upon the conditions which produce them, cannot therefore be inherently absolute in order to exist. Thus the apparent paradox that things must be "empty" in order to exist turns out to be not paradoxical or contradictory at all, but rather a simple statement of the conditional nature of things.

Fourth is the aspect of phenomena being able to show noumenon. But for phenomena, there would be no medium of expression and perception of the principle of relativity—indeed there would be no relativity. Similarly, impermanence is obviously observed only in temporal existence. Thus we find in the Hua-yen scripture such statements as "all things constantly expound the Teaching." The effort of the Buddhist is to bring this awareness to the foreground in order to avoid being confused by appearances.

Fifth is the aspect of removing phenomena by means of noumenon. By bringing the awareness of noumenon or emptiness to the fore, one views the nonabsoluteness or nonfinality of the characteristics or appearances of things. This perspective is used, as mentioned previously, to overcome the tendency to become caught up in things. Instead of seeing specific things—things which vex or delight, things which bring profit or loss, and so on—one sees only a single stream of impermanence; instead of seeing individual people —personalities which may attract or repel or provoke any combination of these or other emotional reactions—one sees only beings who are going to die. These are examples of using noumenon to remove or efface phenomena in order to stabilize the emotions and avoid being controlled by feelings and discriminations.

Sixth is the aspect of phenomena being able to conceal noumenon. This means that the surface of things, the obvious appearances, obscure the noumenon. Thus the scripture says that though all people have the knowledge of Buddhas, nevertheless their attachments and illusions prevent them from being aware of it.

Seventh is the aspect of true noumenon being identical to phenomena. This means that noumenon is not outside of things; it is nothing but the principle of selflessness or lack of inherent identity of things. In other words, this means that emptiness has no existence of its own; it is nothing but the relativity or interdependence of existents.

Eighth is the aspect of phenomena being identical to noumenon. This means that phenomena, originating interdependently, being products of causes and conditions, have no individual reality, no intrinsic nature of their own, and in that sense are identical to the noumenon, emptiness. This is like the conclusion of the Buddhist logicians that since existence is but a continuity of efficient moments, the very existence of a thing is identical to its extinction.

Ninth is the aspect of true noumenon not being phenomena. This means that emptiness qua emptiness is not the characteristics of form. The appearance of discrete phenomena is an illusion; although the illusion is in reality empty, emptiness is not the illusion.

Tenth is the aspect of phenomena not being noumenon. This means that phenomena qua phenomena are not noumenon, that characteristics or appearances are not essence. These last two aspects view noumenon and phenomena as extremes, on the basis of which they are correlative. It must always be borne in mind that these ten aspects of the noninterference of noumenon and phenomena are themselves interdependent: each one implies the others.

In his monumental *Tsung-ching lu*, "Source Mirror Collection," the eminent scholar and meditation master Yen-shou (904–975) deals with the realm of noninterference of noumenon and phe-

nomena from the point of view of mental cultivation. To introduce
the subject, he brings out two facets of the realm of noumenon:

> The reality-realm of noumenon has, generally speaking, two
> aspects. One is the aspect of inherent purity—even when
> shrouded it is not defiled, its nature being eternally pure.
> Though it pervades all, it is not the same as all things; it is like
> the nature of wetness pervading motion and stillness, pervad-
> ing freezing and flowing, without itself changing, always thus
> whether in purity or pollution. Second is the aspect of remov-
> ing defilement: by specific cures barriers are done away with,
> according to the shallowness or depth of the state. Though the
> essence is always pure and still, yet according to conditions
> there is difference.[7]

Thus, from the point of view of noumenon, it is no different
whether or not it is veiled by illusion. As relativity/emptiness, it permeates all things without being the things themselves as existents,
remaining constant and pure regardless of whether or not there are
mental constructions of things as discrete realities obscuring the
noumenal emptiness of things. The aspect of removing defilement
refers to purifying the mind, freeing it from attachments to appearances so that insight into the noumenon may be clarified; while the
noumenon itself has no degrees, nevertheless there are degrees in the
perception of noumenon—hence it is said that there are differences
according to conditions. Continuing this line of reasoning, Yen-shou
goes on to speak of the realm of noninterference of noumenon and
phenomena; this too, he says, has two general aspects:

> One is the aspect of mutual identification without hindrance:
> the reality-realm of one mind includes two aspects—true thus-
> ness and birth-and-death—which interpenetrate without de-
> stroying essence and appearances; it is as if the waves which
> contain the water are not still, while the water which contains
> the waves is not in motion. The second aspect is that of efface-
> ment and nonreliance: this means that without phenomena,
> noumenon is not noumenon, so phenomena are not phenom-
> ena; without noumenon, phenomena are not phenomena, so
> noumenon is not noumenon.[8]

What is here called true thusness of mind is associated with the noumenon, while so-called birth-and-death of mind is associated with phenomena. True thusness of mind means holistic awareness which does not cling to specific appearances but merely perceives the flux of being as simply "thus." Birth-and-death of mind refers to the awareness grasping particulars—thus in effect being born and dying along with the passing of transient phenomena, being born and dying with each thought, each mental construct, each psychological state or phase of personality. The two are said to interpenetrate because discriminating awareness cannot exist without the whole basic awareness underlying it. The sense of effacement and nonreliance is that noumenon and phenomena are interdependent and have no absolute existence; seeing in this way, one ultimately clings neither to the perspective of noumenon nor to that of phenomena. This point is parallel to the teaching of the Ch'an master Pai-chang Huai-hai, who spoke of using the so-called mirror awareness, corresponding to the "true thusness of mind," to avoid being affected by the feelings of the fluctuating mind (the birth-and-death of mind), but he pointed out that abiding permanently in the mirror awareness is not right. Yen-shou goes on to explore in some detail the merging of noumenon and phenomena and the detachment from both views:

By detachment from appearances, phenomena disintegrate and are identical to noumenon. By detachment from essence, noumenon disappears and is identical to phenomena. By detachment from appearances without annihilating appearances, phenomena are identical to noumenon, yet phenomena remain; [what are in terms of absolute reality] not phenomena constitute phenomena. By detachment from essence without effacing essence, noumenon equals phenomena yet noumenon remains; not-noumenon constitutes noumenon. Because detachment from appearances is not different from detachment from essence, phenomena and noumenon negate each other and thought and speech are transcended. Because not annihilating appearances is not different from not effacing essence, this is the first two realms—phenomena and noumenon—existing clearly. Because not annihilating and not effacing is not dif-

ferent from detachment from appearance and essence, it becomes one reality-realm of noninterference of phenomena and
noumenon, causing the subtle truth which transcends seeing
and hearing always to pervade seeing and hearing, and causing the profound meaning which is beyond thought never to
obstruct speech and thought. Since phenomena are merged by
means of noumenon, causing them to be without division, in
accord with the universal permeation of noumenon, one enters
all, and in accord with the inclusiveness of noumenon, all
enter one. Therefore interdependently originated things each
contain the universe without end.[9]

At the conclusion of this passage Yen-shou makes the transition
from the realm of noninterference of noumenon and phenomena to
the realm of noninterference among phenomena. The teaching of
the realm of noninterference among phenomena, of every thing
containing the universe, is presented throughout the Hua-yen scripture, but virtually exclusively in symbolic form; it is often considered the most abstruse of Hua-yen doctrines, but it is really not so
farfetched if properly understood on the basis of the noninterference of noumenon and phenomena. In his "Contemplation of the
Reality-Realm," Tu Shun also deals with this realm in terms of ten
interdependent aspects. The first pair, which forms the basis of this
realm, is still presented in terms of the relation of noumenon and
phenomena; it provides the key to understanding this teaching
device.
    The first aspect of the noninterference among phenomena
which Tu Shun brings up is that of noumenon conforming to phenomena. This notion is based on the premise of the emptiness of
phenomena; since their appearances are nil in terms of absolute
reality, the noumenal nature is manifest in everything—the whole
noumenon *is* phenomena and does not exist outside phenomena.
One verse of the text expresses this aspect in terms of "noumenon
manifesting in conformity with phenomena."
    The second aspect is that of phenomena conforming to noume-
non. This means that phenomena are in essence not different from
noumenon and their noumenal nature is one with the noumenal
nature of all things. In this sense one phenomenon is said to pervade
all phenomena, inasmuch as its noumenal nature is present in all

things; the emptiness of absolute nature and the transience of one thing is in principle the same as the emptiness and transience of all things, and so it may be said in this light that even a minute particle contains the central principle of the whole universe.

The third aspect is that of phenomena containing noumenon and phenomena without interference. This means that things are both empty and apparent. In terms of their phenomenal or apparent aspect, things retain individuality, while at the same time in terms of their noumenal or empty aspect things each pervade and contain the universe. This is why it is said that an atom contains boundless lands without expanding: the containing refers to its noumenal nature; not expanding refers to its characteristics as a phenomenon. Within this aspect Tu Shun goes on to mention four facets of it: one in one, one in all, all in one, all in all. One in one refers to a phenomenon retaining its own phenomenal individuality while noumenally being able to "contain" another one because they are not different in terms of essence or emptiness. One in all means that the multitude do not lose their characteristics as phenomena while at the same time "containing" each individual, which is noumenally not different from the all. All in one, likewise, means that one does not lose its individuality and yet "contains" all in terms of its noumenon being one with the noumenon of the all. Finally, all in all means that all phenomena do not lose their characteristics as phenomena while at the same time they each noumenally contain all others.

Fourth is the aspect of noninterference of universality and limitation. This means that the nonunity of all things with noumenon is identical to nondifference; that is to say, the nonunity of things with noumenon, being their relative existence, is none other than their individual emptiness. Therefore phenomena are noumenally present in all particles of the universe without phenomenally departing from their places. Again, because nondifference of phenomena and noumenon (which means the emptiness of phenomena) is identical to their nonunity (which means the relativity of phenomena), while completely pervading the universe noumenally, phenomena nevertheless do not phenomenally move throughout the universe. Thus "universality" refers to noumenal pervasion whereas "limitation" refers to phenomenal location.

Fifth is the aspect of the noninterference of extension and

restriction. This means that because the nonunity of phenomena with noumenon (that is, the relative existence of phenomena) is none other than nondifference (that is, the individual emptiness of phenomena), therefore an atom, without phenomenally dissolving, can noumenally contain the universe. Thus the atom is noumenally extensive but phenomenally restricted at the same time. This and the fourth aspect are both further ramifications of the third aspect.

Sixth is the aspect of noninterference of pervading and containing. This means that the noumenal nature of a phenomenon may be said to pervade all other phenomena inasmuch as it is one and the same noumenon. At the same time and for the same reason the noumenal nature of a phenomenon may be said to contain all phenomena since the noumenal nature of one phenomenon is itself the whole noumenon.

Seventh is the aspect of inclusion and entry. This means that the totality depends on the individual; therefore, since the individual is necessarily implied in the totality, it is said that one "enters" all or the unit enters the manifold, while the manifold "includes" the unit. At the same time, the unit implies the manifold, since the individual and the totality are interdependent; therefore one is said to include all and also enter all, while each one entering all simultaneously includes all within it. This notion is represented in the scripture as each atom in a universe containing countless worlds, with each atom of those countless worlds also containing countless worlds and so on. While moderns may well see in this concept allusions to the structure of the universe from the macrocosmic to the microcosmic (and certainly the idea of atoms and subatomic particles did indeed exist in the India of the *Avatamsaka* scripture), still in terms of this aspect of the philosophy, worlds within atoms refers to the mutual reflection of the unit and the manifold.

Eighth is the aspect of communion without interference. This refers to one atom or particle looking to or relating to all—"including" all because its relative existence implies that of the totality and also "entering" all because the existence of the totality depends on the units. Tu Shun presents four propositions within this aspect: one includes all; one enters all; all include one; all enter one. Naturally, these four facets are simultaneous and interdependent; they reduce to the interdependence of one and many. Depending has the sense of "entering," as the existence of the dependent is subsumed by or included by that upon which it depends; being depended on has the sense of "including," since it is a necessary correlative of that which depends. On the other hand, depending also has the sense of including, since the existence of that which depends necessitates the existence of that which is depended on, while being depended on also has the sense of entering, because it is always involved in the existence of the dependent. Since one and many are interdependent, both are simultaneously the dependent and that which is depended on—hence the sense of communion without interference.

Ninth is the aspect of mutual inherence or immanence without interference. This means that the all, which includes the individual, enters (is included in) the individual; the all, in which individual units each include the all, enter (are included in) one; the all, which includes the individual, enters all individual units; all, each of which include all, enter all. In other words, each and every phenomenon implies and reflects the existence of each and every other thing; the existence of all is inherent in the existence of one. As we shall see in the translation of Tu Shun's "Contemplation of the Reality-Realm" with Cheng-kuan's commentary, Cheng-kuan illustrates this with the metaphor, devised by Fa-tsang, of ten mirrors reflecting each other. This metaphor presents a step-by-step development of the doctrine known as the net of Indra, a doctrine we find expounded in Tu Shun's "Cessation and Contemplation," Chih-yen's "Ten Mysterious Gates," and Fa-tsang's "Return to the Source," translations of which are included in this volume.

Tenth is the aspect of universal merging without interference. This means that the unit and the totality are simultaneous; one and all coexist interdependently. Basically this summation of the foregoing concludes that all nine aspects are simultaneously inherent in the interrelationship of all phenomena.

These ten aspects of the mutual inclusion of all phenomena as delineated by Tu Shun were further developed by Chih-yen and Fa-tsang into the famous doctrine of the ten mysterious gates. As I later present a translation of Chih-yen's treatise on the ten mysterious gates—the only Hua-yen document dealing exclusively with this teaching device—by way of introduction here I shall present the mysterious gates in the form into which they were later cast by Fa-tsang.

The first gate is called simultaneous complete correspondence.

This refers to the fact that all things come from interdependent origination, simultaneously depending on each other for their manifestation. Since interdependent origination is the nature of all things, all things are simultaneously one whole. This is the total aspect of the universe of the mutual noninterference of phenomena; the rest of the mysterious gates are particular aspects of this total interrelatedness.

The second gate is called freedom and noninterference of extension and restriction, or breadth and narrowness. Since one phenomenon conditions the existence of all phenomena—inasmuch as all are interrelated and interdependent—the power or function of one phenomenon is in this sense unbounded; this is what is called broad or extensive. Yet at the same time it retains its bounds as one phenomenon and does not dissolve its basic status; this is what is called narrow or restricted. So it is that all interdependent things have both these limited and unlimited aspects, in that as conditional individual phenomena they are integral parts of the whole universe. This is called the freedom and noninterference of extension and restriction.

The third gate is called that of one and many containing each other without being the same. In terms of the interrelation of all things, the power of one phenomenon enters into all other phenomena, while the power of all other phenomena enters into one. This notion might be visualized in terms of gravitational force—looking upon each and every particle as the gravitational balance point of the universe (which as a sum of forces requires all its parts to subsist) while at the same time seeing the universe maintaining the relative position of each particle. This may also be looked upon in terms of individual and society, in that the doings of a society affect the individual in that society while the doings of the individual affect the society—this is but two ways of saying that each individual in a society affects, directly or indirectly, every other individual. The functions of things, like the influences of people, interpenetrate, yet unity and multiplicity remain; that is why it is called one and many containing each other without being the same. The unit contains the influences of the manifold, while the manifold contains the influences of each unit; in this sense they merge, yet still retain oneness and manyness, for it is on this very relation that existence depends.

The fourth gate, called mutual identification of all things, is based on the preceding mutual containment of one and many. When the power of one thing enters all things, that one is one thing among all things; since it is a part of all things, it loses its identity and becomes the same as the others—the substance of one thing is wholly all things, so there is no one thing outside of all things. Hence from this point of view the unit is empty while the manifold is substantial. At the same time, all things enter one thing, so they lose their identity to the one; all things are the substance of one thing, so there is no "all things" outside that substance, and therefore from this point of view "all things," the manifold, are insubstantial. Since they are mutually substantial and insubstantial, one phenomenon equals all phenomena and all phenomena equal one phenomenon. This is called mutual identification. In the third gate, singleness and multiplicity are not effaced and the interpenetration of power and function is shown; it is likened to two mirrors reflecting each other. In this fourth gate, the two aspects (one and many) are shown to merge into one suchness; this is likened to water and waves containing each other.

The theme illustrated by these two mysterious gates is spelled out further by Fa-tsang in the fourth scroll of his commentary on the Hua-yen scripture, where he introduces the doctrine of interdependent origination of the universe by saying that all the different conditions in the whole universe form one single interdependent creation. This we may also call conditional origination or relative origination. He goes on to say that each of the conditions, being interdependent, embodies two meanings: one, in terms of substance or entity, is the meaning of emptiness and existence, whence proceeds the mutual identification of conditions (or phenomena); the other, in terms of function, is the meaning of having power and having no power, whence proceeds the mutual interpenetration of conditions and phenomena.

As for the first meaning, the point is that if there is no unit then the totality entirely loses its own being. (If there is no one, there can be no many; and if the manifold is not formed, the many are not in effect conditions.) Therefore when there is one there is all, and when one is denied all are denied. In this case, "all" has the sense of emptiness, whereby it loses itself in "one"—that is, "all" has no identity apart from "one." As "one" then has the sense of existence, it assimilates the other to itself—that is, "one" contains "all" as integral to itself. Looking at this in the opposite way, one becomes empty and loses itself in the all, while the manifold exists and embraces the one in itself. Because both can be seen to exist and both can be seen to be empty, they are never not mutually identical—insofar as one is empty and one existent, able to be seen both ways without interference, there is always this mutual identification. Moreover, because in each individual condition emptiness and existence are not two— empty from the point of view of depending on the manifold, that is, and existent from the point of view of the manifold depending on it —therefore conditions or phenomena identify with the others without losing themselves.

Regarding the second meaning, the point set forth is that conditions arising are not collectively born of a portion of the power of each; therefore each individual condition has both a sense in which it acts or creates totally as well as a sense in which it totally does not act or create. That is to say, if one condition is lacking the rest of the conditions are totally ineffectual in that they cannot produce a unified totality; this is referred to as one having the power and the rest having none. The same can be said from the point of view of the other conditions—if they are not there, the one condition is ineffectual and hence the many has the power and the one has none. In terms of one having power, it is thereby said to be able to contain the many, while the many, lacking power, are said to submerge into the one. Again we can see this from the opposite point of view, the many containing the individual and the individual submerging into the many. Because both have power and both have no power, therefore there is never a time when they do not interpenetrate each other; because when one has power the other does not, without mutual interference, therefore they always interpenetrate.

Moreover, because in each individual condition the facts of having power and not having power are nondual—being but two facets of the same relativity—therefore they always interpenetrate and yet remain external to each other at the same time. Because in interdependent origination there is such a sense of mutual creation, producing one and many, the unit and the manifold produce each other. The scripture says that in one there is infinity while in infinity there is one. It says also that the one and the many are not real, meaning that one is not really of itself one—so it can contain the many—and the many is not really of itself many—so it can be one and can contain one.

The fifth mysterious gate is called the existence of both concealment and revelation. It follows from the foregoing gates that when one thing is identified with all things, then the all is manifest and the one is concealed. When all things are identified with one, then one is manifest and the many is concealed. This amounts to an affirmation of the coexistence and noninterference of both perspectives.

The sixth mysterious gate is called the establishment of mutual containment even in the minute. This gate, based on the second through fifth gates, means that even the most minute particle contains all things, like a mirror reflecting myriad forms. Once again this doctrine merely points out that all elements are integral parts of the whole, while at the same time and for the same reason the whole is, because of the relation of interdependence, an integral part of the existence of each and every element.

The seventh gate is called the realm of Indra's net. The net of Indra is a net of jewels: not only does each jewel reflect all the other jewels but the reflections of all the jewels in each jewel also contain the reflections of all the other jewels, ad infinitum. This "infinity of infinities" represents the interidentification and interpenetration of all things as illustrated in the preceding gates.

To illustrate the net of Indra principle with a simplistic example from everyday life, we might consider the cost of a commodity as representing a nexus of various conditions. For the sake of simplicity, let us say the cost of something reflects (1) the cost of raw materials, (2) the cost of energy required for its manufacture, (3) the cost of labor involved in its production, and (4) the cost of transportation for distribution. Turning our attention to raw materials, the first element, we can see that the cost of raw materials also involves the cost of energy required for their extraction, the cost of labor involved in their extraction, and the cost of transportation of the raw materials to the processing site. The cost of energy involves the cost of raw materials from which energy is produced as well as raw materials for the devices involved, the cost of labor involved in producing energy, and the cost of distribution of energy. The cost of

labor reflects the cost of goods, energy, and transportation necessary for the work force. The cost of transportation involves the cost
of materials, energy, and labor necessary to the manufacture and
operation of transportation systems. Thus each element in this analysis reflects and contains every other element. While this example is
rudimentary, using an oversimplified scheme of analysis and stopping at only one level of subanalysis, it illustrates how the net of
Indra concept may be applied to the development of a balanced
view of a complex of phenomena. The analytic framework may be
usefully applied in economics, socioeconomics, group and individual psychology, and ecology. While it may be said that the net of
Indra does not necessarily reveal anything startlingly new—it is,
after all, merely an articulation of a principle inherent in an interdependent nexus of phenomena—still it is a valuable instrument for
the achievement of balance and depth in understanding and, moreover, for the avoidance of one-sided views.

The eighth mysterious gate is called using a phenomenon to
illustrate a principle and produce understanding. Since one and all
are mutually coproduced, one can be used to illustrate all—that is
to say, for example, that the relativity of one phenomenon reveals
the relativity of all. This concept is often referred to as the Buddhist
teaching being revealed on the tip of a hair or in a mote of dust.
This gate also refers to the use of phenomena as illustrations, such
as the net of Indra.

The ninth mysterious gate is called separate phenomena of the
ten time frames variously existing. The ten time frames are the past,
present, and future of the past, present, and future, and the totality
—that is, the past of the past, the present of the past, the future of
the past, the past of the present, the present of the present, the
future of the present, the past of the future, the present of the future,
the future of the future, and the totality of all of these times. These
time divisions interidentify and interpenetrate. They are interdependent—defined only in terms of each other, not existing absolutely—and yet do not lose order or proportion. Thus the terms
"separate" and "various" are used to signify the subsistence of
order. Since the continuum of time (or the continuum of the network of causality) depends on each link, each link implies the preceding and succeeding link, and so on, so that each link implies the

whole. The universe—or, in Hua-yen terms, the universe of interdependent origination—is at once the totality of causes and the totality of effects; hence its total present at once contains its total past and total future. This is the basis for the Buddha's knowledge of past and future in the present.

The tenth mysterious gate is called that of the principal and satellites completely illumined and containing all qualities. As myriad things are one great interdependent production, looking at it through the perspective of the preceding gates we see that when one thing is made the focus, it becomes the "principal" while everything else is a multitude of "satellites" of the principal. Since this doctrine applies to each individual thing, everything is at once both principal and satellite to everything else. Each thing fulfills and reveals the qualities of all things—hence the terms "completely illumined" and "containing all qualities." Its application in the social sphere too is obvious and provides a theoretical basis for the balanced harmonization of the individual and the community.

In Chih-yen's treatise on the ten mysterious gates, and also in Fa-tsang's treatise on the five teachings, one finds two more gates: the "gate of the purity and mixture of the stores, containing all their qualities," and the "gate of creation only by the operation of mind." The former means that whatever aspect of the teaching is brought up, the other aspects are included in it—in terms of the perfection of generosity, for example, all the teachings are generosity. This is the meaning of "pure," which means "uniform" here rather than undefiled as opposed to defiled. Yet, by the same token, since generosity contains all the teachings, it is "mixed." Since the pure and the mixed do not interfere with each other, all the qualities of the teachings are included.

The gate of creation by the operation of mind alone means that all the teachings are set up by the mind and, moreover, that good and evil come from the operation of the mind. Chih-yen quotes the scripture saying, "Mind creates the Buddhas." He also quotes another saying: "The three worlds [of desire, form, and formlessness] are unreal, just the production of one mind." Chih-yen says that birth-and-death and nirvana are not apart from mind, so they cannot be definitely said to be pure or impure in nature. Thus in essence this gate means that phenomena do not interfere with each other because their sensible existence is but a reflection of mind.

Finally, to conclude this introduction to the Hua-yen realm of noninterference among phenomena, we turn to the teaching of the "six characteristics." This teaching is originally to be found in embryonic form in the beginning of the Hua-yen book on the ten stages, where it refers to six aspects of the mutual interdependence and relativity of the ten stages themselves; later it was applied by the Hua-yen masters to all phenomena. The six characteristics are known as totality, distinction, sameness, difference, formation, and disintegration. To give a succinct explanation of these six characteristics, I turn once again to the "Source Mirror Collection" of Yen-shou, where he gives the following account:

> If you want ultimately to escape the biased extreme views of nihilism and eternalism, you must understand the meaning of the Hua-yen teaching of the six characteristics: then you can abide by the truth in all actions, spontaneously forgetting subject and object; in action and stillness according to conditions, not hindering existence and nonexistence, you have the great spell, ultimately free of error.
>
> The meaning of these six characteristics is analyzing the things of the world freely, without hindrance, properly showing conditional origination and the noumenon, where there is no discrimination. Those who can see attain the spell of wisdom and do not fall into the various existences. It will not do to ignore one and take one; they stand together and vanish together. Though they are all simultaneous, while arising in profusion they do not exist; though each has distinctions, while dark and silent they are not nonexistent. It cannot be known by mindfulness; it cannot be understood by mindlessness. . . .
>
> The six characteristics are (1) totality, (2) distinction, (3) sameness, (4) difference, (5) formation (integration), and (6) disintegration (differentiation). The characteristic of totality may be likened to a house—this is the aspect of totality whereas the beams and so forth are the characteristic of distinction. The various elements, the beams and the like, are joined to make a house—since each does not oppose the other and they

do not make any other thing, it is called the characteristic of sameness. The various elements, the beams and so on, depend on each other and are individually not the same—this is called the characteristic of difference. The various elements such as the beams, single and multiple, one and many, complete each other—this is called the characteristic of formation. The various elements such as the beams each abide in their own states, originally not creating—this therefore is called the characteristic of disintegration. . . .

The one mind of true thusness is the characteristic of totality because it embraces mundane and transmundane things; it gets the name of totality because of embracing all things. It produces various objects, making distinct names; every thing is equal—this is the character of sameness. As their forms are not the same, this is called difference. As they form the objective environment, this is called formation. As they do not move from their own position, this is disintegration.

Also: (1) the characteristic of totality—one combines many qualities; (2) distinction—many qualities are not one; (3) sameness—many meanings do not oppose each other; (4) difference—many meanings are not like each other; (5) formation—because of these many meanings, conditional origination is formed; (6) disintegration—the various conditions each abide in their own nature without moving.[10]

In this discussion we have considered phenomena from the points of view of relativity and emptiness—concepts based on the Buddhist teachings of emptiness and existence, the fictional, relative, and real natures of things, and the realms of noumenon, phenomena, noninterference of noumenon and phenomena, and noninterference among phenomena. This shift of perspective is encouraged by the Hua-yen teaching as a means to develop what is called a "round and clear" understanding, which may also be translated as "complete awareness" or "complete illumination." Having glimpsed something of the contents of the Hua-yen scripture and bared the foundation of Hua-yen metaphysics, we may now turn our attention to original treatises by some of the great interpreters of the Hua-yen to corroborate these points.

First I present two seminal treatises by Tu Shun, the founder of Hua-yen Buddhism, dealing with the basic aspects of pan-Buddhist as well as special Hua-yen theory and practice; then we shall proceed to Chih-yen's elucidation of the ten mysterious gates and his special application of this concept; I conclude with a treatise by Fa-tsang which summarizes and coordinates the philosophy, ethics, and meditation practices of Hua-yen Buddhism.

Cessation and Contemplation in the Five Teachings of the Hua-yen

by Tu Shun

THIS TREATISE BEGINS with an elementary teaching of Buddhism refuting the notion of the body-mind as self. This is done by analyzing the body-mind and showing that it is really an aggregate of elements and cannot be a unified self. This contemplative exercise is carried out basically to stop selfishness and break through the shell of ego by revealing that one's identity is a mental construction and there is nothing real in it to preserve or defend. This is called the teaching of the lesser vehicle of Buddhism.

The next step, after losing the illusions surrounding the notion of self, is realizing that origination is the same as nonorigination. This is referred to as the elementary teaching of the greater vehicle of Buddhism: no true origin of anything can be found; beginnings exist only in terms of demarcations which from the standpoint of ultimate reality are arbitrary. Reality is continuous because it has no opposite; the origin of the definitions which conjure images of things from an infinitely extensive and dense flow of data is the mind. Nonorigination also means emptiness—referring to the emptiness of the independent individual phenomenon. Thus the apparent origination of a phenomenon is identical to the nonorigination of its real nature.

This elementary step of the greater vehicle is divided into two parts: the first is to demonstrate that names and characterizations, by which we define things and their specific signs, marks, or characteristics, do not correspond exactly to real entities but are mental projections formed by habits. Having dismissed the notion that names correspond to realities, the next phase of this vehicle is contemplation of nonorigination. This is done by observing that all things are interdependent, born of causes and conditions, and thus have no independent nature or identity of their own.

The next step in Tu Shun's treatise is the contemplation of the merging of noumenon and phenomena, which is referred to as the final teaching of the greater vehicle. Concentration on the aspect of noumenon, or emptiness, leads to cessation and detachment from existents; concentration on the aspect of phenomena, or conditional existence, forms contemplation ending attachment to nirvana. By harmonizing these two aspects one is able to unite wisdom (whose sphere is emptiness) and compassion (whose sphere is existence), attached neither to being nor nonbeing. To illustrate this point, Tu Shun quotes the scripture saying, "Those who come to realize thusness do not see birth-and-death and do not see nirvana—birth-and-death and nirvana are equal, without distinction."

Tu Shun then goes into the so-called immediate or sudden teaching of the greater vehicle, called the end of language and views. This means transcending all verbalization and conceptualization so that "there is only true thusness and the knowledge of true thusness." This does not mean the absolute cutting off of words and thought, for it includes realizing everything as part of thusness. It does, however, mean that words and thoughts are not clung to as ultimate arbiters of reality.

The final step of uniting the mind with the real universe of thusness, according to this treatise, is the special teaching of the Hua-yen: the flower ornament meditation. This step, called the complete teaching of the one vehicle, refers to the immediate realization of the conditional origin of everything in the universe: everything at once and forever depends on everything else. By seeing the conditional nature of one thing, one realizes the conditional nature of all things.

WHEN THE CULTIVATOR PRACTICES THE WAY, in weeding out the false and entering the true, there are five methodical gates of cessation and contemplation:

1. Elements exist; self does not (the teaching of the lesser vehicle).
2. Origination is identical to nonorigination (elementary teaching of the greater vehicle).
3. Phenomena and noumenon merge completely (final teaching of the greater vehicle).
4. Language and views are both ended (immediate teaching of the greater vehicle).
5. Flower ornament meditation (complete teaching of the one vehicle).

1.

Prescriptions are designed in response to illness; when the illness is ended, the prescription is finished with. Medicine is dispensed to quell attachments; when attachments are gone, the medicine is done with. Since illnesses are manifold, the medicines given are not one. According to potentials, progress and practice differ; therefore techniques are not the same. Now, from just among the five mental stabilizations,[1] I shall explain the analytic contemplation of the elements for those sentient beings who cling to self.

Sentient beings, from beginningless time, have been attached to the physical being and consider it as one, conceiving of self and possessions. But there are two kinds of conception of self. One is to cling to the body as self; the second is to cling to a self apart from the body.

Clinging to a self apart from the body means the non-Buddhists' conception of the separate existence of a spirit self within the body.[2] The details of this conception are refuted throughout the scriptures and treatises, so I need not go into it here.

As for clinging to body as self, the Buddha, in his kindness and compassion, determined to destroy this disease and set out four medicines in all to cure four illnesses. Among them each distinct

approach has medicine and illness as explained below in detail. The
four illnesses are:

1. Grasping the body as one self
2. Grasping the four gross components[3]
3. Grasping the five clusters[4]
4. Grasping the twelve sense media[5]

The four medicines are:

1. The two elements matter and mind
2. The four gross components and the five clusters
3. The twelve sense media
4. The eighteen elements[6]

Next comes an explanation: to those sentient beings who grasp
the body as one self and thus become ill, the two elements of matter
and mind are expounded as medicine. So we could say that here are
two elements, matter and mind—how can they be one self?

Sentient beings, hearing this, then go on and take material
form to be real and it becomes sickness. For them matter is then
divided into four materials—that is, the four gross components.
Mind too is divided into four—that is, four of the five clusters (sensation, perception, coordination, consciousness). Since there are
now four materials and four mental clusters, how can you just
grasp one material form and one mind as one self?

Sentient beings then turn to grasping the four materials and
four mental clusters and become sick, so the Buddha combines the
four gross components into one material form—this is the matter
[form] cluster among the five clusters. And he combines the four
mental clusters into one mind—this is the cognitive medium among
the twelve sense media.

Hearing this, if sentient beings still go on to grasp it and make
it a sickness, the Buddha then analyzes one material form into
eleven materials; that is to say, among the twelve media, the inner
five organs and the outer six data fields—this makes eleven materials. And he analyzes one mind into seven mental elements; that is,
among the eighteen elements, the six consciousnesses plus the intellectual consciousness. Here then are eighteen elements—how can
you just cling to one material form or one mind and consider it to

have self? Sentient beings hearing this are finally enlightened and can enter into emptiness.

But within the eighteen elements there are three kinds: the inner elements, the outer elements, and the elements in between. And within these three kinds, each is divided into two: three of sickness and three of medicine.

As for the three sicknesses, the first is inwardly clinging to the totality of the six sense organs as the self; the second is clinging to the totality of the six outer fields of sense data as the self; the third is to consider the totality of the six sense consciousnesses in between as the self's perception, in the sense of "*I* see, *I* hear, *I* discern, *I* know."

Next, regarding the three medicines, the first is analyzing the inner six organs into six elements—the element of the eye and so forth. This cures the aforementioned sickness of conceiving of a self. The second is analyzing the outer six data fields into six elements—the element of color/form and so forth. This cures the aforementioned sickness of conceiving of them as self. The third is analyzing the "I see, I hear" and so forth in between (organs and data) into six consciousnesses—the element of eye consciousness, the element of ear consciousness, and so forth. This cures the aforementioned sickness of "*I* see, *I* hear," and the like.

These three points combined clarify the representations, divisions, and distinctions of the sets, their individual dissimilarities. Bringing them all up at once under an inclusive rubric, they are named the phenomena of the eighteen elements; "elements" means distinction, and eighteen is their number, so we speak of eighteen elements.

In each of the aforementioned elements there are six levels: one, the name; two, the phenomenon; three, the substance; four, the characteristics; five, the function; six, the cause.

As for the name, "eye faculty," for example, is the term spoken by the mouth. The so-called phenomenon is the illusionary thing immediately associated with the name. The substance is the eight subtleties—hardness, wetness, warmth, motility, color, odor, flavor, and feel. As for the characteristics [form], the eye is spherical. As for the function, it is producing the eye consciousness. Here there are four relevant doctrines: one, the eye consciousness creates the eye faculty; two, the eye faculty produces the eye consciousness; three, the eye consciousness is within the eye faculty; four, the eye consciousness assists the eye faculty. The cause is the seeds of faculties [organs] in the repository consciousness.[7]

The ear organ resembles a sideways handle in form; the nose organ is like an overturned fingernail; the tongue organ is like a scimitar; the body organ is like a standing snake. The organ of cognition, according to the lesser vehicle, is like a lotus; according to the greater vehicle, its characteristic is that it is born together with four delusions. The four delusions are selfish greed, self-conceit, selfish ignorance, and the idea of self.

The substance of the cognitive faculty is the repository consciousness; the phenomenon of it is what is indicated by the name, instantly relating to the inner object of the cognitive consciousness, grasping it as self. Except for the substance and phenomenon of the cognitive faculty, the other faculties [organs] can be known by considering them in the same way as the eye organ.

As for the outer six data fields; each has six aspects. First is the name—the saying of "the field of form/color" in the mouth. Second is the phenomenon—this is what is indicated by the name, that which instantly relates to the eye consciousness. Third, the substance is the eight subtleties. Fourth, the characteristics are blue, yellow, red, and white. Fifth, the function is being that which induces the eye consciousness. Sixth, the cause is the seeds of color and form in the repository consciousness.

The data field of sound has for its characteristics loud and soft sounds and long and short. The data field of odor has fragrance and foulness and so forth as characteristics. The data field of flavor has sour, salt, sweet, pungent, and bitter for characteristics. The data field of feel has characteristics such as cool, warm, sticky, slippery, hard, soft, light, heavy, and the like. The data field of objects has such characteristics as square and round shapes, long and short sizes, and so on. This data field of objects has ignorance as its substance. Except for the data field of objects, the other five data fields are to be considered in the same way as the data field of form/color.

As for the six consciousnesses in between: first, the name is, say, the words "eye consciousness" articulated by the mouth; second, the phenomenon is that which nominal representation cannot reach but which is subtly apprehended, not nil; third, the substance is the matrix of the issue of thusness;[8] fourth, their characteristic is the form of pure spheres; fifth, the function is apprehending objects and perceiving; sixth, the cause is the seeds of, say, eye consciousness within the repository consciousness.

However, the phenomenon of the cognitive consciousness is something that does not correspond to the truth as represented by the name; its characteristic is all extension and limitation. Except for the phenomenon and characteristics of the cognitive consciousness, the other five consciousnesses can be thought of along the same lines as the eye consciousness.

Since the name, phenomenon, and so forth in one element are six in number, with a total of eighteen elements, this amounts to one hundred and eight elements in all; some scriptures speak of this as one hundred and eight afflictions. As the illnesses to be cured are such, so also are the curative medicines: they include the organs [faculties], data fields, and consciousnesses—all of them have the repository consciousness for substance. Therefore the *Laṅkāvatāra* scripture says, "The ocean of repository consciousness always abides; stirred by the wind of objects, the waves of the perceptual consciousnesses are always rising—flying, leaping, arising more and more." This passage can be relied on as testimony of this.

If the practitioner contemplates these eighteen elements, cuts off afflictions such as those mentioned before, and manages to detach from self and possession, this is liberation.

The contemplating mind is knowledge; the object of contemplation has no person—this is called attaining knowlede of the selflessness of person. Although the personal self is gone, attachment to the elements remains—attachment to elements refers to matter and mind.

Question: How does the attachment to elements here, matter and mind, differ from the material form and mind of one self as previously refuted?

Answer: Previously one body was considered to have person, so we brought up matter and mind to refute this view. And so we went on in the same way, further analyzing one body into eleven materials and analyzing one mind into seven minds and so on. At this point it is finally realized that it is born of a combination of many conditions, so the idea of person finally disappears. But the

perception of noumenon is not yet clear, and one holds the conditions to be really existent—there is the difference.

Here I have briefly set forth the lesser vehicle's breaking down
attachment to self and illustrated the analytic contemplation of the
elements.

2. Origination Is Identical to Nonorigination

In this gate of the identity of origination and nonorigination,
we first eliminate names and characterizations and then enter the
gate of nonorigination. First, in eliminating names and characterizations, for the moment we can take something from the world and
question it to do this; suppose we make our investigation in respect
to a headrest.

Question: Without controverting the mundane, what do you
call this?

Answer: It's a headrest.

Question: Then what is this "headrest"?

Answer: It's a name.

Question: What kind of headrest is it?

Answer: It's a wooden headrest.

Question: And what is a "wooden headrest"?

Answer: It's not a name.

Question: If it's not a name, then what do you call it?

Answer: It's a phrase.

Question: What do you call a "headrest"?

Answer: It's not a phrase.

Question: Since it's not a phrase, what do you call it?

Answer: It's a name.

Question: What function does it perform?

Answer: A name is used to call a thing by.

Question: Call it.

Answer: It's arrived.

Then, pointing to what has been brought forth, we ask, "What is
this?" Stop—you can't say anything. This is a silent answer. The
questioning goes on:

Question: What is it for sure?

Answer: It's not a "headrest."

Question: Since it's not a "headrest," where has the headrest gone?

Answer: It's a name.

Question: Where is the name?

Answer: It is that which is spoken in the mouth.

Question: Since this isn't a "headrest," what do you call it?

Answer: It's apart from words.

Question: How can it be known that it's apart from words?

Answer: Because we see with the eye, we use verbal explanation provisionally.

Question: If verbal explanation is used provisionally, what thing do you say it is?

Answer: It is a phenomenon.

Question: There are many kinds of phenomena: they might be the phenomena of characteristics, the phenomena of colors and forms, or the phenomena of principles.

Answer: It is a phenomenon of characterization.

Question: There are also many kinds of characteristics—crooked, square, round, and so on.

Answer: This headrest is square.

Question: There are many kinds of squares. To say there are many kinds means the name is the same but the phenomenon is different.

Answer: This is the "square" associated with the name "headrest."

Question: Among the eight consciousnesses, which mind [consciousness] contains the name, characteristics, and phenomenon?

Answer: They're the name, characteristics, and phenomenon in the sixth, or cognitive consciousness, via the medium of the eye consciousness.

Question: How do we get this name, these characteristics, and this phenomenon suddenly appearing in the cognitive consciousness?

Answer: From seeds.

Question: How do you know?

Answer: Since the name and characteristics of this headrest cannot be taken to be the name and characteristics of a seat, we can know they come from seeds.[9]

Question: Where do the seeds come from?

Answer: They are gotten from false teachers.[10]

Question: How do we get them?

Answer: They come from the influences of seeing and hearing and so forth becoming seeds.

Question: Since these names, characteristics, and phenomena are in the cognitive consciousness, we should behold them inside the mind. Why then do we look outside the mind, in front of us?

Answer: When you look in front of you, these names and characteristics are all in your mind.

Question: How can this be known?

Answer: The eye consciousness just sees form/color; names, characterizations, and phenomena are in the cognizing conscious mind.

Question: As a deluded person, I only see names and characteristics. Since you, the wise one, see form, what is its appearance like? What *is* form?

The question is returned to the deluded one: "Since you see names and characteristics, what is their appearance like?"

The deluded one answers, "The headrest is characterized by four edges and six faces."

The wise one asks, "Look at where the edge is—do you see an edge or do you see form?"

The deluded one thinks carefully and replies, "I only see form, not an edge."

This same question and answer is carried out for the rest of the edges and the faces. The deluded one asks, "Since it's all form, where are the name and characteristics?"

The wise one replies, "The names and characteristics are in your mind." The deluded one does not submit. When the wise one asks why not, the deluded one replies, "As I now see the gates and towers of a monastery, the names and characteristics are in my mind; the names and characteristics of this thing before me must also be in my mind. Why does one person manage to apprehend while another doesn't?"

The wise one retorts, "You've apprehended the name and characteristics?"

The deluded one replies, "I have apprehended them."

The wise one asks, "What things have you apprehended?"

The deluded one replies, "I've apprehended names and characteristics."

Question: Are names and characteristics soft or hard?

Answer: Hard.

The wise one says, "Let go of hardness. Just grasp the name and characteristic—don't grasp 'hard'."

The deluded one replies, "The hardness is found together with the name and characteristics."

Question: Then can you see the hardness?

Answer: It can't be seen.

Question: Then what do you see?

Answer: I just see name and characteristics.

The deluded one then retorts, "Once I have apprehended names and characteristics, I have only apprehended them. Where *are* the names and characteristics?"

The wise one replies, "Names and characteristics are in the deluded one's mind."

When the deluded one refuses to accept that names and characteristics are in the mind, the wise one asks, "Why don't you acquiesce?"

The deluded one answers, "If all kinds of names and characteristics are in my mind, why don't I find them equally hard?"

Answer: If you find something hard, it is name and characteristic of the present. If something isn't found to be hard, that is because it is a name of the past.

Criticism: The cognitive consciousness does not apprehend objects of direct perception—how can there be past objects of direct perception?

Answer: Both kinds of name are in the past. It's a matter of operating alone or not operating alone [having a coexistent referent].[11]

Question: Since the two kinds of names and characteristics are all false consciousness, as a scripture says, how can there be mere images and images with substance?

Answer: What you call "substance" is also a mere image as a mental object—since the characteristic of squareness is an object of inference, it is not an object of direct perception. That is why I now say they are distinct. Because of being together with the eye consciousness or not being together, I say mere images and images with substance are distinct.

Question: Why are the discriminations not the same?

Answer: There are two different kinds of discrimination—manifest comprehension and memory. Therefore there is a difference between discrimination based on solid images and discrimination which is not based on solid images.

The deluded one also asks, "I only see two kinds of names and characteristics—what does the wise one see?"

The wise one replies, "The wise only see material phenomena, not names and characterizations."

This concludes the elimination of names and characteristics; next we consider the entry into nonorigination.

When a wise person examines material phenomena, there is really no discrimination when the eye consciousness apprehends them. It is not that there is no discrimination because of not apprehending; this is the consciousness of the eye of objective reality intimately witnessing matter as it is without differing—but then the cognitive consciousness does not comprehend and wrongly conceives of self and creates artificial discriminations, sinking into false views. Within phenomena, the real and the false are equally construed. Why? The discrimination of the cognitive consciousness is not in accord with things as they are.

As for "real" and "false," as the eye consciousness apprehends it, it is called real; as the cognitive consciousness relates to it, it is false.[12] Reality and falsehood are distinct, not equivalent. Therefore in realization of truth there is no person. A scripture says, "Truth has no discrimination: if you discriminate, this is discrimination, not the search for truth."

As material phenomena are thus, so too are mental phenomena. Considered in the same way, they are no different from material phenomena. Therefore a scripture says, "The objects apprehended by the five [perceptual] consciousness are in their very essence the matrix of the issue of thusness" and so forth. This is a technique for entering the first gate, a subtle door to merging with the natural state. A brief explanation of the general idea has been presented here; it is expounded at length in the scriptures and treatises.

Moreover, all things are of the character of emptiness; none is not null. Herein there are also two contemplations: the first is the contemplation of nonorigination; the second is the contemplation of signlessness.

The contemplation of nonorigination means that things have no nature of their own; they are born of mutual interdependence, so their origination is not really existent. This means they are empty, and there is not so much as the tip of a hair in emptiness. Therefore things are said to be birthless, or without origin. Scripture says they exist because of causes and conditions and they are empty because they have no intrinsic nature. By way of explanation, having no nature means conditionality, and conditionality means there is no inherent nature. Furthermore, the "Treatise on the Mean" says, "Because there is the meaning of emptiness, therefore all things can be."[13] And a scripture says, "If all things were not empty, then there would be no Path and no realization" and so on.

Second, the contemplation of signlessness means that signs [characteristics] are signless. Why? Because things are unconnected to signs. Thus a scripture says, "Reality is beyond signs, because there is nothing to which it is relative." Scripture also says, "All things are empty and have not the slightest sign; they are empty, without discrimination, just like empty space." The discussion on existence says, "The truth of naturelessness is also not so, because everything is empty."[14] When you see things like this, you leave behind sentimental attachments—therefore it is called contemplation.

Question: If all things are empty, how is contemplation possible?

Answer: It is precisely because all things are empty that contemplation is possible. If they were not empty, it would be erroneous and untrue. How then could we manage to contemplate it?

Question: What sickness does the practice of such contemplation cure?

Answer: It cures the sickness of clinging to elements as mentioned above. What does this mean? The elements are not really

existent—only the deluded see them as existent. It is because of delu-
sory, views that it is said that real suchness and nirvana can be
attained and, moreover, that birth-and-death and contrived effort
are to be abandoned. Because of this view, sickness comes to be;
now knowing that things are empty, one is in accord with things as
they are, without error—therefore it is contemplation. Hence scripture says, "Suchness and the universe, enlightenment and the limit
of reality, as well as all kinds of mentally produced bodies, I say are
mental assessments." Scripture also says, "Because of emptiness
without discrimination I speak of contemplation; all things are
empty, no characteristic is not null."

I have briefly set forth the main outline—think of it along these
lines. In the previous gate the knowledge of the selflessness of person
was realized; here bodhisattvas in the elementary teaching realize
the twin emptiness of persons and things. This is also called the
knowledge of the selflessness of things.

3. CONTEMPLATION OF THE COMPLETE MERGING OF PHENOMENA AND NOUMENON

In the complete merging of the two aspects, phenomenal and
noumenal, into unity, there are two gates: one is the gate of true
thusness of mind; the other is the gate of birth-and-death of mind.
The gate of true thusness of mind is noumenon; the gate of birth-
and-death of mind is phenomena. This is to say that emptiness and
existence are nondual. They freely merge but their concealment and
revelation are not the same, though ultimately there is no interference.

Nonduality means that conditionally originated things seem to
exist but are empty. This emptiness is not vacuity but turns out to be
existence. Existence and emptiness are nondual; they are completely merged in one place. Here the two views [of existence and nonex-
istence] disappear, and emptiness and existence have no interference.

Why? Because reality and falsehood reflect each other and
completely contain and penetrate each other. What does this mean?
Emptiness is emptiness which does not interfere with existence; it is
empty yet always existent. Existence is existence which does not

interfere with emptiness; it exists yet is always empty. Therefore existence is not existent—it is apart from hypostasized existence;[15] emptiness is not empty—it is apart from nihilistic emptiness. Since emptiness and existence merge into one, with no duality, emptiness and existence do not interfere with each other; since they can take away each other's appearance, both are apart from either extreme. Therefore the scripture says, "Entering deeply into conditional origination, you cut off all wrong views; there is no further tendency left toward either extreme of existence or nonexistence." The scripture also says, "Because of causes and conditions things are born; because of causes and conditions things perish—whoever can understand in this way will quickly realize enlightenment." Scripture also says, "The most profound matrix of the issue of thusness is always together with the seven consciousnesses. Two kinds of reception are born, and the wise detach from both."[16] And scripture says, "Defiled yet not defiled—this is hard to comprehend; not defiled yet defiled—this too is hard to comprehend."

According to the meaning of this statement, we can therefore have both cessation and contemplation in practice as compassion and wisdom guide each other. What does this mean? As existence is identical to emptiness and not existent, thereby this is called cessation. As emptiness is identical to existence and not empty, thereby this is called contemplation. Because emptiness and existence contain each other and are not two, yet are two, this realization is both cessation and contemplation. Because emptiness and existence cancel each other and are two yet not two, this realization is neither cessation nor contemplation.

Now let us turn to the question of compassion and wisdom guiding each other. Since existence is identical to emptiness yet does not lose existence, compassion guides wisdom and does not abide in emptiness. Since emptiness is identical to existence yet does not lose emptiness, wisdom guides compassion and does not linger in existence. Because of the great compassion that does not dwell in emptiness, one always goes along with existence, thereby rescuing sentient beings. Because of the great wisdom which does not linger in existence, one always rests in emptiness without experiencing extinction. Extinction is nonextinguishing extinction, extinct yet not extinct; birth is birthless birth, born yet not born. Because birth is not birth, signs of birth are profuse but not existent. Because extinction is not extinction, the signs of emptiness are natural and not empty. Because the signs of emptiness are natural and not empty, birth-and-death and nirvana are not one; because signs of birth are profuse yet not existent, nirvana and birth-and-death are not different. Why? Because emptiness and existence merge and are one yet not one.

This practice can also be analyzed into four propositions:

Because existence is emptiness you do not abide in birth-and-death.

Because emptiness is existence you do not dwell in nirvana.

Because emptiness and existence are one whole, both being there, you dwell both in birth-and-death and in nirvana.

Because emptiness and existence cancel each other out and neither remains, you dwell neither in birth-and-death nor in nirvana.

It is like the metaphor of water and waves: the shapes, which are high and low, are waves; the wetness, which is equal, is water. The waves are waves which are none other than water—the waves themselves show the water. The water is water which is no different from waves—the water makes the waves. Waves and water are one, yet that does not hinder their difference. Water and waves are different, yet that does not hinder their unity. Because of their unhindered unity, being in the water is being in the waves; because of their unhindered difference, dwelling in the waves is not[17] dwelling in the water. Why? Because water and waves are different yet not different.

Scripture says, "Sentient beings are themselves the character of nirvana and do not become any more extinct; moreover, attaining nirvana is the nature of sentient beings, which does not undergo rebirth."

Scripture also says, "Those who come to realize thusness do not see birth-and-death and do not see nirvana. Birth-and-death and nirvana are equal and without distinction."

Scripture also says, "In the unconditioned realm is manifest the conditioned realm, yet without destroying the nature of the unconditioned. The same is true of the conditioned realm."

Scripture also says, "It is not the practice of ordinary people, and not the practice of holy ones—this is a bodhisattva's practice." That is to say, the practice of ordinary people is attached to existence whereas the practice of holy ones abides in nonexistence. Now since existence and nonexistence are not two yet two, are two yet not two, therefore both are transcended, both gone—abruptly cutting off the hundred negations,[18] you see the mind independent. Therefore it is called contemplation.

4. THE END OF WORDS AND VIEWS

The end of words and views is what is meant by the scriptural saying, "The path of verbalization ends, the course of mind dies out." That is, in respect to these two aspects, emptiness and existence, the end of words and views means to leave all realms of verbal discussion and mental activity. There is only true thusness and the knowledge of true thusness. Why? Because existence and emptiness merge completely, cancel each other, and transcend all characteristics. Because whatever thoughts are stirred, all is *thus*. Because ultimately there is no subject or object to be "this and that." Because thusness alone is left—manifest and unhindered by defilement. Scripture says, "Only thusness as such and the knowledge of thusness as such alone subsist" and so on.

Scripture also says, "All things are of the character of extinction and cannot be expressed in words."

Scripture also says, "Reality is beyond all contemplative practices."

Scripture also says, "If you understand real truth, there is no enlightenment."

Question: If you say that emptiness and existence merge and verbalization and views both end, then it's divorced from contemplative practice. How then is it possible to realize entry?

Answer: It's not that *not* speaking means silence. It's precisely because speech itself is *thus*, and hence not apart from reality, that there's no language or verbalization. The same is true of contemplative practice. This can be seen by going back to our discussion. Therefore scripture says there were thirty-two bodhisattvas who each explained that duality is not duality, yet dual, calling it entry into the truth of nonduality.[19] Next came Vimalakīrti, who answered silently—silence without any verbal explanation, which is called real entry into the truth of nonduality, Mañjuśrī praised him, saying, "Good, good! Silence without speech is the real entry into the truth of nonduality." To explain: although Vimalakīrti was silent and said nothing, this was in fact expounding the Teaching. Why? Because all the bodhisattvas gained understanding. What does it mean? Verbal explanation and contemplative practice are themselves the Dharma.[20]

Question: The nonduality of emptiness and existence made that great man Vimalakīrti speechless. And, truly as has been explained, the merging of nature and characteristics means there is nowhere to set the contemplating mind.[21] What the student doesn't understand is this: by what technique can one come to realization?

Answer: You can get it by going through the process of elimination in terms of the principles of emptiness and existence. What does this mean? Because emptiness is contained in existence, existence exists yet is not existent; the view of existence ends here. Because existence is contained in emptiness, emptiness is not empty; the attachment to emptiness is utterly gone. Emptiness and existence enter each other, completely interpenetrating; as emptiness and existence are one, nondual, neither view arises. They intermingle without hindrance, yet without preventing both aspects from remaining. They eliminate each other, merging completely, yet without destroying the nonidentity of both and the disappearance of the pair. Thereby you realize the jewel of completeness and are free, unconstrained by any view. You witness the ocean of nature, and there is no carping criticism. You are calm and peaceful, beyond things, transcending feelings and detached from thoughts. You go far beyond hesitation and deliberation and abruptly shut off the hundred negations. Verbalization and visualization are both cut off, causing the ice of the deluded mind to melt and the clouds of opinions to be cleared away. Only experiential realization can comprehend it—how can it be confined to verbal explanation? This is why Vimalakīrti answered with silence—to show that noumenon goes beyond the bounds of word and language. The heavenly maiden spoke volubly to illustrate how nature is not outside words. Nature is *not* outside words—words themselves are no words; noumenon is beyond the bounds of words—not speaking is itself speaking. Because not speaking is speaking, it cuts off the considerations of emotion and thought; because words are no words, it

cuts off the calculations of the intellectually understanding mind.
Thus they merge and dissolve away—how could it be expressed by
pen or speech? Only by experiential realization will you know it for
yourself. Therefore scripture says, "It is like someone drinking cool
water—only he himself knows how cool it is." The meaning of this
is outside of words. Do not cling to words to think about the principle.

Yet the principle does not go out of words, so do not destroy
them to seek the principle. Understand clearly, investigate, examine thoroughly—then it should naturally become obvious of itself.
Polish carefully—then it should become clear. You must simply
make diligent effort with singleminded, unbending determination.
Whether walking, standing, sitting, or reclining, do not let yourself
give up even for a moment. If you work unceasingly for a long time,
white and black will be distinguished by themselves.[22] This you can
deeply believe in. Therefore scripture says, "It is like someone
athirst seeking water. He digs on the high plain, working without
stopping; gradually, seeing moist earth, he realizes water must be
near."

Scripture also says, "It is like a man kindling a fire with a drill
—if he stops before generating enough heat, the force of the fire will
die out accordingly. The same is true of the lazy."

And a treatise says, "It is like a man crossing a river in a
dream; due to his bold and powerful effort he manages to awaken."

If there is any lapse in the application of effort, if you do a little and then rest, your search for enlightenment will of course be
hard to fulfill and you will spend months and years searching in
vain for understanding. Why? The defilement of beginningless habitual actions is thick and difficult to penetrate. Though you have
an awakening, it dies out after a glimpse; if you do not strive diligently with utmost attention, there is no way to develop the practicing mind. Then all day long you will make illusion your state of
mind and wastefully wear out your strength. Practitioners should
keep this in mind and reflect on it.

5. FLOWER ORNAMENT MEDITATION

But the conditional origination of the universe is hard for the
deluded to lead up to: if you do not clean the defiled mind first,

there is no way to ascend to its perfect awakening. Therefore the *Ta chih tu lun* says, "It is like someone having filth under his nose— even fragrance like musk seems foul."

Therefore the *Vimalakīrti* scripture says, "Don't use born and dying mental activities to expound the teaching of the characteristics of reality."

So first it is necessary to strike down conceptual attachments; only then can you enter complete illumination. If anyone sees immediately that all things, like material form, come from conditions, this is at once the conditional origination of the universe—it is no longer necessary to use the preceding techniques. But those who are not able to enter this stage directly should start from the beginning and proceed to the end, questioning everything one by one, to bring about the cessation of confusion and the end of delusion, to eliminate things, cut off words, see the essential nature, and bring about understanding—only then can this be considered getting the meaning.

Question: How can we see such things as material form and thus be able to enter the great universe of interdependent conditional origination?

Answer: Because the basic true reality of all phenomena such as material form has no explanation, it is beyond the scope of the deluded mind. Therefore scripture says, "Verbal explanation is used separately—true reality is beyond words and letters." Therefore, seeing eyes, ears, and such phenomena, we see them enter into the interdependent conditional origination of the universe. Why? All of them are devoid of real substantial nature. And because of their insubstantiality, illusory characteristics come to be. Because they are born from conditions and do not exist of their own nature, it is because of having no intrinsic nature that there can be illusory existence. For this reason nature and characteristics merge, completely contained in the whole. That is how we enter the great universe of conditional origination upon seeing things.

Question: Since you say that emptiness and existence are nondual and thus enter into communion, how can you also say that, seeing the eyes and ears and the like, you then enter into the true universe?

Answer: If you can see emptiness and existence in this way, erroneous views will end. Then you will be able to enter into the true universe in accord with the noumenon. Why? Because the universe is beyond views, without emotions, profusely evolving myriad forms.

Question: Once we know it is so, how can we enter into it?

Answer: The techniques are not the same; in general there are three kinds. One is to question, to cause views to be exhausted, like pointing out something and questioning it—for example, "What is the eye?" This technique has already been analyzed in six ways in the section on the lesser vehicle. If you enter into the teaching that all things are just names, that there is not a single thing that is not a name, then you should further question *how* you know that the eye and so forth are names. In this way you continue progressively to question the reason in order to obliterate names and end interpretation.

The second technique is to point out elements to make you think. There are two approaches to this matter also. One is to strip away delusion: once you have gone through the process of pointing out something with form, odor, taste, feel, and the like, you get rid of false conceptions. Then you will know they are wrong and delusive and that any attachment and grasping is not in accord with things as they are—attachment to conceptions is formed by the beginningless ingrained habits of delusive views of the cognitive consciousness. Without beginning, suddenly they are induced and continue to produce the three worlds,[23] continuously revolving in routines without break. Once you realize that these attachments are themselves conditionally produced, they are birthless. The second approach is to point out elements and cut off attachments. If you do not know the deluded mind first, however, pointing out the elements leads only to error and confusion. If we do not point out elements to show them, the errant mind then becomes attached to emptiness. Therefore we first strip away the deluded mind and only then point out elements to make you see.

The third technique is to show that things are beyond words and understanding. There are two aspects to this approach also: one is stopping sentiments; the other is revealing qualities.

As for stopping sentiments, we ask, "Does conditional origination exist?" The answer is no, because it is identical to emptiness:

conditionally originating things have no essence and hence are
empty. We ask, "Does it not exist?" The answer is no, because it is
identical to existence, since conditionally originating things depend
on nonexistence in order to exist. We ask, "Does it both exist and not
exist as well?" The answer is no, because emptiness and existence
completely merge into one, without duality, since in conditionally
originating things emptiness and existence are one, with no duality.
Think of it as being like gold and gold ornaments.[24] We ask, "Does it
neither exist nor not exist?" The answer is no, because it does not
hinder the presence of both existence and nonexistence, since in
conditionally originating things emptiness and existence remove
each other and yet are fulfilled at the same time. We ask, "Is it
definitely existent or nonexistent?" The answer is no, because emptiness and existence merge into each other and neither remains. In
conditionally originating things, emptiness cancels existence completely, so there is only emptiness, not existence. Existence cancels
emptiness completely, so there is only existence, not emptiness. Thus
they take each other away simultaneously, so that both aspects disappear together.

As for the second aspect, revealing qualities, we ask, "Is conditional origination existent?" The answer is yes, because illusory existence is not nonexistent. We ask, "Is it nonexistent?" The answer is
yes, because having no nature is the same as emptiness. We ask, "Is
it both existent and nonexistent?" The answer is yes, because it does
not hinder the presence of both. We ask, "Is it neither existent nor
nonexistent?" The answer is yes, because they cancel each other out
and both disappear. Moreover, because of conditional origination
things are existent; because of conditional origination things are
nonexistent; because of conditional origination things are both existent and nonexistent; and because of conditional origination things
are neither existent nor nonexistent. This reasoning leads to the fact
that they are one yet not one, both one and yet not one, not one and
not not one, many and not many, both many and not many, not
many and not not many. In this way they are many and they are
one; they are both many and one; they are neither one nor many.
The tetralemma in terms of identity and nonidentity follows the
same pattern. "Stopping" and "revealing" merge without interference, all due to the freedom of conditional origination. One who is

capable of seeing this will then be able to see the truth of conditional origination. Why? Because complete merging into one realm accords with the vision of truth. If one does not see before and after the same, this is wrong seeing, not right seeing. Why? Because seeing separately before and after is not in accord with truth.

Question: Having seen in this way, how can we enter the realm of reality?

Answer: "Means of entry" is found in the context of conditionally originating things. What does this mean? That these conditionally originating things are empty and without inherent nature: it is precisely because they are without nature that illusory existence can come to be. Thus the reality of these things is that their nature is natureless. Therefore these things are without nature and yet do not hinder the presence of forms. If they were not without nature, then conditional origination could not take place, because their inherent natures are unborn, as all come from interdependent conditional origination. Since they are all included, their nature exhausted, the nature is uncompounded and cannot be discriminated—whether they are great or small, the nature is not incomplete in any of them. And the whole of them too is at once the embodiment of the whole nature. Therefore all "that" becomes "this"—that is, nature does not hinder illusory forms. That is why one encompasses the multitude. Even though "that" and "this" completely contain each other, that does not hinder the distinction between "that" and "this." Therefore in "that" there is "this" and in "this" there is "that."

Therefore scripture says, "Things have the same nature, because it is in all things." By way of explanation, "things" refers to conditionally originating things, which have illusory existence. The "same nature" means that, being conditionally produced, they are empty, yet without that preventing their appearances. Therefore "that" is completely contained in being "this," since "that" is empty yet without hindering the appearance of "that." Since "this" and "that" are completely contained in each other's definition, neither is destroyed. Therefore within "this" there is "that" and within "that" there is "this." It is not simply that "that" and "this" include each other—it is so of everything. Scripture says, "In one understand infinity, in infinity understand one; the procession of births is not real—the wise have no fear." It is also said, "In one thing understand many things; in many things understand one thing." Thus, including each other, "that" and "this" enter each other, immediately appearing simultaneously, without before or after. Whichever one completely merges, therefore, wholly contains "that" and "this."

Question: Things being thus, what about knowledge?

Answer: Knowledge accords with things, being in one and the same realm, made by conditions, tacitly conjoining, without rejecting anything, suddenly appearing, yet not without before and after. Therefore scripture says, "The sphere of the universal eye, the pure body, I now will expound; let people listen carefully." By way of explanation, the "universal eye" is the union of knowledge and reality, all at once revealing many things. This makes it clear that reality is known to the knowledge of the universal eye only and is not the sphere of any other knowledge. The "sphere" means things. This illustrates how the many things interpenetrate like the realm of Indra's net of jewels—multiplied and remultiplied ad infinitum. The pure body illustrates how all things, as mentioned before, simultaneously enter each other. Ends and beginnings, being collectively formed by conditional origination, are impossible to trace to a basis—the seeing mind has nothing to rest on.

Now the celestial jewel net of Kanishka, or Indra, Emperor of Gods, is called the net of Indra. This imperial net is made all of jewels: because the jewels are clear, they reflect each other's images, appearing in each other's reflections upon reflections, ad infinitum, all appearing at once in one jewel, and in each one it is so—ultimately there is no going or coming.

Now for the moment let us turn to the southwest direction and pick a jewel and check it. This jewel can show the reflections of all the jewels all at once—and just as this is so of this jewel, so it is of every other jewel: the reflection is multiplied and remultiplied over and over endlessly. These infinitely multiplying jewel reflections are all in one jewel and show clearly—the others do not hinder this. If you sit in one jewel, then you are sitting in all the jewels in every direction, multiplied over and over. Why? Because in one jewel there are all the jewels. If there is one jewel in all the jewels, then you are sitting in all the jewels too. And the reverse applies to the totality if you follow the same reasoning. Since in one jewel you go into all the jewels without leaving this one jewel, so in all jewels you enter one jewel without leaving this one jewel.

Question: If you say that one enters all the jewels in one jewel without ever leaving this one jewel, how is it possible to enter all the jewels?

Answer: It is precisely by not leaving this one jewel that you can enter all the jewels. If you left this one jewel to enter all the jewels, you couldn't enter all the jewels. Why? Because outside this jewel there are no separate jewels.

Question: If there are no jewels outside this one jewel, then this net is made of one jewel. How can you say then that it's made of many jewels tied together?

Answer: It is precisely because there is only one jewel that many can be joined to form a net. Why? Because this one jewel alone forms the net—that is, if you take away this jewel there will be no net.

Question: If there is only one jewel, how can you speak of tying it into a net?

Answer: Tying many jewels to form a net is itself just one jewel. Why? "One" is the aspect of totality, containing the many in its formation. Since all would not exist if there were not one, this net is therefore made by one jewel. The all entering the one can be known by thinking about it in this way.

Question: Although the jewel in the southwest contains all the jewels in the ten directions completely, without remainder, there are jewels in every direction. How can you say then that the net is made of just one jewel?

Answer: All the jewels in the ten directions are in totality the one jewel of the southwest. Why? The jewel in the southwest *is* all the jewels of the ten directions. If you don't believe that one jewel in the southwest is all the jewels in the ten directions, just put a dot on the jewel in the southwest. When one jewel is dotted, there are dots on all the jewels in all directions. Since there are dots on all the jewels in the ten directions, we know that all the jewels are one jewel. If anyone says that all the jewels in the ten directions are not one jewel in the southwest, could it be that one person simultaneously put dots on all the jewels in the ten directions? Even allowing the universal dotting of all the jewels in the ten directions, they are just one jewel. Since it is thus, using this one as beginning, the same is so when taking others first—multiplied over and over boundlessly, each dot is the same. It is obscure and hard to fathom: when one is complete, all is done. Such a subtle metaphor is applied to things to help us think about them, but things are not so; a simile is the same as not a simile—they resemble each other in a way, so we use it to speak of. What does this mean? These jewels only have their reflected images containing and entering each other—their substances are separate. Things are not like this, because their whole substance merges completely. The book on natural origination in the Hua-yen scripture says, "In order to benefit sentient beings and make them all understand, nonsimiles are used to illustrate real truth. Such a subtle teaching as this is hard to hear even in immeasurable eons; only those with perseverance and wisdom can hear of the matrix of the issue of thusness." The scripture says, "Nonsimiles are used as similes. Those who practice should think of this in accord with the similes."

> Vairocana Buddha's past practices
> Made oceans of Buddha-fields all pure.
> Immeasurable, innumerable, boundless,
> He freely permeates all places.
> The reality-body of the Buddha is inconceivable;
> Formless, signless, without comparison,
> It manifests material forms for the sake of beings.
> In the ten directions they receive its teaching,
> Nowhere not manifest.
> In the atoms of all Buddha-fields
> Vairocana manifests self-subsistent power,
> Promising the thundering sound of the ocean of Buddhahood
> To tame all the species of sentient beings.

This is the teaching of cessation and contemplation for practitioners cultivating the Way to weed out error and enter into truth.

Mirror of the Mysteries of the Universe of the Hua-yen

by Tu Shun and Cheng-kuan

THIS IS AN ANALYTIC COMMENTARY by Cheng-kuan on Tu Shun's seminal treatise *Fa-chieh kuan,* "Contemplation of the Realm of Reality," which forms the foundation of Hua-yen dialectics. The treatise begins with a four-part treatment of the identity of form (matter/existence) and emptiness. The first part, on form being identical to emptiness, proceeds thus: (1) Form is not nihilistic emptiness. (2) Characteristics of form are not themselves emptiness. (3) There is no form in emptiness and there is no substance in form. (4) Therefore form is emptiness, being neither the annihilation of form nor the hypostatization of form. Emptiness is not formal characteristics, because it has no mental projection; form, being conditionally originated, has no intrinsic nature and is therefore identical to emptiness.

The second part deals with emptiness being identical to form: (1) Nihilistic emptiness is not form; true emptiness is not different from form. (2) The principle of emptiness is not characteristics of form but is not different from characteristics. (3) Emptiness is that which is depended on, not that which depends. (4) The principle of things having no self is precisely the essence of true emptiness.

The third part treats the mutual noninterference of emptiness and form. If form were solid or inherently real, it would obstruct emptiness; if emptiness were nihilistic voidness, it would obstruct form. Since form is illusory form, it does not obstruct emptiness; since emptiness is emptiness of reality, it does not obstruct form.

The fourth part concerns the disappearance of form and emptiness and the realization of independence. True emptiness cannot be said to be identical to form, since if emptiness were form, sages would see illusory form the same as ordinary people, and ordinary people would see true emptiness the same as sages, and there would not be two levels of reality. Yet one cannot say that emptiness is *not* identical to form, because if they were not identical one would see emptiness outside of form—then there would be no basis for development of wisdom and the ordinary and the wise would be forever separate, because sagehood could not be achieved by the ordinary. Moreover, form cannot be said to be identical to emptiness because then the delusion of ordinary people seeing forms would be the same as the wisdom of sages seeing emptiness and there would no longer be two levels of reality. Then again one cannot say that form is *not* identical to emptiness, because if it were not empty then ordinary people would not be deluded in seeing form and the forms they see would be forever distinct from true emptiness and they would never become sages.

After this discussion of form and emptiness, Tu Shun's treatise goes on to bring out ten aspects of the relativity of noumenon (emptiness) and phenomena (existence) and ten aspects of the universal mutual inclusion of phenomena; these aspects I have explained in the Introduction. This treatise by Tu Shun is the source of the key Hua-yen doctrines of the four realms of reality and the ten mysterious gates. Cheng-kuan's commentary, a typical example of his style of work, was composed in response to requests from his students who found the immense volume and range of his scriptural commentary too vast and needed a more concise statement of Hua-yen philosophy.

TU SHUN'S CONTEMPLATION: Cultivating the contemplation of the realm of reality of the Great Universally Extensive Buddha's Flower Ornament. There are, in brief, three levels. By the Buddhist monk Fa-shun of Mount Chung-nan, whose lay surname was Tu.

CHENG-KUAN'S ANALYSIS: The six words "Great Universally Extensive Buddha's Flower Ornament" refer to the scripture on which this work is based. The word "scripture" is omitted. "Contemplation of the realm of reality" is the contemplation based on the scripture. First we shall briefly analyze the name of the scripture. "Great Universally Extensive" is the reality realized by all enlightened ones. "Buddha's Flower Ornament" conjoins the realm of reality and the person who realizes it. The reality is analyzed into substance, characteristics, and function: in the person there is cause and effect. "Great" means the immensity of the substance, which is the profound realm of reality, the mind-substance of Buddhas and sentient beings: all-inclusive like space, still and silent, permanent, the appellation "great" is forced on it. Therefore the scripture says, "The nature of reality is everywhere—all beings and lands of all times are all in it; yet it has no graspable forms." This is the meaning of "great."

As for "universally extensive," characteristics and function being omnipresent is the characteristic of the substance; the boundlessness of the realities which are its characteristic qualities is the function of the characteristics. The active function is infinitely extensive. These three have no mutual obstruction—bring up one and all are included.

The object of enlightened knowledge is the realm of reality which is realized. "Buddha" is the fruition, in which myriad virtues are complete and manifest. "Flower" symbolizes cause, myriad practices gloriously shining; "ornament" applies to both subject and object and has two levels. First, the "flower" cause is that which ornaments and the fruition "Buddha" is that which is ornamented. By the cause of the ten transcendent ways[1] are perfected the result of the ten bodies;[2] no practice is not fulfilled, no virtue not complete. Second, the "flower" is that which adorns and the "great universal" is that which is adorned. Adorning with the substance, characteristics, and function produces the three qualities of Buddhahood: adornment in conformity with the substance shows the quality of real eternity; adornment according to characteristics elucidates the quality of cultivated development; cultivating adornment based on the function completes the quality of the great function. The universal adornment of the quality of suchness and the quality of completeness is the boundless flower ornament. Thus in the title as a whole there is substance, characteristics, and function; the person has cause and result. The person and the teaching are both in the title; principle and metaphor are brought up at once. The threefold greatness of the one scripture is all "great and universally extensive";[3] the fivefold pervasive cause and effect is all together the "Buddha's flower ornament."[4]

The seven characters of the title each have ten meanings. I shall explain them briefly. As for the ten meanings of "great," the seven characters all are "great." (1) "Great" is the greatness of the substance, because the realm of reality is always omnipresent. (2) "Universal" is the greatness of the characteristics, because the natural qualities are boundless. (3) "Extensive" is the greatness of the function, because the function in accord with the substance is all-pervasive. (4) "Buddha" is the greatness of the result, because the ten bodies all extend throughout the universe. (5) "Flower" is the greatness of the cause, because the practice and vows of Samantabhadra are inherently universal. (6) "Ornament" is the greatness of knowledge, because the Buddha's knowledge is like space and can be an adornment. (7) "Scripture" is the greatness of the teaching, because an ocean of ink cannot write even a single line. (8) There is the greatness of meaning, because the realization of the preceding six words is in accord with nature. (9) There is the greatness of the sphere, because totality of the seven words has all living beings as its sphere. (10) There is the greatness of the work, because the message of this teaching extends everywhere throughout time and space, without pause. Because it includes these ten infinities, it is called great.

As for the ten meanings of "universally extensive," the characteristics conforming to the substance and the function in accord with the substance are ten great functions of all things in the ten directions.[5]

We come now to the ten meanings of "Buddha." (1) The "great" is the reality body—the Buddha has reality for a body, because the reality-body fills the universe. (2) "Universal" is the body of knowledge, because knowledge is in accord with truth. (3) "Extensive" includes the third and fourth bodies: the emanation body—because one body extends everywhere, without measure; and the mentally produced body—being one or many at will reaching everywhere. (4) "Buddha" contains the fifth and sixth bodies: the body of enlightenment, because enlightenment is realized under the tree of enlightenment; and the body of power, because the first realization of enlightenment overshadows the bodhisattvas. (5) "Flower" contains the seventh and eighth bodies: the seventh is the body of virtue, the myriad virtues practiced in past, present, and future, the ocean of cause, which cannot be exhausted; the eighth is the body of vows, Vairocana's vows, as causes, pervading the universe. (6) "Ornament" is the body adorned with distinguishing marks and refinements, adorned by the marks and refinements of ten lotus blossom treasuries.[6] (7) "Scripture" is the body holding the ten powers—the relics, the universal sound's teachings, are inexhaustible.[7] Thus the seven characters of the scripture title all constitute Buddhahood.

We come now to the ten meanings of "flower ornament." By means of the flower ornament of the ten transcendent ways making adornments for the ten bodies, each is different and so there are ten ornaments. The word "scripture" is omitted, so we omit the ten meanings of scripture too. This is inclusive, this is pervasive, this is constant, this is the norm—all should be known. The ocean of inexhaustible teachings is not beyond the seven words. Therefore the method of contemplation is based on this scripture.

We come now to "cultivating contemplation of the realm of reality has in brief three levels." To summarize the essentials, the word "cultivate" is cessation and contemplation applying to the whole title; it is training, practical study, and attainment. "Realm of reality" is the mystic source of the whole scripture, because the whole thing has the inconceivability of the reality-realm of interdependent origination as its source. The characteristics of the realm of reality are essentially only three in number, but in all it has four kinds: first is the reality-realm of phenomena; second is the reality-

realm of noumenon; third is the reality-realm of noninterference of
noumenon and phenomena; fourth is the reality-realm of noninterference among phenomena. Now we are dealing with the latter
three realms. The phenomenal reality-realm is impossible to set
forth in all its particulars, since the characteristics of each individual phenomenon can form a contemplation; therefore I shall not
explain them. The totality makes the substance on which three contemplations are based. The phenomena contain, briefly speaking,
ten pairs: (1) doctrine and meaning; (2) principle and phenomena;
(3) object and knowledge; (4) practice and state; (5) cause and result; (6) objective and subjective; (7) substance and function; (8) person and teachings; (9) retrogression and progression; (10) sense and
response. Each phenomenon becomes the very substance on which
are based three contemplations.

CONTEMPLATION: Number one: contemplation of true emptiness. Number two: contemplation of noninterference of noumenon
and phenomena. Number three: contemplation of universality and
inclusion.

ANALYSIS: This lists the three names. "True emptiness" is
the reality-realm of noumenon. The second is as the name indicates. The third is the reality-realm of noninterference among phenomena.

First, "true emptiness" is not nihilistic emptiness or emptiness
apart from material form. Therefore existence reveals emptiness
although there is no appearance of emptiness—which is why it is
called true emptiness. This idea is fully encompassed in the text.

Second, as for the noninterference of noumenon and phenomena, noumenon has no form but is completely within forms; because they interrelate and mutually negate each other, both affirm-
ing and denying, it is called noninterference. This too is fully
encompassed in the text.

Third, as for universality and inclusion, phenomena basically
obstruct each other, being different in size and so forth; noumenon basically includes everything, like space, without obstruction:
merging phenomena by noumenon, the totality of phenomena is
like noumenon—even a mote of dust or a hair has the capacity of
including the totality. These two, in interdependence, produce ten
facets which also are explained below.

In naming a phenomenon a "realm," by "realm" we mean

division—referring to phenomena in terms of the divisions of infinite differentiations. In naming noumenon a "realm," by "realm" we mean nature, because infinite phenomena have the same unitary nature. The reality-realm of noninterference contains both senses of division and nature. Without destroying phenomena and noumenon, there is still no interference between them; therefore the four reality-realms also contain both meanings, because nature merges phenomena but individual phenomena do not lose their forms—in accord with nature they merge, multiplied and remultiplied without end.[8]

CONTEMPLATION: First is the method of contemplating true emptiness: therein are made, in sum, four statements and ten aspects.

ANALYSIS: This tells what the chapter is about. The first two statements each have four aspects; adding the third and fourth statements makes ten aspects.

CONTEMPLATION: First: the contemplation of resolving form into emptiness. Second: the contemplation of clarifying the identity of emptiness to form. Third: the contemplation of the noninterference of form and emptiness. Fourth: the contemplation of effacement and nonreliance.

ANALYSIS: Here he lists the names.

CONTEMPLATION: In the first approach we make four propositions. One: form is not identical to emptiness, because it is identical to emptiness. Why? Since form is not nihilistic emptiness, it is not emptiness; since the totality of form is true emptiness, we say "because it is identical to emptiness." It is precisely because it is true emptiness that it is not nihilistic emptiness; that is why we say because it is emptiness it is not emptiness.

ANALYSIS: Each of the four contemplations has three stages: statement, analysis, conclusion. According to the following text, the first three propositions eliminate conceptions by means of principle and the fourth reveals the true principle. The three propositions eliminating conceptions are the same in title but different in analysis of meaning. Now we shall clarify what the three propositions eliminate. What they eliminate are three: (1) identity and distinction are eliminated; (2) wrong ideas are eliminated; (3) forms and appearances are eliminated. In the first place, to speak in general terms, all three propositions eliminate identity and distinction; to speak in terms of major divisions, the first proposition explains that emptiness is not apart from form, thereby eliminating distinctness from form; the next proposition explains that emptiness is not identical to form, thereby eliminating extreme identification; the third proposition explains both nonidentity and nondistinctness, thereby eliminating coexistence of identity and distinctness. Proceeding from the elimination of these three conceptions, the fourth proposition reveals the true principle. In the second place, we eliminate wrong ideas. This means, as the *Ratnagotra-śāstra* explains, that bodhisattvas before the stages have three wrong ideas of emptiness; because they do not know that birth-and-death and nirvana are equal in the matrix of the issue of thusness, they grasp three kinds of emptiness. First is emptiness because of annihilation; the first proposition [that form is not nihilistic emptiness] eliminates this. Second is emptiness outside of form; the third proposition [that emptiness is the emptiness of form] eliminates this. Third is considering emptiness to exist; the second proposition [that emptiness has no form] eliminates this. Having eliminated the three untrue kinds of emptiness, the fourth proposition [that form is itself emptiness] explains true emptiness.[9]

Next we shall correctly analyze the passage. To begin with, there are three parts to the first proposition. First is the statement; second, the text following "why" presents the analysis or explanation, which here eliminates emptiness as apart from form and nihilistic emptiness. "Apart from form" means emptiness existing outside of form. And "outside of form" also has two meanings: the first is emptiness as annihilation of form—as in digging a well, removing earth to get emptiness, where it is necessary to get rid of the material form, this is what is being eliminated here. This is why the "Treatise on the Mean"[10] says, "Previously existing then subsequently not existing is considered annihilation." Non-Buddhists and Buddhists of the two vehicles both have annihilation: non-Buddhists, annihilated, return to the "great void"; those of the two vehicles, annihilated, return to nirvana. Therefore Seng-chao says, "There is no greater illusion than having a body—therefore they annihilate the body to return to absence of toil; there is no greater trouble than having knowledge—therefore they cut off knowledge to sink into the void." He also says, "Knowledge is mixed poison; corporeality is bondage. Therefore they reduce the body to ashes and extinguish knowledge, rooting them out entirely."[11] If you think that entering extinction is the same as the "great void," you are the same as a non-Buddhist. Therefore the *Laṅkāvatāra* scripture says, "If the substance of the mind perishes, that is no different from the nihilistic view of outsiders, because it is a false doctrine."[12] The present text says, "Not nihilistic emptiness."

Next, the text following "since the totality of form . . ." explains the statement above "because it is identical to emptiness." Therefore, what follows "precisely because" forms the third part or conclusion. First the conclusion is based on the meaning; because of identity to true emptiness form is not nihilistic emptiness. Then, after "that is why," the conclusion is completed by naming the proposition.

CONTEMPLATION: Two: form is not identical to emptiness, because it is identical to emptiness. Why? Since the characteristics of blue and yellow and so forth are not the principle of real emptiness, we say "not identical to emptiness." Blue and yellow have no substantiality and are all empty, however, so we say "identical to emptiness." Indeed, because the emptiness of the insubstantiality of blue and yellow is not identical to blue and yellow, we therefore say "not identical to emptiness."

ANALYSIS: Again we have a statement, an explanation, and a conclusion. The explanation eliminates two delusions. First, it eliminates extreme identification: hearing that form is empty but not knowing emptiness of nature [emptiness of inherent essence or identity], one will grasp characteristics of form as real emptiness. Since it is necessary to eliminate this, he says that the characteristics blue and yellow are not the principle of true emptiness. This only eliminates the delusion of the ordinary, because those of the lesser vehicle [Hinayana Buddhism] do not consider form to be identical to emptiness.

Next, the text following "Blue and yellow have no . . ." makes it clear that there is no nature apart from characteristics. Essentially, as blue and yellow have no substance they are real emptiness. The second part also uses the preceding statement to eliminate, among the three erroneous ideas of emptiness, the idea that emptiness is existent. Those who hold this idea think there is something distinct which they affirm as the entity of emptiness; hence this idea is now eliminated. Therefore the "Ten Stages" scripture says that existence is nondual and inexhaustible.[13] This one line of scripture eliminates the three wrong ideas of emptiness: with "existence" it eliminates nihilistic emptiness; with "nondual" it eliminates emptiness as different from form; with "inexhaustible" it eliminates considering emptiness an existent. This does not mean that the substance of existence perishes. The present application of "inexhaustible" means that if emptiness were a thing it would eventually perish, in which case it would have birth-and-death, whereas the empty character of things as presented here is not born and does not perish—how then could it have existence? Therefore the ["Heart"] scripture on transcendent wisdom says, "This empty character of things is not born and does not perish" and so on.[14] Moreover, since the characteristics of blue and yellow are still not true emptiness, they must have no nature—how then could emptiness be considered existent?

Finally, the text following "indeed, because . . ." concludes that emptiness is not formal characteristics—since emptiness is not existent, how could it have form?

CONTEMPLATION: Three: form is not identical to emptiness, because it is identical to emptiness. Why? Since there is no form in emptiness, it is not identical to emptiness. Since the totality of form has no substance, it is identical to emptiness. It is precisely because the totality of form is ultimately empty that there cannot be form in emptiness: because form is emptiness, therefore, form is not emptiness. The preceding three propositions have eliminated conceptions by principle.

ANALYSIS: Here the text is twofold: first it explains the proposition at hand; then it concludes the foregoing three. In the first part there are also three stages: first is the statement; second is the analysis. In the analysis it first does away with both identity and distinction. Because there is no form in emptiness, form is not identical to emptiness; because there is no substance apart from form, emptiness is not apart from form—not identical yet not apart, this finally is true emptiness.[15] It then eliminates the wrong idea of emptiness as different from form, the idea which clings to an existent emptiness outside of form and considers it different from form, like the previous explaining of emptiness in contrast to form. Here it explains that since there is no form in emptiness, how could there be an emptiness existing in contrast to form? Furthermore, the totality of form is insubstantial and is therefore said to be identical to emptiness—is there emptiness outside of form which contrasts to form? An ancient said, "Form gone, not leaving emptiness, emptiness does not abide in the realm of being."[16]

Third, the text following "is emptiness" concludes that the preceding "is not emptiness." It is precisely because the whole of form is empty that there cannot be form in emptiness.

CONTEMPLATION: Four: form is emptiness. Why? Because material things are necessarily not different from emptiness and because material things necessarily lack inherent nature. Therefore form is emptiness; since form is empty, so too are all things. Ponder this.

ANALYSIS: Here there are two parts: bringing out the meaning of real emptiness and then applying it to all things. In the first part again there are three stages: first is the statement; second is the explanation. Since forms come from conditions, they must lack inherent nature or identity—their lack of inherent nature due to dependence on something else is identical to the completeness of real emptiness.[17] And third, after "therefore," is the conclusion. Since it is not annihilation of form and is not different from form, is not identical and is not distinct, it is therefore none other than true emptiness. Emptiness is not the characteristics of form, because there is no mental fabrication in it.[18] The lack of inherent nature in that which is conditionally produced is the lack of inherent nature or identity in that which depends on something else. The true principle of naturelessness or identitylessness is identical to completeness.[19] Therefore this true emptiness contains and permeates both nature and characteristics.

In the second part, the text following "since form is empty" concludes with an application to all things. The foregoing four propositions only explain the emptiness of form. Because form is the chief characteristic of phenomena and the first of the five clusters,[20] whenever the various scriptures and treatises expound the ultimate truth, they do it first in terms of form. In the great scripture on transcendent wisdom and others, eighty-odd categories from form on up to the knowledge of specifics are all therefore exemplified by form; the present work too uses form to exemplify all things. If we were to sum them up, things are not beyond the ten pairs previously mentioned—the phenomena which provide the basis are all identical to emptiness. Conceptions about all of them should be eliminated by means of this teachings, which reveals that phenomena are identical to noumenon.

CONTEMPLATION: Second approach: explaining the contemplation of emptiness being form. Here too there are four aspects.

ANALYSIS: This is the general heading. These four aspects in sum are simply the reverse of the four in the preceding part. Here again the first three propositions eliminate conceptions by means of principle, and the fourth proposition reveals the principle of the teaching. In the elimination of conceptions, reverse the foregoing form and emptiness and its meaning is about the same, though the wording is a bit different. The headings too are the same, but the analyses of meaning are different.

First comes a general refutation, which also has three meanings: (1) refuting identity and difference; (2) eliminating wrong ideas; (3) eliminating shape and color. To begin with, the first proposition explains that real emptiness is not apart from present form; the second proposition explains that real emptiness is not identical to the characteristics or appearances of form; the third proposition explains that real emptiness is neither identical to form nor apart from it. Then comes elimination of the three wrong ideas: the first proposition explains that nihilistic emptiness is not actual substantial form. The second proposition explains that the existence of appearances is not real emptiness—this eliminates the idea of the real existence of appearances or characteristics. The third proposition explains that that which is depended on is not that which depends—this eliminates that which depends.[21]

CONTEMPLATION: One: emptiness is not identical to form, because emptiness is identical to form. What is the reason? Nihilistic emptiness is not identical to form, so we say it is not form; real emptiness cannot be other than form, so we say it is identical to form. Since true emptiness is identical to form, this essentially causes nihilistic emptiness not to be identical to form.

ANALYSIS: This proposition too has three parts: first is the statement; second is the explanation. Analyzing the two meanings, the first is that nihilistic emptiness is not actual form; this corresponds to the statement that actual form is not nihilistic emptiness as presented in the previous section on form being identical to emptiness. The second meaning is that real emptiness is not different from form; this corresponds to the previous elucidation of emptiness as not apart from form. Although it includes both identity and difference, the second meaning brings up the truth while the first is the conception that is eliminated—the conception that emptiness is apart from form. Moreover, in terms of eliminating wrong ideas, it points out that nihilistic emptiness is not actual form, corresponding to the statement in the previous contemplation of reducing all form to emptiness that actual form is not nihilistic emptiness. And third, in the text following "Essentially, since true emptiness . . . ," the conclusion is made by bringing up the true conclusion with the second meaning, the first being the conception to be eliminated.[22]

CONTEMPLATION: Two: emptiness is not identical to form, because emptiness is identical to form. What is the reason? Because the principle of emptiness is not blue or yellow and so forth, we say that emptiness is not identical to form. Because true emptiness which is not blue or yellow cannot be other than blue and yellow, however, we say that emptiness is identical to form. Because it is not different from blue and yellow but not identical to blue and yellow, we say that emptiness is identical to form and not identical to form.

ANALYSIS: This proposition too has three parts. First is the statement. In the explanation, first identity and difference are eliminated: explaining that true emptiness is not identical to the appearance or characteristics of form with the statement that emptiness is not identical to form eliminates overidentification or extreme identification. This corresponds to the statement, presented in the previous contemplation of resolving form into emptiness, that appearances or characteristics of form are not true emptiness. After that, the text beginning "Because true emptiness which is not blue or yellow cannot be other than blue and yellow" explains that emptiness which is not identical to form is also not completely outside of form. This corresponds to the previous denial of emptiness being apart from the existence of characteristics. Then, to eliminate conceptions, it eliminates the supposition that emptiness is existent. Since the principle of emptiness is not blue and yellow and so forth, how could it be existent? This corresponds to the previous statement that true emptiness is not the existence of appearances or characteristics. Third, the text following "Because it is not different . . ." concludes by bringing up the truth of nondifference to settle the foregoing conception of extreme identification.

CONTEMPLATION: Three: emptiness is not identical to form, because emptiness is identical to form. What is the reason? Since emptiness is that which is depended on, not that which depends, it is not identical to form. Since it necessarily serves as that which is depended on for that which depends, it is form. It is precisely because it is that which is depended on that it is not form; yet since it is that which is depended on, it is form—therefore because it is not form it is form. These three propositions have also eliminated conceptions by means of principle.

ANALYSIS: In this passage too there are two parts: explaining this proposition and then concluding the foregoing three propositions. In the former part are another three stages. First is the statement, or heading; in the second stage, the explanation, comes the elimination of both identity and difference, which is obvious. Previously these were eliminated in terms of there being no form in emptiness; here, however, they are eliminated in terms of that which depends not being that which is depended on. Moreover, to contrast properly to the former it should obviously say "Because in form there is no emptiness," but it does not say this: one finds "in emptiness there is no form" in the reasoning and expressed in the text, but there is no passage or reasoning stating that "in form there is no emptiness." This is because, there being no form in emptiness, since phenomena are identical to noumenon, noumenon is void of appearances, so form must have emptiness—because form without emptiness is not actual. Therefore it does not reverse the former statement but instead interprets the meaning in terms of that which depends and that which is depended on. Therefore it is eliminating form which is different from emptiness, in contrast to the previous elimination of the explanation of emptiness different from form.

Third, in the text following "It is precisely because . . ." comes the conclusion, which sums up both nonidentity and nondifference by means of one point: "that which is relied on." The sense of it is this: since it is emptiness which is depended on, it surely is not form, which depends on it, so it says emptiness is not identical to form. Moreover, since it is that upon which form depends and thus not a basis for something else [other than form/existence], it is not apart from form.

As for settling wrong ideas, since emptiness is necessarily that upon which dependent form depends, this explanation makes it clear that form is not outside emptiness. This meaning is coordinate with the previous statement that emptiness is not outside form.

CONTEMPLATION: Four: emptiness is identical to form. Why? Because true emptiness is necessarily not other than form. Since this principle of the absence of identity or self in things is not nihilistic emptiness, therefore emptiness is form. As with emptiness and form, so it is of all things. Ponder this.

ANALYSIS: This passage too has two parts: explaining the fourth proposition and then concluding by aligning all things [with the principle]. Now the first part also has three stages: first is the statement; second is the explanation. "Since this principle of the absence of identity or self in things . . ." puts forth the reason. Selflessness is emptiness; hence the emptiness of things is the selflessness of things, wherefore emptiness is form. And third, "Therefore emptiness is form" concludes this proposition. Then, "As with emptiness and form" concludes by bringing up the four propositions or aspects; since emptiness is form, accordingly emptiness is all things. Is it not that upon which the ten pairs [mentioned at the outset of the treatise] depend?

CONTEMPLATION: Third approach: the contemplation of the noninterference of form and emptiness. This means that the whole of form is none other than emptiness. Because it is entirely the emptiness which is the totality of form, therefore emptiness appears without form being ended. Emptiness as a whole is none other than form; because it is entirely the form of the totality of emptiness, therefore emptiness is identical to form yet emptiness is not eclipsed. Thus when bodhisattvas contemplate form, in no case do they not see emptiness; when they contemplate emptiness, in no case are they not seeing form. Without obstruction or interference, form and emptiness are one uniform reality. If you think about it you can grasp it.

ANALYSIS: This contemplation has three parts: the name or heading, the analysis or explanation, and the summary or conclusion. Following the second sentence, "This means that the whole of form . . . ," where the explanation says "it is entirely the emptiness of the totality of form," there is a version of the text which does not have the words "of the totality of form," only saying, "it is entirely empty"—yet the meaning of the explanation still comes across. But because it does not match the following passage ("it is entirely the form of the totality of emptiness") and the principle is not wholly revealed, I am basing my analysis on the version which does contain the words "of the totality of form."

However, "form" is a different name, or a particular appellation, applying to existence in general, so emptiness and form simply means the two aspects emptiness and existence. Emptiness and existence each have two meanings. The two meanings of emptiness are "empty" and "not empty." The two meanings of existence are "existent" and "not existent." We speak of emptiness in emptiness because emptiness must exhaust existence.[23] We say it is not empty because it has no feature or characteristic of emptiness, and also because it does not interfere with existence. We speak of existence in existence because existence must exhaust emptiness. We speak of nonexistence because the characteristics of existence are removed,[24] and also because it does not hinder emptiness.

Now, in explaining the noninterference of form and emptiness, first to be explained is how form does not hinder emptiness, taking the given sense of emptiness as the whole of form; next to be explained is how emptiness does not hinder form, taking the given sense of form as the whole of emptiness. Their mutual noninterference is the meaning of "the whole of" and "is entirely."[25] The sense of detachment from or removal of the appearance of [both] emptiness and form is in the fourth approach, on effacement.

In this section of the text there are three propositions each about form and emptiness: in each case the first statement is the heading or proposition of noninterference, after which are set forth the characteristics of noninterference. In setting forth the characteristics within form, he says that emptiness is manifest without form being ended, because since form does not hinder emptiness, form does not end;[26] since this is none other than the emptiness which is the whole of form, emptiness is manifest. In setting forth the characteristics [of noninterference] in emptiness, where it says that emptiness itself is identical to form and yet is not eclipsed, because emptiness does not hinder form, therefore emptiness is identical to form; yet because this is emptiness which is the whole of form, emptiness is not hidden. If we were to summarize the matter, it says simply that the totality of form is emptiness, so form does not come to an end; and since it is identical to emptiness, therefore emptiness is manifest. The same reasoning applies to emptiness: because the totality of emptiness is form, emptiness is identical to form; and since emptiness is form, emptiness is not hidden. If we interpret the version without the words "of the totality of form" on this basis, the meaning and principle also carry; in that case we should have to eliminate the words "of the totality of emptiness" in the following sentence. Here I go by the version which has the words in question.

Finally, the text after "Thus" concludes with the establishment of noninterference. The preceding text was the explanation of what is contemplated; here it shows the contemplator—therefore it says, "when bodhisattvas contemplate form" and so on.

CONTEMPLATION: Fourth approach: the contemplation of effacement and nonreliance. This means that the emptiness which is contemplated cannot be said to be identical to form or not identical to form; nor can it be said to be emptiness or not to be emptiness. No doctrines are appropriate. "Not appropriate" is not appropriate either, and this statement too is not accepted—transcending absolutely, with no resort, it is not within reach of speech or understanding. This is called the sphere of practice. Why? Because if you arouse the mind and stir thoughts you turn away from the essence of truth and lose right mindfulness.

ANALYSIS: This fourth contemplation is divided into two major parts: the first explains this fourth contemplation; the latter part deals with the preceding three contemplations, assembling the explanation into a whole. The portion of the text we are analyzing now belongs to the first of these parts. There are three steps: first, indicating the name; second, the text following "This means" explains the features of the contemplation; third, the text following "Why?" brings forth the conclusion. The overall intent here is simply to sweep away the tracks and reveal the whole in its entirety. If we analyze in detail, the interdependence of form and emptiness has multiple meanings. One is the meaning of merging the two truths [conventional and real]:[27] the first contemplation, resolving form into emptiness, makes it clear that the conventional truth is therefore identical to the real truth; the second contemplation, showing that emptiness is identical to form, reveals that the real is identical to the conventional; the third contemplation, concerning the noninterference of form and emptiness, makes it clear that both truths are revealed together; the fourth contemplation, concerning effacement with no resort, shows that both truths are effaced together.

If we explain in terms of the threefold truth,[28] the first is the real truth, the second is the conventional truth, the third is the ultimate truth of the Middle Way. In terms of the three contemplations,[29] the first is the contemplation of emptiness, the second the contemplation of conditionality, the third and fourth the contemplation of the Middle Way. The third shows the middle in the revelation of both emptiness and conditional existence, while the fourth shows the middle in the effacement of both. Though there is the meaning of the three contemplations, it merely shows that the three contemplations merge as true emptiness.

Moreover, in the interdependence of form and emptiness there are four propositions in all, each differing slightly in form of expression. In the first contemplation, resolving form into emptiness, the first three propositions explain that form is not different from emptiness; the fourth explains that form is identical to emptiness. As for the four propositions in the second contemplation, of emptiness being form, the first three explain that emptiness is not different from form whereas the fourth explains that emptiness is identical to form. The third contemplation simply conjoins the previous two. The fourth sweeps away the characteristics of the four propositions, revealing the character of true emptiness, unborn, undying, and so on, including having no knowledge and no attainment—thus the contemplation of true emptiness is complete.[30] In terms of the three contemplations, going to the purport of the "Heart" scripture, "form is not different from emptiness" makes it clear that the conventional is not different from the real; "emptiness is not different from form" makes it clear that the real is not different from the conventional; the identity of form and emptiness makes it clear that this is the Middle Way. Hence these four propositions [reconciling form and emptiness] constitute the three contemplations of the real, the conditional, and the middle. The meanings are the same, but the expression is slightly different.

Finally, there are in all three meanings in the interdependence of form and emptiness: complementarity, noninterference, and mutual destruction. This point is fully expounded in the second contemplation of the noninterference of noumenon and phenomena. Here the text contains the three previous contemplations: the first two are the meaning of mutual identification—complementarity or mutual creation; the third, the contemplation of the noninterference of form and emptiness, clarifies the meaning of noninterference. The fourth contemplation here is the meaning of mutual destruction, because form and emptiness destroy each other and both disappear. Although there are thus three meanings, all simply reveal the meaning of true emptiness.

Now let us break down the passage at hand into particulars. The statement that emptiness "cannot be said to be identical to form or not identical to form" sweeps away the second contemplation preceding—namely the contemplation of emptiness being identical to form. "It cannot be said to be identical to form" sweeps away the fourth proposition of the contemplation while "it cannot be said to be not identical to form" sweeps away the first three propositions. Because emptiness is not emptiness, it cannot be said to be identical or not identical to form. This is because noumenon is fundamentally beyond speech, and because based on contemplation the mind merges with the true ultimate. Only thus can the contemplation of inconceivable form be accomplished.

Next it says: "Nor can it be said to be emptiness or not to be emptiness"—this sweeps away the first contemplation, of resolving form into emptiness. "It cannot be said to be emptiness" properly sweeps away the fourth proposition of the contemplation, while "it cannot be said not to be emptiness" sweeps away the first three propositions. Because form too is not form, it cannot be said to be identical to emptiness or not identical to emptiness. Because phenomena themselves are identical to noumenon, because noumenon is fundamentally beyond speech, because mind merging with the true ultimate is identical to no-mind, only thus can the contemplation of true emptiness be.

Moreover, the previous contemplation of resolving form into

emptiness is free from the repudiation [of truth] by exaggeration; that which reveals how emptiness is identical to form is free from the repudiation by underestimation; the noninterference of form and emptiness is free from the repudiation by specious argument denying both; the present contemplation, of the nonexistence of anything that can mutually identify, is free from the repudiation by contradiction. Since these four repudiations[31] are absent here, the hundred negations[32] are cut off and thus one transcends absolutely with no resort to depend on.

And when it says that all doctrines are inappropriate, this is to sum up categorically and totally efface all. When I say sum up categorically, I mean that it is not only formal or material things which constitute the three contemplations, sweeping them all away—sensation, conception, action, consciousness, and the myriad things produced are all the same as form. When I say totally efface, I mean totally wiping away the preceding three contemplations, resolving form into emptiness and so on; all are inappropriate. Moreover, because there are no four statements to cut off or three contemplations to efface, it says that " 'inappropriate' is also inappropriate." As for when it says that "this statement too is not accepted," if you accept inexplicability and say this is right, then you are accepting something, and when you accept something you have thought, and having thought is all traces of speech in the mind. Transcending absolutely, with no resort, once the dual extremes are left behind, the Middle Way does not remain and both mind and objects vanish; and as they vanish utterly, with no resort or reliance, transcendent wisdom appears. If you arouse the mind and stir thoughts it is all out of harmony with the noumenon. Because "the path of speech ends," language cannot reach it; because "the sphere of mental activity vanishes," understanding cannot reach it. The statement "this is the sphere of practice" ties together the foregoing practices. But there are two meanings. One is that the foregoing is the sphere of the practitioner: now mind merges with objects, knowing unites with the spirit; forgetting words and emptying the heart, silencing the mind and dismissing intellection, only then can one reach this sphere. This is because it makes it clear that only practical application can reach it—that it is not in the realm of intellectual understanding. The second meaning is that the aforementioned merging of mind and knowledge [with objects and spirit] is true practice because practice is the realm of action in that sphere. In the third part of this passage, the text following "Why?" explains practice in terms of its contrary.

CONTEMPLATION: In the preceding four approaches, the first two contemplations with eight facets, all eliminate conceptions and expose understanding; in the third contemplation, understanding is finished and we proceed to practice; it is in the fourth contemplation that the body of practice is developed.[33] If one does not clearly comprehend the foregoing understanding, there is no way to proceed to accomplish this practice. If one does not understand the principle of this practice, one nullifies the former understanding and has no way of attaining true understanding. If one clings to understanding without relinquishing it, one has no way of entering into this right practice. Therefore practice is based on understanding; but when practice is developed, understanding ends.

ANALYSIS: This is the second summation of the four approaches. In the fourth approach above he only summed up that approach into practice; now he sums up all four approaches.[34]

There are three statements here. The first properly distinguishes understanding and practice. Second, following "if one does not clearly comprehend," the text shows that understanding and practice support each other just as eyes and feet help each other. Herein first practice is accomplished by means of understanding; next, following "if one does not understand," understanding is cut off to accomplish true understanding; finally, in the text following "if one clings," understanding is relinquished to accomplish practice. The third statement, following "therefore," unites dualities into a holistic contemplation of true emptiness without signs— inside and outside merge and object and contemplation are both annulled.

CONTEMPLATION: Second is contemplation of the noninterference of noumenon and phenomena.

ANALYSIS: This is the reality-realm of noninterference of noumenon and phenomena.

CONTEMPLATION: The merging of noumenon and phenomena, subsistence and disappearance, opposition and accord, has in all ten aspects.

ANALYSIS: This article of the contemplation has three parts:

first, the general heading; second, explanation of particulars; third, conclusion and exhortation. This passage is the first part—the general heading with the name of the contemplation. In all it comprises ten aspects. Basically, in the previous contemplations form and emptiness are identical to phenomena and noumenon but do not bear these names. There are four meanings in this: one is because although there is form-phenomena, turning out to be emptiness-noumenon, the noninterference of form and emptiness is true emptiness; second is because noumenon only shows emptiness—it does not yet reveal the subtle existence of real thusness; third is because in effacement without resort there are no phenomena or noumenon; fourth is because the former contemplations do not extensively reveal the characteristics of noninterference—uncreated yet created, formless yet with form, the characteristics of phenomena and noumenon clearly manifest as they merge into each other without interference. For these four reasons, the name of this contemplation of noninterference of noumenon and phenomena could not be given until this point—here alone is it acceptable. Therefore it is now presented in the heading. It includes the ten aspects given below; on the basis of noninterference they merge. This merging is total inclusion of the ten aspects given below: it is like a furnace for casting images —"merging" means melting, in the sense of first resolving the meanings, and it also means melding, in the sense of ultimately becoming one meaning. Merging phenomena by noumenon, phenomena fuse with noumenon, two yet not two. The ten aspects have no interference because their meanings are the same. Furthermore these two, noumenon and phenomena, merging, each must pervade the other because mutually pervading they melt into each other.

Next, "subsistence" is the ninth and tenth of the ten aspects: the reason is that real noumenon is not a phenomenon and phenomenal things are not noumenon—the characteristics of both subsist.

"Disappearance" is the seventh and eighth of the ten aspects: the reason is that real noumenon is identical to phenomena and phenomena are identical to noumenon—as each loses itself assimilating to the other, each itself disappears.

"Opposition" is the fifth and sixth aspects: the reason is that real noumenon removes phenomena—noumenon is opposed to phenomena; phenomena can conceal noumenon—phenomena are opposed to noumenon.

"Accord" is the third and fourth aspects: the reason is that, based on noumenon, phenomena become—noumenon accords with phenomena; phenomena reveal noumenon—phenomena accord with noumenon. Therefore these two statements of noumenon and phenomena altogether contain ten aspects, finally establishing the meaning of the noninterference of phenomena and noumenon, forming the second contemplation. Thus the noninterference of phenomena and noumenon is properly the contemplated and contemplating this in the mind is called the contemplator. This contemplation separately explains the contemplation of the conventional, which is contemplation of phenomena, the contemplation of the real, which is contemplation of noumenon, and the contemplation of the noninterference of phenomena and noumenon, which forms the contemplation of the Middle Way.

Moreover, contemplating phenomena involves compassion whereas contemplation of noumenon is wisdom; the noninterference of these two is compassion and wisdom guiding each other, accomplishing the practice of nondwelling.[35] Also they are simply the contemplation of the conditional, of emptiness, and of the Middle Way.

CONTEMPLATION: First is the aspect of noumenon pervading phenomena. This means that the pervading noumenon is by nature undivided whereas the pervaded phenomena are differentiated in division and position. In each individual phenomenon noumenon pervades in its totality—it is not a part [of noumenon] pervading. Why? Because real noumenon cannot be divided. Therefore each individual particle contains the boundless real noumenon completely.

ANALYSIS: This is the first aspect. Hereafter the ten aspects should be considered as ten, but to analyze the two meanings [of noumenon and phenomena] they are all considered selectively and therefore divided into five pairs: first, the pair of noumenon and phenomena pervading each other; second, the pair of noumenon and phenomena completing or making each other; third, the pair of noumenon and phenomena destroying each other; fourth, the pair of noumenon and phenomena identifying with each other; fifth, the pair of noumenon and phenomena denying each other, also called the pair of nonidentity.

These five pairs all explain noumenon first, since noumenon is considered important. Still, in all of them noumenon and phenomena are interdependent: in the first, third, fifth, seventh, and ninth, noumenon looks to phenomena; in the second, fourth, sixth, eighth, and tenth, phenomena look to noumenon.

The first pair is twofold: first comes the analysis proper; then comes discriminating assessment. In the beginning are two aspects, so it is divided into two; this part is the first. In the text there are three parts. The first part indicates the name. The second part, following "This means the pervading . . . ," explains the characteristics of phenomena and noumenon—the real noumenon of inherent emptiness has one characteristic, which is absence of characteristics, or signlessness, and therefore cannot be divided, so it has no boundaries; phenomena rely on interdependent origination, so their divisions and relative positions have myriad distinctions. The third part, following "In each individual phenomenon . . . ," explains the characteristic of pervasion; since noumenon is not outside of phenomena, it must pervade phenomena. As the scripture says, "The nature of things is universally present in all places, all beings, and all lands."

Next, the text following "Why?" explains the reason for pervasion in totality. It means that it must pervade in its totality or else noumenon would be divisible. It is not like clouds which fill the sky but can be divided according to location. Following "Therefore" points to a particular phenomenon to illustrate the characteristic of pervasion: because a particle contains the noumenon it shows that the noumenon pervades as a totality.

CONTEMPLATION: Second is the aspect of phenomena pervading noumenon. This means that the pervading phenomena have boundaries whereas the pervaded noumenon must have no boundaries. These bounded phenomena must be wholly the same, not partly the same, as the unbounded noumenon. Why? Because phenomena, having no substance, are after all like noumenon. Therefore a single atom pervades the universe without dissolving. As does one atom, so do all things. Ponder this.

ANALYSIS: This passage too has three parts. First is the heading. Second, the text following "This means that the pervading . . ." indicates the characteristics of the pervader and the pervaded. Third, the text following "These bounded . . ." shows the characteristic of pervading the noumenon: therein, first is the explanation proper, giving total sameness the name "pervasion"; next, the text following "Why?" explains the reason for sameness—because bounded phenomena are as a whole like noumenon—if they were not pervasively identical [to noumenon], phenomena would have separate substance. Next, the text following "Therefore" sums up with an indication of the characteristic of pervasion. Finally, the text following "As does one atom" generalizes all things. This pair is the basis of the following four pairs; because of mutual pervasion there are mutual creation and so forth.

CONTEMPLATION: This aspect of total pervasion transcends conception and is difficult to see. It is difficult to depict by conventional metaphors.

ANALYSIS: Third is a consideration of the preceding two aspects. Therein are three parts: first is the heading of difficulty of description; second is a particularized illustration based on metaphor; third is an explanation based on questions and answers. This passage is the first part; when it says that it is difficult to see, it is because the principle is deep. One version says it is beyond perception—beyond perception has the meaning of transcending conceptions. To say that it is difficult to see admits the possibility of seeing; therefore the following metaphor is used to clarify the difficulty. It merely says that it is hard to depict by conventional metaphor. As for the reason why it is hard to depict by metaphor, phenomena and noumenon differ and yet pervade each other—because noumenon pervades phenomena, it is formless and yet totally within forms; because phenomena pervade noumenon, one atom is boundless. Since one atom is boundless, how can there be anything which matches commonsense conceptions? Since formlessness is totally within forms, when has the ultimate truth ever been distant? Forms themselves are formless, even the five eyes can hardly see;[36] as for a phenomenon containing the whole of noumenon, how can conventional things be similes for this? Therefore the scripture says, "It is like the reality-realm pervading all but you cannot apprehend it as all." It also says, "Nothing at all in the world, existent or nonexistent, can be a simile for this." Even the metaphor of the ocean given below is just a partial metaphor.

CONTEMPLATION: It is like the whole ocean being in one wave, yet the ocean is not small; it is like one small wave extending over the whole ocean, yet the wave is not large. Though it simultaneously pervades all waves, the ocean is not differentiated; though each extends over the ocean at the same time, the waves are not the same. When the whole ocean is in a single wave, moreover, that does not prevent it from being entirely in all the waves. And when one wave extends over the whole ocean, all the other waves also extend completely over it without interfering with each other. Ponder this.

ANALYSIS: This second part explains by way of metaphor. To raise a metaphor when it is conceded that it cannot be likened to anything is to use a partial metaphor temporarily to convey the mysterious meaning, to cause those of developed perceptivity to see the great by way of the small, to forget words on comprehending the message.

In this passage are three levels of noninterference. First, relating the ocean to a wave, it illumines the noninterference of great and small. This is brought up as a metaphor for the two senses of the mutual pervasion of phenomena and noumenon, as explained above. The passage simply brings up the metaphor and does not match it to the principle. To match them in general terms, the ocean symbolizes noumenon whereas the waves symbolize phenomena. If you substitute these terms in the appropriate places in the passage, it can be understood, but the meaning is still hard to see. How can the ocean be wholly in one wave? It is because the ocean has no duality. How can the whole noumenon be in one phenomenon? It is because noumenon has no duality. How can one wave extend over the whole ocean? Because it is the same as the ocean. How can one atom totally pervade the noumenon? Because phenomena are the same as noumenon.

Second, the text following "it simultaneously pervades all" relates one ocean to multiple waves and illumines the noninterference of unity and difference. In terms of principle, the one noumenon relates to multiple phenomena, clarifying noninterference. Moreover, the foregoing is "not large, not small," while this is "not one, not different." Their characteristics of unity and difference and so forth, as well as the questions and answers below, reveal their own reasons.

Third, the text following "When the whole ocean is in a single wave" relates the ocean both to one wave and to multiple waves, depending on each other, equally pervading without interference. In terms of the principle, the text relates the one noumenon to one phenomena and multiple phenomena, depending on each other, equally pervading without interference.

CONTEMPLATION *(Question):* Since noumenon is in its entirety present in one atom, why is it not small? And if it is not small like an atom, how can it be said that its whole is in one atom? If one atom extends throughout the noumenal nature, moreover, why is it not large? If it is not vast like noumenon, how can it pervade the noumenal nature? This is contradictory.

ANALYSIS: The third part is a question-and-answer explanation. It explains both the principle and the metaphor, but the text speaks only in terms of the principle, thus making the metaphor understood by analogy. In the preceding simile the text had three sections, but here they are joined to make a double question and answer. The first question is in terms of large and small, but the answer also includes unity and difference. The second question is in reference to the aforementioned relation of the ocean to both one and many waves, depending on each other and equally pervading without interference.

In the former, first there is the question and then the answer; the passage we are considering now is the first question. There are two parts to the passage. First is a question based on noumenon as seen in phenomena. In terms of the simile, it is the previous "the whole ocean is in one wave, yet the ocean is not small"—so it says, "Since noumenon is in its entirety present in one atom," thereby questioning smallness based on immanence. Following "And if it is not small like an atom," the text questions immanence based on not being small. Second, in the text following "If one atom extends throughout . . ." questions are based on the dependence of phenomena on noumenon. First it questions largeness, based on one atom; next, following "If it is not vast as noumenon," it questions pervasion, based on not being large. In terms of the simile, it is the aforementioned "one wave extends over the whole ocean, yet the wave is not large." "This is contradictory" concludes the challenge.[37]

CONTEMPLATION *(Answer):* Noumenon and phenomena are relative to each other; they are neither one nor different. Therefore they can completely contain each other without destroying their original status.

ANALYSIS: From this point on is the answer. Within it are two parts: first it introduces both; then it explains both. This is the first part. The foregoing question only asked about size, while this part actually answers in regard to unity and difference but includes size. Because noumenon and phenomena depend on each other, it says they are neither one nor different.

CONTEMPLATION: First, in the relativity of noumenon to phenomena there are four points: (1) because real noumenon is not different from phenomena, the totality of real noumenon is one phenomenon; (2) because real noumenon is not one with phenomena, the noumenal nature is eternally boundless; (3) because nonunity is nondifference, the boundless noumenal nature is totally in one atom; (4) because nondifference is nonunity, the noumenal nature of one atom has no bound or limit.

ANALYSIS: This explains noumenon relative to phenomena. Among the four points, the first two properly clarify the characteristic of being in an atom yet not being small; the first point is being in an atom, the second is not being small. The third and fourth points respond to difficulty: the sense of the challenge is that being in an atom and not being small are mutually contradictory—how can they interpenetrate? The third point explains that the great noumenon is totally in one atom. The fourth point explains that even though it is in one atom it is not small—its having no bound or limit is not being small. Hence it answers both the challenge to being in an atom and the challenge to not being small. Though there are two parts, the point is just uniform pervasion.

CONTEMPLATION: Next, the relativity of phenomena to noumenon also has four points: (1) because phenomena are not different from noumenon, a single atom extends throughout the noumenal nature; (2) because phenomena are not one with noumenon, it does not dissolve the individual atom; (3) because nonunity is identical to nondifference, one small atom pervades the boundless real noumenon; (4) because nondifference is identical to nonunity, though pervading the boundless noumenon, the atom is not big. Ponder this.

ANALYSIS: Answering in terms of phenomena relative to noumenon is the answer to the question "If one atom pervades the noumenon, why is it not large?" and so on. Moreover, the first two points clarify the characteristic of pervading noumenon without being large: the first point is that one atom pervades noumenon; the second explains its not being large. Again the third and fourth points respond to the challenge of contradiction. The third point explains that one small atom pervades the vast noumenon, moreover, and the fourth explains that although it pervades the noumenon, yet the atom is not large. The text simply explains that phenomena and noumenon are not one and not different; these two meanings are hard to penetrate.

CONTEMPLATION *(Question):* When the boundless noumenal nature is wholly in one atom, is there noumenal nature in other things or not? If there is noumenal nature outside that atom, then it is not in its entirety in the one atom; if there is no noumenon outside that atom, then it does not wholly pervade all things. This doctrine is utterly contradictory.

ANALYSIS: What follows is the second pair. To begin with, the question and answer are based on the simile of the ocean in relation to one wave and all waves, interdependent and equally pervading without interference. Now this is the question; the previous simile said that although the ocean is entirely in one wave, that does not prevent the whole thing from being in all the waves, and when one wave extends throughout the ocean, so do all the waves, without mutual interference. In the text, first the question is posed and then the answer is given. The text following "If there is noumenal nature outside that atom" sums up the objection. If we posed the question in terms of the simile, we should say this: when the whole ocean is in one wave, is the ocean in the other waves or not? If there is an ocean outside the wave, then it is not entirely in one wave; if there is no ocean outside the wave, then it does not as a whole pervade all waves. This is obvious by comparison to the text of the challenge.

CONTEMPLATION *(Answer):* Because of merging by the one noumenal nature, because manifold things have no interference, noumenon can be complete inside [a phenomenon] yet complete outside, without hindrance or interference. Therefore each has four points.

ANALYSIS: Here follows the answer, in which both aspects [noumenon and phenomena] are presented: "because of merging by the noumenal nature" introduces four points based on phenomena. The rest is obvious.

CONTEMPLATION: First consider the four points in terms of noumenon. (1) When the noumenal nature is entirely in all phenomena, that does not interfere with its being complete in one atom; therefore being outside is identical to being inside. (2) When the whole [noumenon] is in one atom, that does not prevent the whole from being in other phenomena; therefore being inside is identical to being outside. (3) The nondual nature [of noumenon] is individually in all complete; therefore it is both inside and outside. (4) Because the nondual nature is not all things, it is neither inside nor outside. The first three points explain that it is not different from all things; the fourth point explains that it is not one with all things. Precisely because it is not one and not different, being inside and outside have no interference.

ANALYSIS: This passage dealing with noumenon is one unit: first it explains; then it sums up with noninterference.[38] The first point answers the question of whether or not there is noumenal nature in other things when the whole of the boundless noumenal nature is in one atom. The second point answers that it is in other places—thus explaining how the whole ocean in the simile being in one wave does not prevent the whole ocean from completely permeating all the waves. The first point also explains that when it is in everything it is also complete in one atom. Before this the question is omitted; if we were to formulate the question, we should say, "When the noumenal nature is totally in all things, is it complete in one atom or not?" Now this explains that it is complete in one atom —how could we eliminate the atom, because it pervades all things? The third point explains that noumenon wholly pervades inside and outside [one atom]. Because this is the constant principle, again there is no question; if we were to ask the question, we should say, "Does it equally pervade [one and many] or not?" The fourth point denies both; and as it is not the doctrine of pervasion, there is no question for it.

Because there is no obstacle in the meaning and principle, these four points are presented together. After that, the text following "The first three points . . ." concludes with the establishment of noninterference and also replies to the previous challenge of contradiction—since noumenon is inside and outside [one atom] without interference, there is no contradiction.

CONTEMPLATION: Next, consider the four points in terms of phenomena. (1) When each individual phenomenon completely pervades the noumenon, that does not prevent all phenomena from completely pervading also. Therefore being inside is identical to being outside. (2) When all phenomena pervade noumenon, that does not prevent one atom from completely pervading it also. Therefore being outside is identical to being inside. (3) Because all phenomena individually pervade noumenon at the same time, therefore noumenon is completely inside [each phenomenon] and also outside, without any hinderance. (4) Because the individual phenomena do not dissolve, noumenon and phenomena depend on each other and noumenon is neither inside nor outside. Ponder this.

ANALYSIS: These four points in terms of phenomena reflect what was not in the preceding question but was in the preceding simile, which said that when one wave extends throughout the ocean, so do all the other waves, without mutual interference. Because first one wave is related to the ocean, these are four points in terms of phenomena, so a previous statement said, "because manifold things have no interference." If we were to pose a specific question for it, we should ask, "When one phenomenon pervades noumenon, do other phenomena also pervade noumenon? If they do, then noumenon is multiple; if not, then manifold phenomena are not in accord with noumenon." Therefore the answer now says that manifold phenomena are in accord with noumenon and are the same as noumenon, so there is no multiplicity in pervasion. Why? Because noumenon is nondual. It is simply that phenomena, being the same as noumenon, have no bounds and are therefore said to pervade [noumenon]. Now the first point herein is that one phenomenon pervading does not hinder manifold phenomena pervading. The second point is that manifold phenomena pervading do not hinder one phenomenon pervading. The third point is that all things pervade at once. The fourth is that the characteristics of one and many are clear.

Question: With noumenon being considered relative to phenomena, being in one phenomenon is called being inside and being in manifold phenomena is called being outside. Here phenomena are considered relative to noumenon—what is considered as inside and outside?

Answer: In this case too one phenomenon is considered inside and manifold phenomena are considered outside.

Question: Then how is it different from the previous aspect of noumenon relative to phenomena?

Answer: In the previous aspect, noumenon pervading phenomena was brought up first; this is called noumenon relative to phenomena. Here phenomena pervading noumenon is brought up first; this is called phenomena relative to noumenon. Hence the division into two aspects with their own proper meanings. If we simply ask if manifold phenomena pervade noumenon, then does one phenomenon pervade noumenon, the former approach answers this. If we also ask if one phenomenon pervades noumenon, then do manifold phenomena pervade, then this approach is used to answer it. Throughout, phenomena are taken as inside and outside, so in the former approach there is only one question—that is, in the first point, since one phenomenon entirely pervades noumenon, therefore noumenon is inside, and since that does not hinder each phenomenon from also pervading noumenon, noumenon is outside. The one and the many are all identical to noumenon. Therefore it says that total pervasion does not mean that there are many noumena pervading phenomena. Therefore it says in the fourth point that noumenon and phenomena are relative to one another, neither inside nor outside. Before, we spoke in terms of noumenon; in the fourth point, just because [noumenal] nature is not all things, it abides neither inside nor outside. Now this is in terms of phenomena depending on noumenon; noumenon has no inside or outside—how then can there be "neither unity nor difference"? Therefore we say that since it does not destroy characteristics, it must be that in one phenomenon it is not all phenomena, and in all phenomena it is not one phenomenon—only thus is the fourth point established. Therefore it must be that each is relative to the other, neither inside nor outside. This finishes the explanation of the first pair: mutual pervasion.

CONTEMPLATION: Third is the aspect of the formation of phenomena based on noumenon. This means that phenomena have no separate substance and must depend on real noumenon to be established. This is because all things which are interdependently originated have no inherent nature of their own and, moreover, because phenomena can only come to be from the noumenal principle of lack of inherent nature. It is like waves accomplishing movement by means of water, because water, in relation to the waves, is that which forms them. You should know that the possibility of the existence of all things based on the matrix of the issue of thusness is also like this.[39] Ponder this.

ANALYSIS: Following is the pair of mutual formation. In the following eight aspects first the name is presented, followed by the explanation, with no further considerations. In this pair, first to be explained is noumenon relative to phenomena, which is the third aspect. First comes the explanation proper; then, following "This is because," the reason is presented. The reason is twofold: one, it is because of lack of inherent nature; two, it is because true thusness goes along with conditions.[40]

But the passage has three parts. The first part explains that phenomena come to be because they have no inherent nature: the "Treatise on the Mean" says, "All things can be because there is the sense in which they are empty. If there were no emptiness, nothing could be." The great scripture on transcendent wisdom says, "If all things were not empty, there would be no Path and no realization." The second part, following "It is like waves," gives a simile which has two meanings: the first symbolizes lack of inherent nature— because water does not stick to its own identity it can form waves; the second symbolizes becoming due to true thusness going along with conditions—that is, if there were no water there would be no waves; if there were no real thusness, what thing could be? The third part, following "the possibility of the existence of all things based on the matrix of the issue of thusness," joins with the foregoing, symbolizing true thusness going along with conditions. Hence the *Śrīmālāsiṁhanāda* scripture says, "Based on the matrix of the issue of thusness there is birth-and-death; based on the matrix of the issue of thusness there is true thusness." This means that if there were no true thusness, by what means could illusion coalesce into birth-and-death? Because all things have no being of their own apart from the true mind, the matrix of the issue of thusness is the true thusness of the fact of birth-and-death. Therefore, in the [Hua-yen] book on asking for clarification, Mañjuśrī questions, "The nature of mind is one—why are there seen to be various differences?" Chief in Awareness answers, "The nature of things is fundamentally birthless, yet it gives the appearance of the existence of birth." This is the answer that true thusness goes along with conditions.

CONTEMPLATION: Fourth is the aspect of phenomena being able to show noumena. This means that we apprehend noumenon through phenomena; therefore phenomena, being empty, are noumenon. Truly, because phenomena are empty, the noumenon which is completely in phenomena stands revealed. It is like the waves: because their characteristics are insubstantial they cause the body of the water to be revealed—the principle here is the same. Ponder this.

ANALYSIS: This fourth aspect is looking at noumenon from phenomena. In this passage the principle and the simile are together. To explain it, it is established in pursuit of the previous aspect; that is, if there were not the third, then there would be phenomena apart from noumenon—then how could this fourth aspect show noumenon? It is like the nonexistence of waves apart from water—the arising of waves shows the water. Since phenomena are based on noumenon, they can manifest the noumenon. Because phenomena come from conditions, they have no inherent nature; thus the noumenon of absence of inherent nature establishes phenomena, and phenomena necessarily have no inherent nature—therefore deriving from conditions and having no inherent nature is none other than ultimate reality. In the [Hua-yen book] "Verses in the Suyama Heaven" it says, "Analyzing the physical and mental elements, we find their nature to be fundamentally empty; because they are empty, they cannot perish—this is the meaning of birthlessness." Only by way of the phenomena of the physical and mental elements is inherent emptiness revealed. Inherent emptiness is the birthless real noumenon. And in the "Verses on Mount Sumeru" it says, "Understand that the inherent nature of all things has no existence —thus understanding the nature of things, one will see the Buddha." "All things" means phenomena; having no existence is true noumenon.

CONTEMPLATION: Fifth is the aspect of removing phenomena

by means of noumenon. This means that since phenomena are based on noumenon, ultimately that causes all the characteristics of phenomena to be void—only the equality of the one true noumenon appears. This is because apart from true noumenon not a single thing can be apprehended. It is like the water taking away the waves, all the waves being void; this means that the water remains, having abolished the waves.

ANALYSIS: Beginning here he discusses the pair showing mutual destruction. Mutual destruction means the taking away of their forms so that both [phenomena and noumenon] disappear. This is the fifth aspect; by looking at phenomena from noumenon, noumenon takes away phenomena. In the passage are both the principle and a simile. Moreover, this fifth aspect can be realized by apprehending the third; because the whole of noumenon constitutes phenomena, phenomena are fundamentally extinct.

First comes the explanation proper; the text following "apart from true noumenon" presents the reason. Because there are no phenomena apart from reality, it therefore takes away phenomena. It is like making waves of water—the waves are only moisture; they themselves are void. Therefore the [Hua-yen] book on the appearance of the Buddha says, "Even if all sentient beings attain enlightenment in an instant, that is no different from not attaining enlightenment. Why? Because enlightenment has no forms or formlessness." Everything being formless, the noumenon thus is manifest —"sentient beings" and "Buddha" both vanish.

CONTEMPLATION: Sixth is the aspect of phenomena being able to conceal noumenon. This means that real noumenon, conforming to conditions, forms phenomena; since these phenomena differ from noumenon, however, that causes the phenomena to be apparent after all and the noumenon not to be evident. It is like water: when it makes waves, movement is apparent and stillness is concealed. The scripture says [in the book "A Bodhisattva Asks for Clarification"], "The reality-body [of Buddha] circulating in the five paths of mundane existence is called 'sentient beings'."[41] Therefore when sentient beings are manifest the reality-body is not manifest.

ANALYSIS: This is looking to noumenon from phenomena. The passage has three parts. First is the explanation proper; this too derives from the third aspect: since the whole of noumenon forms phenomena, and since phenomena have physical characteristics whereas noumenon has none, and since phenomena cover noumenon, therefore "since these phenomena differ from noumenon" noumenon is concealed. There is a version which says that since they pervade phenomena they do not quite oppose it. Second is a simile for manifestation, taking "water" to represent stillness, because the meaning of concealment is clear. Third, the scripture is quoted for testimony, in which the noumenon is the reality-body. Following this should be further explanation: when the bodhisattva Chief in Riches also says, "All worldly philosophy is discrimination—there has never been anything or any doctrine by which it is possible to enter into the nature of things,"[42] this is because phenomena conceal noumenon.

CONTEMPLATION: Seventh is the aspect of real noumenon being identical to phenomena. This means that real noumenon is necessarily not outside of phenomena. This is because it is the principle of selflessness of things; moreover, phenomena must necessarily depend on noumenon, and noumenon is empty, without substance. Therefore this noumenon as a whole is entirely phenomena—only thus is it the real true noumenon. It is like water being waves—without movement it is not wetness, so the water is waves. Ponder this.

ANALYSIS: Beginning here he discusses the fourth pair: mutual identification. The preceding pair elucidated concealment and cancellation: phenomena conceal noumenon, yet noumenon does not perish; noumenon cancels out phenomena, yet phenomena remain. Although it is said that it cancels out phenomena entirely, the meaning is in the emptiness of the characteristics or forms of the phenomena; it is not that there are no phenomena. Here is elucidated mutual identification, losing self and assimilating to the other; in each case they are but one. Now in this seventh aspect noumenon is seen in phenomena; again there is both the principle and a simile. In dealing with the principle, first comes a brief explanation; then the text following "because it is the principle of the selflessness of things" sets forth the reason. If it were just emptiness outside of phenomena, it would not be identical to phenomena; since it is the principle of things having no self or inherent identity, how could this principle, or noumenon, exist outside of phenomena? Therefore noumenon is empty and without substance—taking phenomena as a whole, their fundamental emptiness is simply the real noumenon. The statement in the simile that without movement it is not wetness is based on phenomena being identical to noumenon; the idea is that the whole of the wetness is the movement—therefore noumenon is simply identical to phenomena.

CONTEMPLATION: Eighth is the aspect of phenomena being identical to noumenon. This means that interdependently originating things necessarily have no individual intrinsic nature of their own; and because they have no inherent nature of their own they are entirely identical to reality. That is why it is said that sentient beings are *thus* without awaiting extinction.[43] It is like the waves' appearance of movement being in totality the water—therefore there is no sign of difference.

ANALYSIS: This is phenomena seen in noumenon. Again there is both principle and simile. The "Treatise on the Mean" says, "If things are born from conditions, then they have no inherent nature of their own. If they have no inherent nature, how can these things exist?" Absence of inherent nature is the true noumenon. Therefore phenomena are identical to noumenon. The passage "that is why it is said that sentient beings are *thus*" indirectly quotes the *Vimalakīrti* scripture—that scripture's chapter on Maitreya says, "All sentient beings are *thus*." It also says, "If Maitreya attained extinction and deliverance, so should all sentient beings. Why? All sentient beings are features of true thusness and do not become any more extinct." All forms and appearances are stamped by impressions of a single reality; whatever you encounter is real. Without destroying provisional names the character of reality is explained. When the simile is brought up this becomes obvious. Thus in this eighth aspect the nullity of sentient beings is the reality-body; in the seventh, the reality-body going along with conditions is called sentient beings. "Sentient beings" and the "reality-body" are one in substance but different in name. There has never been movement or stillness, and no concealment or revelation. Because the names are different, there is mutual interidentification, there is mutual concealment and cancellation; because they are one substance, they can interidentify and can conceal and reveal each other. Because of this interidentification the two truths, real and conventional, have never been contradictory. In the "Verses in the Suyama Heaven" it says, "Just as gold and gold color are in essence not different, so are things and nonthings—their essential nature has no difference."[44] Because noumenon is identical to phenomena, though empty it is not annihilation; because phenomena are identical to noumenon, though existing they are not permanent. Because noumenon is identical to phenomena, outside of knowledge there is no thusness for knowledge to enter into; because phenomena are identical to noumenon, outside of thusness there is no knowledge that can realize thusness.

CONTEMPLATION: Ninth is the aspect of real noumenon not being phenomena. This means that the noumenon is identical to phenomena and yet is not phenomena. This is because reality and illusion are different, because the true is not the false, and because that which is depended on is not that which depends. Although water is identical to waves, it is not waves, because motion and wetness are different.

ANALYSIS: Beginning here he discusses the fifth pair: mutual negation. This is identical to the meaning of coexistence: if they do not coexist there is nothing that can mutually produce, mutually identify, conceal, cancel, and so forth. This aspect concerns conforming to conditions: the reality-body which is not existent is always manifesting, not differing from phenomena. The subsequent aspect is extinction or nullity: sentient beings which are not nonexistent always exist, not differing from reality. That is to say, in this aspect noumenon is relative to phenomena, while having three pairs: the first, noumenon is the real; in the second, it is the true; in the third, it is that which is depended on—this reveals the tenth aspect, in which phenomena are illusory, false, and that which depends.

CONTEMPLATION: Tenth is the aspect of phenomena not being noumenon. This means that phenomena, which are the whole noumenon, are as phenomena forever not noumenon, because essence and characteristics are different and because that which depends is not that which is depended on. Therefore the whole being is noumenon, yet phenomenal characteristics are clearly evident. It is like waves: although they are the whole of the water as waves, they are not the water, because the meaning of motion is not wetness.

ANALYSIS: This tenth aspect is phenomena vis-à-vis noumenon. But there are two pairs: the first explains that phenomena are in characteristics, reflecting the ninth aspect where noumenon is in essence or nature, with a total of four oppositions; the second is that which depends and that which is depended on, which is no different from the preceding aspect, which can be seen from the text. If we were to place them in reference to the two truths [real and conventional] based on this, then in terms of truth these ninth and tenth aspects are always inherently two; the seventh and eighth, in terms of understanding, are always inherently one; the fifth and sixth are two yet not two; the third and fourth are not two yet two. Based on the first pair, all the meanings may be made to complement and form each other.

CONTEMPLATION: The ten meanings given above are the same one interdependent origination. In terms of noumenon vis-à-vis phenomena, there is formation and disintegration, there is identity and difference; in terms of phenomena vis-à-vis noumenon, there is revelation and concealment, there is unity and distinction. One may go back and forth freely without hindrance; they all arise at once. Thinking deeply in order to cause the views to appear clearly is called the contemplation of noumenon and phenomena completely merging without interference.

ANALYSIS: Third is the conclusion and exhortation. There are two parts: first it summarizes the foregoing meanings; then it urges cultivation of contemplation.

The first part begins with a general statement: if one meaning is lacking, it is not true interdependent origination. Then, in the text following "In terms of noumenon . . . ," it separately categorizes the ten aspects, making eight characterizations. Aspects one, three, five, seven, and nine are noumenon vis-à-vis phenomena; two, four, six, eight, and ten are phenomena vis-à-vis noumenon.

In terms of noumenon vis-à-vis phenomena, "there is formation" refers to the third aspect, forming phenomena based on noumenon; "there is disintegration" refers to the fifth aspect, true noumenon canceling phenomena; "there is identity" refers to the seventh aspect, noumenon being identical to phenomena; "there is difference" refers to the ninth aspect, noumenon not being phenomena.

In terms of phenomena vis-à-vis noumenon, "there is revelation" refers to the fourth aspect, phenomena being able to reveal noumenon; "there is concealment" refers to the sixth aspect, phenomena being able to conceal noumenon; "there is unity" refers to the eighth aspect, phenomena being identical to noumenon; "there is distinction" refers to the tenth aspect, phenomena not being noumenon.

However, formation and disintegration and so on are presented in terms of function; to say there is formation means that noumenon can form phenomena, not that noumenon makes itself. The same thinking applies to the other seven. So in each aspect there is the meaning of phenomena and noumenon without interference. The fact that mutual pervasion is not included has three meanings: one is because it is the general characteristic—the subsequent eight characterizations [formation and disintegration and so on] come to be based on this mutual pervasion; second is because mutual pervasion has no distinctions—it is not like the differences of formation and disintegration, concealment and revelation, and so on; third is because the overall characteristic of sameness is mutual identity and inclusion.

As for "one may go back and forth freely," in the interdependence of noumenon and phenomena there are two accords and two oppositions each: in the third aspect, formation, and the seventh, identity, noumenon accords with phenomena; in the fourth, revelation, and the eighth, identity, phenomena accord with noumenon. In the fifth, cancellation, and the ninth, nonidentity, noumenon opposes phenomena; in the sixth, concealment, and the tenth, nonidentity, phenomena oppose noumenon. The expression of mutual pervasion also means accord. When you want formation there is formation, when you want disintegration there is disintegration, when you want revelation there is revelation, when you want concealment there is concealment—therefore it says "freely." Formation does not interfere with disintegration, disintegration does not interfere with formation, and so on—thus it says "without hindrance." Because the very time of formation is none other than the time of disintegration and so on, it says "at once"; because the five pairs have no order of succession, it says they "all arise at once."

In relation to the foregoing four oppositions, moreover, noumenon vis-à-vis phenomena has only formation and the like and no revelation and the like, whereas phenomena vis-à-vis noumenon have only revelation and the like and no formation and the like. Since phenomena are based on noumenon, we could say they form noumenon, but it is not newly existing, so we can only say that phenomena reveal noumenon; since phenomena, having been formed, must perish, we can say they disintegrate, but real noumenon is permanent, so we can only speak of its concealment. Because noumenon is formless, it can only identify with phenomena; phenomena, having myriad distinctions, can merge with noumenon. Therefore we can speak of one noumenon; because it is beyond all forms, we can say it is distinct from phenomena. Because phenomena have differences, we speak of different characteristics.[45] This nonsameness exists in terms of the distinction in meaning [of noumenon and phenomena]: if we sum it all up, they form only five pairs; among these five, the first four show that phenomena and noumenon are not separate, while the last one shows that phenomena and noumenon are not identical—nonidentity and nonseparation is precisely the characteristic of interdependent origination.

Furthermore, within the five pairs are altogether three meanings. The pair of formation and revelation has the meaning of noumenon and phenomena making each other. The two pairs of cancellation/concealment and nonidentity have the meaning of phenomena and noumenon opposing each other. The two pairs of mutual pervasion and mutual identity have the meaning of phenomena and noumenon not interfering with each other.

Furthermore, because they mutually pervade there is mutual creation; because there is mutual creation there is mutual identification. Because they differ there is nonidentity; and if there were no nonidentity, there would be nothing to interidentify or mutually pervade. It is due to mutual pervasion that the other four pairs exist. Therefore we speak of true emptiness and inconceivable existence each having four meanings.

In terms of noumenon vis-à-vis phenomena there are four meanings of true emptiness: (1) losing self and becoming the other —this is the aspect of forming phenomena based on noumenon; (2) effacing the other and revealing self—this is the aspect of real noumenon canceling or removing phenomena; (3) self and other coexisting—this is the aspect of real noumenon not being phenomena; (4) self and other both disappearing—this is the aspect of true noumenon being identical to phenomena. Also, from the first and third meanings there is the aspect of noumenon pervading phenomena; because self exists it entirely becomes the other and therefore pervades the other.

Next, in terms of phenomena vis-à-vis noumenon, there are four meanings to inconceivable existence: (1) revealing the other, the self being null—this is the aspect of phenomena being able to reveal noumenon; (2) revealing self and concealing the other—this is the aspect of phenomena being able to conceal noumenon; (3) self and other coexisting—this is the aspect of phenomena not being noumenon; (4) both self and other disappearing—this is the aspect of phenomena being identical to noumenon. Again, from the first and third there is the aspect of phenomena pervading noumenon; because they themselves exist they can reveal the other, so they pervade each other.

In terms of existence, therefore, being and nonbeing are without interference, because true emptiness is concealed or revealed freely. Thus opposition and accord, going back and forth from one to the other, are free, without hindrance or interference.

In the second part, following "Thinking deeply" he exhorts cultivation of contemplation. Studying without thinking is the same as not comprehending anything. When one thoroughly comprehends in the mind, the ordinary person becomes a sage.

CONTEMPLATION: Third is the contemplation of complete pervasion and inclusion.

ANALYSIS: This is the reality-realm of noninterference among phenomena.

CONTEMPLATION: Phenomena, in conformity to noumenon, merge, pervading and containing each other without interference, communing freely. I shall briefly elucidate ten aspects of this merging.

ANALYSIS: This contemplation has three parts: first, the general heading of the category; second, specific demonstration of the characteristics of the contemplation; third, conclusion and exhortation to cultivate the practice. This passage is the first part—that is, the meaning's overall name, which is based on the noninterference among phenomena. If we see only in terms of phenomena, then they obstruct one another; if we see only in terms of noumenon, there is nothing which can mutually obstruct. Now in this case, merging phenomena by noumenon, phenomena are therefore without obstruction—therefore it says that phenomena, in conformity with noumenon, merge. Now, noumenon contains myriad existents; there is nothing to which it may be likened exactly, but it is something like space. We take in general two senses of space: one is the sense of complete pervasion as it universally pervades all places, material and immaterial; the other is the sense of inclusion—in principle it contains all with nothing outside, there being not a single thing which goes outside of space. Noumenon, like space, also has these two senses, because it is all-pervasive and all-inclusive. Since phenomena conform to noumenon, even a fine particle can contain and pervade. Therefore it says "Phenomena, in conformity to noumenon, merge, pervading and containing each other without interference." Containing has the meaning of including and admitting. Noninterference has two meanings: one is that pervasion does not interfere with containment; the other is that containment does not interfere with pervasion. All phenomena can contain and pervade, equally with interference—their communion is free. Again this communion is covered by ten aspects.

CONTEMPLATION: First is the aspect of noumenon conforming to phenomena. This means that since phenomena are empty their characteristics are all null and the real body of noumenal nature appears in everything. Thus in phenomena there are no particular phenomena—that is, the whole noumenon is phenomena. Therefore, though bodhisattvas' contemplation of phenomena is itself contemplation of noumenon, nevertheless when speaking of these phenomena they do so as if they were not noumenon.

ANALYSIS: The ten aspects unfolded from here on successively produce one another. The mutual conformity of phenomena and noumenon is much like the aspects of mutual pervasion as set forth in the previous contemplation. These two aspects of mutual conformity are the overall meaning and can produce the following eight aspects. These two still include noninterference of noumenon and phenomena; because there are these two there can be the meaning

of noninterference of phenomena, so they are included in the realm
of phenomena.

There is a version which says "noumenon manifests in conformity with phenomena; phenomena pervade in conformity to
noumenon." As we look over commentaries, many are based on the
meaning of pervasion and manifestation. If we consider carefully,
however, this becomes a limitation, because with only pervasion
and manifestation the other meanings are lacking. Most versions do
not have the words "pervasion" and "manifestation" here; without
them the meaning is wider, so I now follow the versions which do
not have them. Now "noumenon conforming to phenomena" means
manifestation as phenomena, limitation as phenomena, differentiation as phenomena, greatness and smallness, unity and multiplicity
as phenomena, and so on. Therefore, in the latter aspect of phenomena conforming to noumenon, it is not just pervading as noumenon
—it also means that as noumenon they are signless, unhindered,
neither inside nor outside, and so on. Moreover, if the text has the
words "pervade" and "manifest," it would be like the mutual pervasion of phenomena and noumenon in the contemplation of the noninterference of phenomena and noumenon; thus not having the
words "pervade" and "manifest" is correct in terms of the meaning.

For each of the ten aspects first the name is presented and then
it is interpreted. In this first aspect of noumenon conforming to phenomena, first comes the explanation proper: since phenomena are
empty and noumenon is real, the body of noumenon is manifest.
Thus true noumenon is as the emptiness of phenomena; emptiness is
called the real body. Emptiness being reality is called the nonexistence of particular phenomena, or separate phenomena.

Next, the text following "Therefore, though bodhisattvas" is
based on people's realization: due to seeing the reality of phenomena, seeing phenomena is seeing noumenon. After that, following
"nevertheless when speaking of these phenomena" he explains that
bodhisattvas do not destroy characteristics: if characteristics were
destroyed, to what would noumenon conform? Therefore true noumenon is great and small in conformity to the characteristics of
phenomena.

CONTEMPLATION: Second is the aspect of phenomena conforming to noumenon. This means that phenomena are not different

from noumenon, so phenomena, in accord with noumenon, are completely pervasive, thus ultimately causing a single atom to pervade the universe completely. When the whole body of the universe pervades all things, this single minute atom too, in conformity with its noumenal nature, is completely present in all things. And as this is true of one atom, so is it true of all phenomena.

ANALYSIS: This passage, based on the first explanatory passage, seems only to elucidate the meaning of pervasion. Pervasion is another name for noumenon, because its characteristic is boundlessness. As one atom in its totality is in all things, it is also like noumenon in terms of indivisibility. The passage first presents the basis: since phenomena are not different from noumenon, and accepting the preceding aspect of noumenon conforming to phenomena, phenomena can be entirely in conformity with, or like, noumenon. As for "pervade . . . completely," because phenomena have no division their pervasion is complete, and because their substance is omnipresent, therefore they pervade. The text following "ultimately causing" separately points out the characteristic of pervasion—it means pervading the reality-realm of noumenon. The text following "the whole body of the universe" elucidates the dissolving of pervading phenomena: because an atom is in conformity with noumenon, it pervades all things. Next, the text following "as this is true of one atom" brings up an atom as representing all things—that is, all things pervade. Therefore each thing is multiplied and remultiplied without obstruction.[46]

CONTEMPLATION: Third is the aspect of phenomena containing noumenon and phenomena without interference. This means that because phenomena and noumenon are not one, while keeping one thing intact it still has the capacity of universal inclusion. It is like one atom: its form is not large, yet it can contain the boundless universe. Since phenomena, such as lands and so on, are not apart from the universe, therefore all of them appear in a single atom; as in a single atom, so it is in all things. This is because phenomena and noumenon fluidly interpenetrate, being neither one nor different. There are four points in all here: (1) one in one; (2) one in all; (3) all in one; (4) all in all. Each has a reason—think of it.

ANALYSIS: This passage has three parts: first, the explanation proper; second, summary and generalization; third, merging. Now in the first part, because as previously stated a single phenomenon contains the noumenon, and because all other phenomena are essentially not distinct from that noumenon which is contained [in one phenomenon], in terms of the noumenon contained all are in one phenomenon. As for his saying that phenomena are not one with noumenon, in the preceding aspect they are not different from noumenon, pervading the same as noumenon; this aspect is also conformity with noumenon, and because of phenomena containing noumenon they are also not different [from noumenon]—only because of not destroying the characteristic of oneness can there be the capacity to contain; it is to contrast to the previous statement of nondifference that it says here they are not one. Later, in dealing with the noninterference of the universal and the restricted, he demonstrates that the second aspect [phenomena in conformity to noumenon] still does not destroy characteristics.

The text following "It is like one atom . . ." sets forth the aspect of phenomena containing. Next, the text following "as in a single atom . . ." concludes and generalizes. Merging and permeating, in terms of the aspect of universal inclusion or containment, has four aspects [one in one, one in all, all in one, all in all]: that which contains and that which is contained do not go beyond the one and the many; interrelating, they are four. As for that which contains, they all contain both meanings of not being one with noumenon and not being different from noumenon: because phenomena are not one [with noumenon] they have substance, which is that which contains; because they are not different [from noumenon] they have function [of relating] by which they can contain. As for that which is contained, they are only based on the meaning of phenomena not being different from noumenon.

Take the first point, "one in one": because the first "one" does not lose its characteristics, it has substance, which contains; because it is numenally not different from the second "one," it can contain the second "one." Meanwhile, since the second "one" is numenally not different from the first "one," in accord with the contained noumenon it is in the first "one," because there is no phenomenon outside of noumenon.

Second, as for "one in all," because all do not lose their characteristics, they have substance which contains; being numenally not different from the one, they can contain the one. Because the one is noumenally not different from the all, in accord with the principle of its own oneness the one is in the all.

Third, as for "all in one," because one does not lose its characteristics, it can be that which contains, while because it is noumenally not different from the all it can contain all. The all which is contained is noumenally not different from the one, so in accord with the noumenon inherent in all it is in the one.

Fourth, as for "all in all," because the first "all" do not lose their characteristics they have substance which contains; noumenally not being different from the second "all," they therefore contain the second "all." Because the second "all" noumenally are not different from the first "all," in accord with the noumenon of the second "all" they are in the first "all." Therefore in the conclusion he says each has a reason.

The first two aspects are the meaning of universal pervasion; the third aspect is the meaning of containing or including. These have already fully accounted for the name of this contemplation; the subsequent seven aspects are not beyond the two meanings of universal pervading and containing.

CONTEMPLATION: Fourth is the aspect of noninterference of universality and limitation. This means that the nonunity of all things with noumenon is identical to nondifference,[47] therefore causing phenomena to be present in all atoms of the ten directions without leaving one place. Because nondifference is identical to nonunity, while completely pervading the ten directions phenomena do not move: one position is far and yet near, all-pervading and yet stationary, without obstruction or interference.

ANALYSIS: This aspect further interprets the second aspect. In the second aspect all pervade: now, not obliterating characteristics, there is also the sense of not pervading. Pervading is universality; not pervading is limitation. In the passage, "nonunity with noumenon" is limitation and "nondifference" is universality. The text following "is far" concludes; pervasion is universality, remaining stationary is limitation.

CONTEMPLATION: Fifth is the aspect of noninterference of extension and restriction. This means that because the nonunity of phenomena with noumenon is none other than nondifference, without dissolving an atom it can contain the oceans of worlds of the ten directions; because their nondifference is identical to their nonunity, while containing the whole universe the atom still is not large. Thus the phenomenon which is one atom is at once extensive and restricted, at once large and small, without mutual interference.

ANALYSIS: This further interprets the third aspect, which elucidates containing in conformity to noumenon. Because in phenomena there is the sense of not being one with noumenon, without destroying the restricted form of one atom yet it can extensively contain the universe. In this passage, because phenomena are not one with noumenon they are restricted as individual phenomena, and because they are not different from noumenon they are extensive as all-pervasive noumenon. First it explains that nonunity is none other than nondifference, thereby explaining nondissolution of individuality. The passage beginning "while containing" reverses the above; the passage beginning "Thus the phenomenon which is one atom" is the conclusion.

CONTEMPLATION: Sixth is the aspect of noninterference of pervading and containing. That is to say, this one atom is relative to all; because universal pervasion is none other than universal inclusion, when it is ubiquitous within all at the same time it also contains all things within itself. Moreover, because universal containing is none other than universal pervasion, this causes the one atom also to be omnipresent within all the different things within itself. Therefore when this one atom itself pervades the others, the others pervade it; able to contain and able to permeate, it simultaneously pervades and includes without interference. Ponder this.

ANALYSIS: This aspect combines the fourth and fifth aspects, and also combines the second and third aspects, because the fourth and fifth explain the second and third. Universal containing and universal pervasion are not apart from each other, so "pervasion" means universal pervasion and "containing" means universal containing. In the explanation, first is the heading, then the explanation, then the conclusion. This is the first. Because one is relative to many, there is the meaning of pervasion and containment. Because there is the many which can be pervaded, this one can contain. If the many depends on one, there is no pervasion and containment, because the one which is depended on cannot be said to pervade—

the many which depends on one contains the one, which cannot be said to be universal containing.[48]

Next, the text following "because universal pervasion" has two pairs in the explanation: first, pervading is containing—there is only one pervading, one containing; second, after "Moreover, because" containing is pervading—again there is only one containing, one pervading. In the first, regarding pervading being containing, when the one pervades the many, it also contains within itself the many which is pervaded. It is like one mirror reflected in nine mirrors: the one mirror also contains [reflections of] the nine mirrors. Next, containing being pervading is the converse of this statement. It is like one mirror containing [reflections of] many mirrors: the containing mirror is also reflected in the reflection of the many mirrors which are contained in it. Therefore it says one atom is also omnipresent within all the different phenomena within itself. The text following "Therefore" is the conclusion, which is self-evident.

CONTEMPLATION: Seventh is the aspect of inclusion and entry. This means that the all depends on one thing; because entering the other is identical to including the other, when all completely enter into one, that causes the one also to be within all that are within itself, simultaneously, without interference. Moreover, because including the other is identical to entering the other, when one thing is completely in all, that causes the all to be always in the one, simultaneously, without interference. Ponder this.

ANALYSIS: In the explanation, first comes the heading and then the analysis. To begin, it speaks merely in terms of the many depending on the one. "Inclusion" here is the same as the "containing" of the previous aspect; "entry" is the previous "pervading." But before, "one" was the pervader and "many" the pervaded; here "entry" is only entry into one—it cannot be called pervasion. In the previous aspect there was the many being contained, so he could speak of containing; here one has no many which can be contained, so he speaks only of inclusion.

Next, the text following "because entering the other is identical to including the other" separately explains their characteristics. Here again there are two pairs. In the first pair, the many is that which enters; therefore it also includes the one which is entered within the many which enters—like nine mirrors entering into one mirror, including the one mirror which is entered in the many mirrors which enter. The second pair simply reverses this, making the many which enters the many which includes—this means that when the many includes the one, the many is that which includes while the one is that which is included, yet the many is that which enters, so this many also enters into the one phenomenon which is included, like nine mirrors, while being that which contains, being reflected in that one mirror whose reflection is contained in them. So in the foregoing two pairs, that which enters and that which includes, the identity of inclusion and entry is in reference to the many, calling this inclusion and entry without interference; as for the one, it can only be that which is included and that which is entered—it cannot be called that which includes and that which enters. Only at the eighth aspect can it be able to include and enter.

Finally, "simultaneously, without interference" is the conclusion, summing up the foregoing point that when the many is that which enters it is at the same time that which includes—thus it says "simultaneously."

CONTEMPLATION: Eighth is the aspect of communion without interference. This means that one phenomenon is relative to all; there is inclusion, there is entry, with four steps in all: one includes all, one enters all; all include one, all enter one; one includes one phenomenon, one enters one phenomenon; all include all, all enter all. They commune simultaneously without interference.[49]

ANALYSIS: In the explanatory passage there are also three parts: first it indicates the basis, next it explains, finally it concludes. The first part is only "one is relative to the many; there is inclusion, there is entry." Next, the text following from "with four steps [or expressions] in all" explains. Because one is relative to many, one is in the beginning. But the sixth aspect is also one relative to many; it only has the two expressions of "containing" and "pervading," without "inclusion" and "entering." The seventh aspect is only many relative to one, with inclusion and entering; this aspect has only two expressions. In this eighth aspect, although one is relative to all, yet both the one and the many are that which includes and that which enters—hence it gets the name of "communion." As for communion, in the preceding seventh aspect the many includes the one, so the many is also that which enters. Now in this eighth aspect, the many includes the one, while the one included also includes the many, so the including many is also the included; therefore it enters the one, hence the term "communion." Since one and many are both that which includes and that which enters, there are four expressions; though there seem to be eight expressions, they go by pairs, so there are only four. These four all contain inclusion and entering. The first expression says "one includes all, one enters all" —the "one" of the first clause is that which includes, the "all" is that which is included; yet the included "all" can also be that which includes, so the "one" which includes is also that which is included —therefore the first-mentioned "one" thus enters "all," so it says "one enters all."

The second expression says "all include one, all enter one"— the "all" of the first clause is that which includes, while the "one" is that which is included; yet the included "one" can also be that which includes, and so the first-mentioned "all" thus becomes the included and "all enter one." This is just the reverse of the first expression. The third expression relates one to other ones; the fourth is within the third, all relating to all the others. Because these four expressions, in reference to the including are the same as noumenon containing, and in reference to the entering are the same as noumenon pervading, and because the four expressions all derive from phenomena being neither one with noumenon nor different from noumenon, then because of not being one with noumenon there is the substance of one and many which can include and enter, and because of not being different from noumenon they can include and enter.[50]

If we use the example of ten mirrors [arrayed in a circle or sphere so that all face all the others] as a simile, one mirror is the one, nine mirrors are the many. As the first expression states, "one includes all, one enters all," we should say that one mirror includes in it [reflections of] nine mirrors, meaning that one mirror is that which includes and nine mirrors are that which is included—yet because the nine mirrors also are that which includes [because they contain the reflection of the one mirror], the aforementioned one mirror which includes also enters the nine mirrors, so one mirror enters nine mirrors. The next three expressions follow this pattern. The second expression says, "all include one, all enter one"—we should say that nine mirrors include in them one mirror, nine mirrors enter one mirror. That is to say, the first-mentioned nine mirrors are that which includes, so the one mirror is that which is included; because the included one also includes, the aforementioned including nine mirrors enter the one mirror, so nine mirrors enter one mirror. As for the third expression "one includes one thing, one enters one thing," we would say that one mirror includes one mirror, one mirror enters one mirror. This means that the first one mirror includes in it [the reflection of] a second one mirror, and the [reflection of the] first one mirror also enters the second one mirror. As for the fourth expression, which says "all include all, all enter all," we would say that the ten mirrors each include in them [reflections of] nine mirrors, and [reflections of] ten mirrors all enter nine mirrors. That the entered and the included are only said to be nine mirrors is to leave one to include and enter.

CONTEMPLATION: Ninth is the aspect of mutual inherence without interference. This means that all are relative to one, also involving both entry and inclusion. Again there are four steps or expressions: (1) including one, entering one; (2) including all, entering one; (3) including one, entering all; (4) including all, entering all. They simultaneously merge with no hindrance or obstruction.

ANALYSIS: First is the presentation of the name. "Mutual inherence" or immanence means that the individual, including phenomena,[51] enters into other phenomena, and the other phenomena also include phenomena within themselves. Therefore they are said to be inherent in each other. This can be seen in the succeeding statements.

In the explanation there are also three parts: the heading, the explanation, and the conclusion. The first part, the heading, says that all are relative to one—the placing of "all" first is opposite to the eighth aspect. The second part, following "Again there are four expressions," explains. In explaining the four expressions, since the heading says that all are relative to one, which involves four expressions or statements, at the beginning of each expression there should be the word "all" as that which includes, but here it is omitted—it only takes that which is included and that which is entered to make four statements.

These four statements are completely different from the previous ones, however. For example: previously "one includes one phenomenon, one enters one phenomenon" simply explained each one relating to other individual ones—that when each one includes another one it also enters the other one. Statements of the ninth aspect are not like this. That is to say, when it says in the first expression, "including one, entering one," this means that all include each single phenomenon and, including each phenomenon, enter one phenomenon. To explain it in terms of the ten mirrors, all take nine mirrors as that which includes. As for the first expression, nine mirrors include in them [reflections of] the first; [the reflection of] one mirror enters into the second mirror. Second, including all entering one: this means that the nine mirrors, each including in them [reflections of] nine mirrors, enter into one mirror. Third, "including one, entering all" means that the nine mirrors, each including one mirror, enter into all [the other] nine mirrors. Fourth, "including all, entering all" means that the nine mirrors, all including nine mirrors, each enter [the other] nine mirrors. Because each one, with the reflections it includes, enters into the other ones, and also includes each other one in the many reflections in it, and so on, therefore it is called mutual inherence or immanence.

In terms of phenomena, each one is the agent. Now speaking in terms of the Buddhas vis-à-vis sentient beings, taking the Buddhas as the all, that which includes and contains, sentient beings would be that which is contained or included and that which is entered. The first proposition would be the Buddhas contain one sentient being and enter into all sentient beings; in the second, the Buddhas, containing all sentient beings, enter into one sentient being; in the third, the bodies of the Buddhas, containing one sentient being, enter into the hairs on the bodies of all sentient beings; in the fourth, the Buddhas, each containing all sentient beings, enter into all sentient beings. The relativity of other things, one and many, are also like this.

The third part, from "They simultaneously merge" on, is the summary conclusion. Because of this mutual inclusion and mutual immanence, there is the sense of multiplication and remultiplication, as in the net of Indra.[52]

CONTEMPLATION: Tenth is the aspect of universal merging without interference. This means that all and one are simultaneous;

relative to each other, each contains all of the aforementioned two sets of four expressions, all merging without interference. Think about this along the foregoing lines.

ANALYSIS: This tenth aspect totally merges the preceding nine. More immediately it includes three. The eighth aspect looks at all from the standpoint of one; the ninth aspect looks at one from the standpoint of all—this tenth includes these two. By looking at all from the standpoint of one, there are the four statements of the eighth aspect [one includes all, one enters all; all include one, all enter one; one includes one, one enters one; all include all, all enter all]. By looking at one from the standpoint of all, there are the four statements of the ninth aspect [all including one, entering one; all including all, entering one; all including one, entering all; all including all, entering all]. Although the seventh aspect does not contain four statements, it is subsumed within all including one; therefore the tenth aspect immediately includes three aspects [the ninth, eighth, and seventh].

As for the statement that the tenth aspect includes all the previous nine, it is because the nine aspects do not go beyond one and many: because of the first aspect, noumenon conforming to phenomena, one can be many; because of the second aspect, phenomena conforming to noumenon, many can be one; the second and fourth represent pervasion in conformity with noumenon, the third and fifth represent containing in conformity with noumenon; the second represents duality being nondual, the fourth is nonduality being dual, because of not destroying characteristics; the third represents nonvastness being vast, the fifth is vastness not being vast, also because of not destroying characteristics; the sixth contains both one and many containing and pervading without obstruction; the seventh is including and entering freely; the eighth contains one and many commingling, the ninth contains including and entering freely; so the tenth merges them all into one.

The tenth aspect is identical to the aspect of simultaneous complete interrelation; the ninth is the aspect of the realm of the net of Indra; in the eighth, in communion there is mutual exchange of roles of subject and object, so there is the aspect of concealment and revelation; the seventh is the aspect of mutual identification and interpenetration; the fifth is the aspect of extension and restriction;

in the fourth, pervading all without leaving one place, is the aspect of mutual identification; in the third, because phenomena contain both noumenon and phenomena, there is the aspect of minute [containment and establishment]; the sixth contains both aspects of mutual identification and extention and restriction; since the first three entirely create all the aspects, with phenomena and noumenon conforming to each other, there is the aspect of purity and mixture; since any of the ten can be the main one, there is the aspect of principal and satellites; in time there is the aspect of the ten time frames, so the beginner ultimately includes many eons in an instant, with faith fulfilled, the Path complete, in an instant comprehending the stage of Buddhahood; because all things are thus [in accord with the noninterference among phenomena], there is the aspect of using phenomena [to illustrate principle]—hence the ten mysteries also derive from here.[53]

CONTEMPLATION: Cause complete illumination to become manifest in accord with the realm of practice, without hindrance or obstruction.[54] Reflect deeply on this, causing it to become evident to you.

ANALYSIS: The third part is the concluding exhortation to practice. It means that if "complete illumination" is in the mind, then in accord with understanding it produces practice; when practice arises understanding ends, but though understanding ends it is manifest as understanding and practice merge into each other, cultivating without cultivation. Not only the one aspect of universal pervasion but also the three contemplations [of the conditional, emptiness, and the mean] are equally consummated. With no-mind embracing the ultimate, constantly practicing without interruption, what hindrance is not dissolved, what thing can obstruct?[55] When this contemplation is manifest, is sagehood remote? Embody it and you are spiritualized. Its essence is not of the provisional greater vehicle or of the lesser vehicle—even saints can hardly conceive of it.[56] Therefore when Buddha was first born in a royal palace, his nobility the highest, ministers assisted; if you develop contemplation apart from this, how can you reach this mystery?[57]

I have long searched deeply into the mystic scriptures and concentrated meditation on the Hua-yen. This one contemplation has been at length consummated. Not mirroring an individual heart and vainly turning away from the essential spirit, I therefore call it the mirror of the mysteries of the reality-realm. The original text concludes with "The Mysteries of the Reality-Realm of the Hua-yen," in one scroll. Now I include the original text and give it a separate title: "Mirror of the Mysteries of the Reality-Realm of the Hua-yen."

Ten Mysterious Gates of the Unitary Vehicle of the Hua-yen

by Chih-yen

THIS TREATISE BY CHIH-YEN, the second patriarch of the school, is another seminal text of Hua-yen philosophy. According to the traditional attribution of authorship, it is based on the explanation of Tu Shun; as has already been pointed out, the roots of the ten mysterious gates are to be found in Tu Shun's "Contemplation of the Realm of Reality."

I have already explained the general principles and significance of the ten mysterious gates in the Introduction; here I might reemphasize that, as aspects of interdependent origination, they are all interrelated. Chih-yen's presentation particularly stresses the relativity of the Buddhist teachings themselves—to each other and to those who are taught—and the overall unity of the teachings in what is called the unitary vehicle or comprehensive school of the Hua-yen.

Multiplicity within unity and unity within multiplicity are represented in this treatise not only in terms of the interdependence or mutual definition of numbers but also in terms of a holistic view in which every part includes the whole by virtue of being inextricably related. By emphasizing the relationship of teacher, teaching, and student, as well as the interdependence of phenomena and principles, Chih-yen establishes this very principle of relativity as the central and pervasive principle of the comprehensive, unitary teaching of the Hua-yen. Thus the Hua-yen teaching subsumes all the Buddhist teachings, specifically and generally, into a whole which transcends, without obliterating, the multitude of differences in the doctrines and practices of Buddhism.

CLARIFYING THE MEANING OF THE UNIVERSE of the own-being of interdependent origination according to the unitary vehicle is not the same as interdependent origination according to the greater vehicle and the two vehicles,[1] by which one can only remove such errors as attachment to eternity or annihilation. The Hua-yen school is not thus: in the Hua-yen teaching, no error is not removed, no thing is not the same [as everything else].

If for the moment we turn to this Hua-yen scripture alone to explain the interdependent origination of the universe, we find that it is not beyond the cause and result within its own being. "Cause" means cultivation of appropriate techniques, investigating thoroughly with the whole body, and fulfilling all the stages [of enlightenment]: this is what is represented by the bodhisattva Samantabhadra. The "result" means the complete result of ultimate dispassion and extinction of own-being, the realm of the ten Buddhas, where one is identical to all: this means the ten Buddhas' oceans of worlds and the meaning of the ten Buddhas as explained in the Hua-yen book on detachment from the world.[2]

Question: Mañjuśrī too is a personification of cause: why do you only say that Samantabhadra is the personification of cause?

Answer: Although the beginning starts from subtle wisdom [as represented by Mañjuśrī], the fulfillment is in comprehensiveness [as represented by Samantabhadra]. Therefore it is hidden in Mañjuśrī and we speak only of Samantabhadra. It is also possible to thoroughly explain interdependent origination based on the beginning and end.

Now to clarify these two aspects, cause and result, the complete result is beyond explanation, so it cannot be clarified by verbalization. As for cause, it shows the conditional cultivation of appropriate techniques for enlightenment, so we briefly explain.

Question: In the book on the inconceivable qualities and elsewhere, it also explains the qualities of the result—how can it be explained in the realm of cause?

Answer: Although these are expositions of the qualities of result, they present an explanation of result in relation to conditions, not the ultimate result of complete dispassion. That is why it is explained in the same congregation as cause.

Now, to clarify interdependent origination in the context of own-being according to the Teaching, there are two parts: one is to bring up a metaphor in order to elucidate the doctrine; the other is to analyze the doctrine in order to comprehend the principle. As for citing metaphor to elucidate, let us turn to an example. In the book on bodhisattvas gathering like clouds in the assembly in the Suyama heaven, it says, "It is like the principle of counting ten, adding ones up to infinity—all are the original number, but are differentiated by the intellect."[3] Now in bringing up this metaphor of counting to ten, there are also two aspects: one, different being; two, same being. Within the aspect of different being, there are again two aspects. (1) Many is in one, one is in many; as the scripture says, "In one understanding infinity, in infinity understanding one—they produce each other and are not real, so the wise have no fear."[4] This is speaking in terms of forms. (2) One is identical to many, many is identical to one; as it says in the scripture in the seventh of the ten abodes, "One itself is many, many is identical to one; in essence null and void, all are equal. Divorcing delusive characterizations of oneness and difference is called the bodhisattva's abode of nonregression."[5] This is speaking in terms of principle or noumenon.

Now to explain "many in one, one in many" according to the count of ten: if you count forward from one to ten you go up; if you count backward from ten to one you go down. As for "one," it exists dependently, so in one there is ten, which is why "one" can be; without ten there can be no one, because it has no inherent identity and is dependent. Because the implication of ten in one is how one is established, so are two, three, four, and so forth all established. If one remained in its own identity, ten could not be formed; and if ten is not established, neither is one.

Question: Since each individually has no inherent identity, how can they make one and many?

Answer: This depends on the power of the interdependent origination of the actual qualities of the universe, which accords with the realm of Samantabhadra. Therefore one and many always exist, without increasing or decreasing. As the *Vimalakīrti* scripture says, "All things are established from a nonabiding basis."[6] And the "Treatise on the Mean" says, "It is because there is the meaning of emptiness that all things can be established."[7]

Question: As far as this aspect embraces the universe, is it exhaustive or inexhaustible?

Answer: There is a sense in which it is exhaustive and a sense in which it is inexhaustible. Why? One in ten is exhaustive; ten in one, if fully expounded, is inexhaustible. You must realize "one" and "ten" both include the senses of exhaustive and inexhaustible.

Next, to explain "one is identical to many, many is identical to one," it is the same as going up and going down, as previously explained. Just as one is identical to ten because they are interdependently established, and if one were not ten, then ten could not be, so going from higher to lower is the same: ten is identical to one because they are interdependently established; so if ten were not one, then one could not be established.

Question: How is it that if only one is not established, ten also is not established?

Answer: It is like this: if pillars are not a house, then there is no house: if there is a house, there are pillars—so, because the pillars are identical to the house, when there is a house there are pillars. Because one is ten and ten is one, the establishment of one implies the establishment of ten.

Question: If one is ten and there is no ten without one, how can you speak of one and ten and say they can be established because of their identity?

Answer: One being ten is not one: this is not the commonsense meaning of one—it means one as interdependently established. This is because the interdependently established one is not the one of common sense [which is thought to exist of itself]. Therefore the scripture says, "One is not even one."[8] This is intended to break through numbers: those of shallow intellect cling to things, and when they see "one" they take it to be in and of itself one.

Question: Before you explained ten in one. Here you explain the identity of one and ten. What is the difference?

Answer: In the previous explanation of ten in one, apart from one there is no ten, yet ten is not one. As for this explanation of the identity of one and ten, apart from one there is no ten, and ten itself is one, because they are interdependently established.

Question: If one and many must await interdependent establishment, are they simultaneous or is there precedence and succession?

Answer: Because of their interdependent establishment, they are always simultaneous yet successive. Why? Since one is ten and ten is one, they are always simultaneous, yet because of counting up and down they are successive.

Question: Since there is clearly counting up and counting down, then there is increase and decrease—how can you call it not moving from their original characteristics?

Answer: Although they are successive, they are always unmoving. Therefore the scripture says, "Coming with no characteristic of coming."[9] It is like this: one is many yet without displacing its oneness. Such oneness is also not the commonsense idea of one. It is the same with many: though the many is one, that does not destroy its aspect of multiplicity. This again is not the commonsense idea of many.

Question: Since this one and many are interdependently established, and not the same as the commonsense conceptions, do you consider this one and many to be primordially existent or do they have an origin?

Answer: Is this question of primordial existence or nonexistence intended to clarify primordial existence in terms of knowledge or in terms of the being of one and many itself? If you are merely trying to clarify it in terms of the being of one and many itself and not considering knowledge or cognition, that being itself is beyond all discussion because it is the same as the ultimate complete result and is beyond verbalization. Now if we were to analyze one and many in terms of knowledge, the scripture says, as previously noted, "They are differentiated by intellect." The scripture also says, "the wise have no fear." Therefore we speak of one and many according to knowledge.

Question: If they are primordially existent in terms of knowledge, is it not a fact that because knowledge is aware of them they preexist?

Answer: It is like the space in a room—when you open the door and look, this space is preexistent. It is like the saying of the *Nirvāṇa* scripture, "When you have seen the Buddha-nature, it is not contained in past, present, or future."[10]

Question: Can they also be originated?

Answer: When you see, only then do you say it exists—if you do not see, you do not speak of existence. Therefore it can also be spoken of as having an origin.

Question: If the being of one and many depends on perception by knowledge, and thus includes both preexistence and prior nonexistence, can this perception by knowledge include both perception and nonperception?

Answer: Because of preexistence, knowledge is not perception;[11] because of prior nonexistence, it depends on knowledge. So we know that perception includes both perception and nonperception. All things are like this.

Next is the aspect of same being [of one and many]: this, like the previous aspect, clarifies many in one, one in many, one is many, and many is one. Now to explain in terms of the aspect of "within one," we clarify counting up and down, wherein there is backwards and forwards, each containing ten aspects. Suppose we summarize the process. Speaking in terms of ten and one, as in one there is ten, because they are interdependently established—for if there is no ten, one is not established—so also are two and three and so on. The same is so of ten being identical to one.

Question: What is the difference between this aspect of same being and the preceding aspect of different being?

Answer: In the aspect of different being or entity, we say ten in one because it depends on or looks to the succeeding nine. In this aspect, if we say ten in one there is already nine in the one, so we say ten in one.

Question: If there is nine in the one, what is different from the "one in ten" of the previous aspect of different being?

Answer: Here when we speak of one having nine, there is in itself nine, and yet one is not nine. In terms of the foregoing aspect of different being, one is identical to the different being of ten, and ten is not apart from one.

Question: If there are inherently nine in one, this must not be interdependent establishment.

Answer: If they are not interdependently established, how can there be nine?

Question: How can the being of one have nine?

Answer: If there is no nine, there is no one.

Next, to explain the identity of one and ten in the aspect of same being, when we speak of one that one is interdependently established, so one is ten. Why? If ten were not one, one could not be established. Just as one is ten, so one is two and three and so on. Going back and forth, the ten aspects are all like this.

Question: Here you say that one itself is identical to ten. How is that different from ten in one according to the aspect of same being?

Answer: Previously we explained that in the same being there is ten in one, yet one is not ten; here we explain that one is ten—the difference is that one is identical to ten.

Question: Here you explain that the being of one is ten. Does this include all things exhaustively?

Answer: Depending on the difference in how it is known, it is exhaustive and also inexhaustible. If one includes ten, that is called exhaustive; if expounded completely, it is inexhaustible.

Question: Is it inexhaustible in itself or because it includes the other aspects [of two to ten]?

Answer: If one is inexhaustible, so are the others; if the others are not exhausted, neither is one. If you establish one, all are established; if you do not establish one, none are established. Therefore including all things is inexhaustible, and then the inexhaustible also fulfills the meaning of one. In respect to three or four, the meaning [of one] is dependent, empty like space, so this is exhaustive without including others. Therefore it is called inexhaustible because it includes both exhaustiveness and nonexhaustiveness.[12]

Question: Since you say that one includes all, does that just include the ten in that one or does it also include tens elsewhere?

Answer: Including other tens also has exhaustive and nonexhaustive meanings. Why? Because there is no self apart from other. One including other places is infinite, yet the infinite fulfills the meaning of one. The meaning of tens elsewhere is like empty space, so there is exhaustiveness.[13]

The foregoing has been a figurative metaphor based on the ten numbers. Below we use the doctrine to understand the principle. There are ten aspects:

1. Simultaneous complete interrelation—this is explained in reference to the interrelation of forms and characteristics, without before or after.

2. The realm of the net of Indra—this is explained in terms of metaphor.

3. Latent concealment and revelation both existing—this is explained in terms of conditions.

4. Minute containment and establishment—this is explained in terms of forms and characteristics.

5. Separate phenomena of the ten time divisions variously existing—this is explained in terms of time divisions.

6. The purity and mixture of the repositories containing all virtues—this is explained in terms of practice.

7. One and many containing each other without being the same—this is explained in terms of noumenon.

8. All things freely identifying with each other—this is explained in terms of function.

9. Creation only by the operation of mind—this is explained in terms of mind.

10. Using phenomena to illustrate the Teaching and produce understanding—this is explained in terms of knowledge.

In each of these ten gates are also ten, all together making a hundred. These ten are: (1) doctrine and meaning; (2) principle and phenomena; (3) understanding and practice; (4) cause and result; (5) person and dharma; (6) divisions of sphere and stage; (7) teaching and knowledge, teacher and disciple; (8) principal and satellites, objective and subjective realms; (9) retrogression and progression, substance and function; (10) adaptation to the faculties, inclinations, and natures of beings.

As for (1) doctrine and meaning, doctrine is the teachings of the three and five vehicles,[14] their common and particular characteristics. By particular doctrines are expounded particular meanings; so when the principle is realized, forget about the doctrine. If you enter this comprehensive [Hua-yen] school, doctrine is meaning because they simultaneously interrelate.[15]

As for (2) principle and phenomena, in the doctrinal analyses of the three vehicles, different phenomena demonstrate different principles, as when the various scriptures mention different things as similes for different principles. In the Hua-yen school, phenomena themselves are principle, or noumenon. This is like the words of scriptures such as "Entering the Cosmos of Truth": the essential reality is the principle, or noumenon, while the manifestation of characteristics and forms is phenomena.

As for (3) understanding and practice, it is explained in the three vehicles: understanding without practice is like saying a person's name without knowing the person. According to the explanation of the comprehensive school, practice is identical to understanding: it is like seeing the face without saying the name, yet knowing by oneself. The characteristics appear as practice, and the aftermath of reaching the ultimate is understanding.

As for (4) cause and result, the characteristics and qualities of practice are the cause whereas the union with the ultimate is the result.

As for (5) person and dharma, Mañjuśrī illustrates wisdom and Samantabhadra illustrates comprehensive practice; this shows that the person is the dharma.[16]

As for (6) divisions of sphere and stage, they commune without confusion, each abiding in its stage; this is division of sphere and stage.

As for (7) teaching and knowledge, teacher and disciple, that which develops is the teacher whereas that being developed is the student.

As for (8) principal and satellites, objective and subjective, bring up one as principal and the rest are satellites. The principal is taken to be the subjective, the satellites the objective.

As for (9) retrogression and progression, substance and function, this is the meaning of becoming and decay.[17]

As for (10) adapting to the faculties, inclinations, and natures of beings, as it says in the *Nirvāṇa* scripture, "Here the moon is seen full, while elsewhere it is seen half; yet the moon really has no waning or waxing."[18] According to the explanation of the Hua-yen school, there is always increase and decrease without there ever being increase or decrease, because they simultaneously interrelate.[19]

The substance of these ten aspects has no linear succession, however. Since interrelation has these ten aspects, so also do the other gates, Indra's net, and so forth. And it is not only these ten aspects—each one therein pervades the universe. This is why we bring up ten aspects: to form the sense of inexhaustibility.

Now to explain the first gate: simultaneous complete interrelation. This shows the aforementioned ten aspects—doctrine and meaning, principle and phenomena, and so on—simultaneously. How is this possible? It is due to the powerful function of the concentration which is like the ocean reflecting and the nature of things, whose actual qualities are interdependently originated. It is not attained by conditional practice of expedients—that is why it is simultaneous.

Now let us speak for the moment in terms of simultaneity of cause and effect. According to the teaching of cause and result in the lesser vehicle, the cause is developed to produce the result—only when the cause disappears is the result completed. According to the greater vehicle, cause and result can also be simultaneous, but the infinity of it is not brought to light. It is like the various interdependent elements of a house forming a house—the cause and result simultaneously become and do not form anything else. Because there is nearness and remoteness of causes, the product is finite.[20] If we explain cause and result by the comprehensive school, we introduce remote causal factors into the near; therefore when the house is complete, everything is produced at once.[21] If there is a single thing that is not established, this house is not established either. It is like this: if the first step arrives, all steps arrive. If the first step does not arrive, then all steps do not arrive. Therefore the scripture says, "Though one fulfill perfect enlightenment, one does not give up the initial inspiration."[22] And as the great scripture on transcendent wisdom says, "It is not at the beginning, yet not apart from the beginning; not the aftermath, yet not apart from the aftermath."[23] This is an explanation of enlightenment.

Question: Since you speak of arrival in one step, what is the need for a second step?

Answer: When you speak of arriving in one step, do you consider many identical to one? And when you say what is the need for a second step, do you consider this second step as one being identical to many? If the first step is one of many and the second step is a multiple of one, how can you say that arrival in one step does not need the second step? If one is not one of many and many is not many of one, not only can one step not arrive—even if you walk many steps you can never arrive. So we know that one step and many steps always contain the meaning of arriving and not arriving. Since it is thus in the cause, in result there is also the sense of no result. Therefore the *Nirvāṇa* scripture says, "The wise should definitely say both there is and there isn't."[24]

Now when we mention arriving in one step, it means the power of the concentration of oceanic reflection of the interdependent origination of the universe—speaking of arriving and not arriving [in terms of the oceanic reflection] is not the same as speaking of arriving and not arriving in terms of commonsense conception.[25] Therefore the scripture says that only those who are ready to be liberated can see it. This concentration does not lose sight of the relation of cause and effect and does not fall into nihilism or eternalism. Therefore the scripture says that we should abandon all false views by entering deeply into interdependent origination—that is what this means.

Question: If cause and result are simultaneous, then the cause becomes the result. But if the cause becomes the result, how can you say the relation of cause and effect is not lost?

Answer: As the "Treatise on the Ten Stages" says, "According to two different meanings of condition, there are two kinds of time. Based on the meaning of cause it is called cause; based on the meaning of result it is called result."[26] How can you say the cause and effect relation is lost? And since you say cause and result are simultaneous, how can you say they are lost? If they were lost, how could it be called simultaneity of cause and result?

Such being the simultaneity of cause and result, so in the same way doctrine and meaning, principle and phenomena, and so forth are also simultaneous.

Question: Since you speak of simultaneous interrelation, as you now bring up one matter, cause and result, does it include all the aforementioned ten aspects, such as doctrine and meaning?

Answer: We brought up the ten aspects just now to establish their inexhaustibility. If we discuss the complete merging of the worlds of past, present, and future, it is not only that each thing contains these ten aspects—it also contains innumerable laws, as extensive as the space of the universe, making it infinite infinities. If we spoke only in terms of a separate thing,[27] it would not establish infinity and would only be the same as the greater vehicle.

The second gate is the realm of the net of Indra. This gate uses a metaphor for illustration and also includes all the ten aspects such as doctrine and meaning. Just as the "Net of Brahma" scripture takes the net in the palace of Brahma for its simile,[28] now when we speak of the net of Indra we are taking the net of the palace of Indra as a metaphor. For this purpose we must first know what this net of Indra is like. It is like many mirrors reflecting each other: the reflections of all the mirrors appear in one mirror, and in these reflections are also reflected all the mirrors, and in each of these reflections too are reflected all the mirrors—thus the multiplied and remultiplied reflections make an infinity of infinities. Therefore, as it says in the scripture in the praises on the seventh stage, "In each atom [Buddha] shows countless Buddha expounding the Teaching."[29] This is the knowledge correctly awakening the world. In the same part of the scripture it also says, "In one atom he manifests countless Buddha-lands, with polar mountains and adamantine surrounding mountains, yet the world is not crowded." This illustration is based on the material world. It also says, "In one atom he shows there existing the three evil paths, gods, humans, and titans, each experiencing the consequences of their actions."[30] This illustration is based on the world of sentient beings. It also says, "What is shown in one atom is likewise shown in all atoms; therefore lands are manifested in an atom and also manifested in the atoms of those lands."[31] Therefore it makes an infinity of infinities. These illustrations represent the interdependent origination of the universe. According to knowledge and according to principle, its real qualities are like this—this is not said in terms of miraculous transformations or specific techniques. The explanation according to the greater vehicle says that the great and small can interpenetrate by virtue of transformation by psychic power,[32] or it says that they interpenetrate through a bodhisattva's power, or that they interpenetrate because they are nondual. This is not the same as the explanation of the unitary vehicle.

Question: If this school demonstrates interpenetration without question of psychic power and says that it is always inherently so, then there are no boundaries at all, no beginning or end. On what basis, then, can you elucidate cause and result, doctrine and meaning, and the like?

Answer: By differentiation according to cognition we bring up one as the principal, and the rest become satellites—just as in the net of Indra we bring up one jewel as the main one, and all the jewels are reflected in it: as it is with one jewel, so it is with all the jewels reflecting. Therefore in the aforementioned scripture one bodhisattva is mentioned as the principal surrounded by all the bodhisattvas—each one of the bodhisattvas is also like this.[33] It is also like in the scripture when bodhisattvas come from all directions to testify to the truth, all having the same name—so do all in the ten directions witness the truth in the same way.[34] Therefore they make infinite infinities, yet without losing the order of cause and effect, before and after, while at the same time there is no increase or decrease in the substance. Therefore the scripture says that even if all sentient beings become Buddhas the realm of Buddhahood does not increase and the realm of sentient beings does not decrease, while if not a single sentient being becomes a Buddha, the realm of sentient beings does not increase and the realm of Buddhahood does not decrease.

Third is the gate of latent coexistence of concealment and revelation. This is explained in terms of interdependent origination. It too includes the aforementioned ten aspects such as doctrine and meaning. "Concealment and revelation" means the same as the "half word" and "full word" in the *Nirvāṇa* scripture:[35] in the past the half word was expounded, so the half word was revealed and the full word was concealed; in the present the full word is expounded, so the full word is revealed while the half word is concealed. This is explaining concealment and revelation according to conditions. Also it is like the chapter on the metaphor of the moon saying, "Here it appears as half, elsewhere it appears full, yet the moon in essence has no waning or waxing. Because it is seen according to conditions, it seems to wax and wane."[36] This is an explanation belonging to the greater vehicle schools: if we explain according to the comprehensive school, it does not depend on expounding or not expounding—it is always half and always full; concealment and revelation are simultaneous. It is like the nature of the moon being always full yet always half, half and full having no different time. Therefore the Buddha fulfills the eight aspects of attaining the Way[37] in a single instant—the time of birth is identical to the time of death, because they simultaneously come into being together.[38] That is why it is called latent. It is like the count of ten: insofar as one is ten, one is revealed, while two, three, four, up to ten, are concealed. Also, "entering right concentration in the eye faculty" is revelation; "arising from concentration in forms" is called conceal-

ment.[39] Yet this concealment and revelation is essentially not successive; therefore it is called latent.

Fourth is the gate of minute containment and establishment.
This is explained in terms of forms and characteristics. An atom
is the small form, for example, while innumerable Buddha-lands,
polar and surrounding mountains, and so forth are the large forms.
By the unobstructed freedom of the actual qualities of interdependent origination they are made to contain each other; because they
are not made by men or gods, they are securely established. It is like
this: there are defiled lands in one atom, while in the very same
atom there are innumerable pure lands which exist there without
interfering with the defiled lands, and without the pure lands losing
their characteristics. There are even lands shaped like banners, tri-
angles, parallelograms, and so on in the one atom,[40] never impeding
each other. Therefore the book on Samantabhadra says, "All worlds
enter a single atom, yet the worlds do not pile up, nor do they dis-
perse."[41] If one can universally relate to them and unite with them,
one can see innumerable lands in a single atom, without confusion,
without increase or decrease. How can "containing a mountain in a
mustard seed" be considered difficult?[42] The establishment and mutual containment of principle and phenomena, and the other ten
aspects, are also like this.

Question: What difference is there between this gate of mutual
containment and the previous gate of Indra's net?

Answer: The interrelating reflection of the various aspects mutually revealing each other, producing multiplication and remultiplication ad infinitum, pertains to the gate of the net of Indra. If all
the aspects are together revealed at once without impeding each
other, this pertains to the mutual containment.

Fifth is the gate of various becoming of separate things in the
ten time frames. This is explained in terms of the three time frames
[of past, present, and future]. As it says in the book on detachment
from the world, "The ten time frames are the past of the past, the
future of the past, the present of the past, the present of the present,
the future of the present, the past of the present, the future of the
future, the past of the future, the present of the future, and considering the three time frames as one instant,"[43] summing up the preceding nine, making ten. In this way, the ten time frames, by virtue of

interdependent origination, mutually identify and even mutually interpenetrate, yet without losing the three time frames. It is like the five fingers making a fist yet not losing fingerhood: though the ten time frames are simultaneous, yet the ten time frames are not lost. Therefore the scripture says, "Past eons enter the future, the present eon enters the past, future eons enter the present."[44] It also says, "Long eons enter short eons, short eons enter long eons, existent eons enter nonexistent eons, nonexistent eons enter eons."[45] It also says, "The past is the future, the future is the past, the present is the past—bodhisattvas comprehend it all." It also says that inexhaustible, countless eons can be one moment, not long, not short: the sphere of liberated people is like this.[46] The ten time frames interpenetrate and interidentify, yet without losing the characteristics of succession and duration: therefore it is said that separate things variously become. The ten aspects of doctrine and meaning, principle and phenomena, and the like mutually interpenetrate and identify, yet without losing their characteristics of succession and distinction—that is why it is called "various becoming."

Sixth is the gate of all repositories being pure and mixed, containing all virtues. This is explained in terms of the ways of transcendence.[47] What does it mean? It is like this: if we speak in terms of the first way, giving, then everything is called giving—therefore it is called "pure." And yet this way of giving contains the practices of all the ways of transcendence, so it is called "mixed." In this way purity and mixture do not interfere with each other—therefore it is called "containing all virtues."

According to the explanation in the book on one instant in the great scripture on transcendent wisdom, from beginning to end does not go beyond a single moment of thought—this is called "pure." Yet in this one moment of thought are included myriad practices—this is called "mixed."[48] Nevertheless, it is different from the meaning of purity and mixture here. Why? The "one moment" spoken of in that scripture means that they all are one with nonapprehensibility—it does not clarify the function of interdependent origination. As we explain purity here, if we do so in terms of giving, all is giving; if we speak of the way of tolerance, all is tolerance. Speaking of the way of tolerance, all actions are like space—this is called "pure." Yet this way of tolerance fully includes all the ways, so it is called "mixed." Purity and mixture do not disturb each other, so it is called "containing all virtues." Therefore it is not the same as the book on one instant.

Question: What is the difference between this and the meaning of mutual inclusion of the six ways of transcendence?[49]

Answer: The meaning of the mutual inclusion of the six ways of transcendence is like including all the ways in giving, yet the other ways are not giving. According to our explanation, when including all the ways in giving, none of the ways are not giving, by virtue of interdependent origination. Therefore it is not the same as the mutual inclusion of the six ways of transcendence.

Therefore one includes nine and ten, and nine and ten and so forth are all one—for this reason it is called "pure." Then again, within one are included nine and ten and so on, so for this reason it is also called "mixed." Thus we know it is not the same as the meaning of mutual inclusion.

Question: And what is the difference between this and the doctrine of the great scripture on transcendent wisdom of mutual support? In that case, if one of the supports is missing, mutual support cannot be established; here, if the count of ten lacks one, it too cannot be established—so what is the difference between them?

Answer: When that scripture speaks of mutual support [of the transcendent ways], still the subject [supporter] is not the object [supported]. Now we say ten makes one and one is ten—therefore it is not the same as the doctrine of mutual support.

Seventh is the gate of one and many containing each other yet not being the same. This is explained in terms of noumenon. Because one enters many and many enter one, it is called "mutual containing." Because their being itself is not successive, yet does not lose the characteristics of one and many, it is called "not the same." This is the real quality of interdependent origination and is not something cultivated by gods or humans. Therefore the scripture says, "With one Buddha-land the ten directions are filled; and the ten directions also enter one completely. And yet the original characteristics of the worlds are not destroyed. This can be so because of the sovereign power of free vows."[50] Also, as it says in the book on Samantabhadra, "The bodies of all sentient beings enter the body of one sentient being; the body of one sentient being enters the bodies of all sentient beings."⁵¹ It also says, "All worlds are made to enter an atom; the worlds do not pile up or become mixed."⁵² The mountain and the mustard seed are not explained here.

Eighth is the gate of freedom of mutual interidentification of all things. This is explained in terms of function and involves—in terms of the ten aspects of doctrine and meaning, principle and phenomena, and so forth—apprehending the freedom of the three kinds of worlds merging unhindered.⁵³ Therefore one includes all, making an infinity of infinities. Because they are inexhaustible, they interidentify and interpenetrate. This is said in reference to function.

Question: Here you explain their infinite infinity, interidentifying and interpenetrating—how is it different from the previous gates of the net of Indra and mutual containment?

Answer: It is as we explained in the metaphorical exposition of the aspect of same being. If we speak in terms of interrelated reflections mutually showing each other, multiplied and remultiplied, making them infinite, then this pertains to the gate of Indra's net. If all aspects simultaneously appear together without mutual interference, this pertains to the gate of mutual containment. If we deal with the three worlds merging with unhindered freedom, interidentifying and interpenetrating, becoming an infinity of infinities, then this pertains to this gate.

Question: If in this way they interidentify and thus also interpenetrate, making their infinity infinite, then they are undifferentiated, with no boundaries. What then is the beginning, what the end, what is cause, what is result?

Answer: This becomes infinite to the power of infinity based on the nature of the substance of the interdependent origination of the universe: therefore the succession of cause and result is not lost. Although succession is not lost, yet "before" and "after" mutually identify and interpenetrate: therefore it becomes infinite. Because before and after imply each other and also interpenetrate, perfect enlightenment is fulfilled at the time of the first determination for enlightenment. It is like the previous gates: one is all—it is infinite to an infinite degree, and the same is true of two and three. Therefore this scripture, in praising the virtues of the first determination, says, "The virtues of that moment [of thought directed to enlightenment] are profound and boundlessly vast; a Buddha could not explain them all in particular even in an eon."[54] This illustrates the one being all, making the all infinite. It also says, "How much the more so to cultivate fully the virtues and practices of the ways of transcendence and stages of enlightenment, over immeasurable, countless, boundless eons."[55] This goes from two and three to nine and ten, all being infinite. Therefore, from the first mind of the ten grades of faith to the ten abodes, ten practices, ten dedications, and ten stages,[56] all clarify the fulfillment of Buddhahood, because the beginning and end interidentify and also interpenetrate, becoming infinite.

Question: According to your previous explanation, the qualities of the result [Buddhahood] are utterly beyond speech. How then can the final mind of the ten grades of faith contain the virtues and function of the fruition of Buddhahood? If the ten grades of faith are the same as the qualities of the result, then the qualities of the result are expressible characteristics, so how could they be inexplicable?

Answer: To say the bodhisattvas in the state of cause have the qualities of the result indicates the inexpressibility of the qualities of the result. Therefore a passage extolling virtues says, "Bodhisattvas abiding in this one stage embody the virtues of all the stages."

Question: If one stage includes the virtues of all the stages, and one is all and the beginning includes the end, then one stage should be complete—what is the need for the other stages?

Answer: Without the rest of the stages, one stage could not be. It is like one *sheng* measure including a *tou* measure [1 *tou* = 10 *sheng*]: if there were no individual *sheng*, this *tou* would not be.

Question: Suppose there is no *tou* without *sheng*. If we now scoop up a *sheng*, will we get a *tou?* If we cannot get a *tou* with a *sheng* measure, then one practice cannot include all practices.

Answer: Ten *sheng* together make one *tou*—when there is no *sheng*, how can we make a *tou?* Therefore we know that without *sheng* there is no *tou*, and since there is *sheng* there is *tou*. Now when we bring up the identity of *sheng* and *tou*, we mean that outside of the *sheng* of *tou* there is no *tou* of *sheng*—it is like the ungraspability of turtle hair and rabbit horns. In fulfilling Buddhahood in the first determination, outside of fulfillment there is no separate cultivation; its characteristics are like space. Therefore when we say that one attains Buddhahood in the first inspiration, it does not mean that all virtues are not included. As it says in the scripture,[57] the youth Universal Adornment in one lifetime saw the Buddha and heard the Teaching and attained concentration; then, later, he saw other Buddhas after the prior Buddhas had passed away, and he attained further concentration. In the first lifetime he was able to see and hear; as he practiced what he learned in the second life, he accomplished its understanding and application; and in the third life he entered the ocean of fruition: it was all one great tree of interdependent origination, and these three lifetimes were in but a single moment. It is like a long journey whose arrival lies in the first step: yet the arrival in this first step does not mean there are no subsequent steps. This makes it clear that when this youth entered the ocean of fruition it was not that he had not planted roots of goodness for a long time.

Question: Since you say he attained only upon long cultivation, how can you say he attained in one instant?

Answer: To speak of long cultivation of roots of goodness is in the province of the three vehicles: entering from the three vehicles into the one vehicle is the beginning and end complete in one instant. That is why the scripture says, "One attains true enlightenment at the time of one's first determination, fulfilling the body of wisdom, not understanding depending on another."[58] It is like myriad streams entering the ocean; as soon as it enters, a single drop pervades the entire ocean, having no beginning or end; as for the depth of the water of the rivers outside the ocean, it cannot reach that of the one drop which has entered the ocean. Therefore, using the cultivation in the three vehicles, the many eons of the three vehicles do not equal the one moment in the one vehicle.[59] Therefore afterward we explain that when Sudhana set out from Mañjuśrī's place to seek teachers, passing through a hundred and ten cities, this still did not compare to the instant he saw Samantabhadra Bodhisattva.[60] So we know that when one manages to enter this great ocean of interdependent origination, does one not attain Buddhahood in an instant? As for those who begin to sit and concentrate and just grasp the quiet mind and immediately say they have attained Buddhahood, this too is still called attainment of Buddhahood, but it cannot be complete ultimate attainment. The rivers may also be water, but they cannot yet be the same as the water of the ocean.

Here we have generally explained the meaning of attaining

Buddhahood in an instant: according to the explanation of the lesser vehicle it requires three incalculable eons and a full hundred eons of practice and embellishing works before one can attain Buddhahood. If the practice is not fulfilled, even though one may desire to attain Buddhahood one cannot. Therefore there is no doctrine of attaining Buddhahood in an instant [in the lesser vehicle].

As for the doctrine of attaining Buddhahood in an instant as explained in the greater vehicle, there are two general kinds. The first is by understanding conditions and entering true nature, where there is no much or little.[61] Therefore it explains the doctrine of attaining Buddhahood in an instant. This is like the meaning of the book on one instant in the great scripture on transcendent wisdom. The second is practice—once practice is fulfilled, that final moment is called attaining Buddhahood. It is like someone on a long journey, where the final step becomes arrival. This second kind also partially invokes interdependent origination, and it also elucidates the three incalculable eons of practice of the Way: before the stages is one incalculable eon; from the first to the seventh stage is the second incalculable eon; and from the eighth to the tenth stage is the third incalculable eon. But still this doctrine does not definitely rest on the existence of attainment of Buddhahood in an instant, so we know it is indefinite.

If we explain attainment of Buddhahood in an instant according to the unitary vehicle, it is like the greater vehicle reaching the final moment, attaining Buddhahood, and thereupon entering the unitary vehicle. Because the end depends on the beginning, the first moment is completion. Why? Because cause and result imply each other and simultaneously correspond. Therefore if we want to talk about the fulfillment, the fulfillment is fulfilled, and that fulfillment is again fulfilled. If sentient beings are going to be later in fulfilling Buddhahood, being later is also later and that being later is later again. Therefore the book on inconceivables says that it is not that the Buddhas are not enlightened before—for the sake of sentient beings in every instant they again and again sever bonds anew, yet do not stay in the state of learning but fulfill true enlightenment.[62] Therefore the fulfillment in one instant we are now bringing up is being of the same status as Buddha but not yet seeing the ultimate— thus there is also difference in shallowness and profundity. It is like someone who has just gone out the gate and one who has long been traveling abroad—although they are both out in the open, there is a distinction between far and near. Therefore while we speak of attaining Buddhahood in each of the grades of faith, the abodes, and so forth, yet we distinguish shallowness and depth. This should be carefully considered.

Ninth is the gate of creation only by the operation of mind. This is explained in terms of mind. "Only by the operation of mind" means that the various aspects previously mentioned—doctrine and meaning and so on—all are established by the pure true mind of the nature of the matrix of the issue of thusness.[63] Good or bad is according to the operation of the mind—which is why it is called creation by the operation of the mind. Since there is no separate objective realm outside of mind, we say "only mind." If it operates harmoniously, it is called nirvana; that is why the scripture says, "Mind makes the Buddhas."[64] If it operates perversely, it is birth-and-death; therefore the scripture says, "The triple world is illusory —it is only made by one mind."[65] Birth-and-death and nirvana do not go beyond the mind, so we cannot definitely say that their nature is pure or impure. Therefore the *Nirvāṇa* scripture says, "The Buddha-nature is not pure and not impure."[66] Purity and impurity are both only mind; therefore apart from mind there is nothing else. Hence the *Laṅkāvatāra* scripture says, "Outside mind there is no objective realm, no illusory views of sense data."[67]

Question: If there are no objects outside of mind and existence and nonexistence are both creations of mind, when someone has seen something outside a screen and then someone else takes it away, the former person thinks it is there but in reality it is not. How then can you say it is created by mind?

Answer: If we go along with the operation of the false mind, this thing outside the screen also goes along with the being or nonbeing of the mind; then again the mind goes along with removing the thing or not removing the thing. If we speak in terms of the real pure mind of the matrix of the issue of thusness, the substance of this thing relates to everything in the ten directions while not moving from its original place. Its essence is constant and always in operation [in the nexus of interrelation]. Even if the thing is moved to another location it never moves from its original place. This is

the power of freedom of interdependent origination—it is not done
by magic. Therefore, although [in the Hua-yen scripture] Buddha is
said to have appeared in seven places in nine meetings, he never left
the quiescent site of enlightenment. This is what is meant by the
statement in the *Vimalakīrti* scripture, "Mañjuśrī comes with no
sign of coming, sees with no sign of seeing."[68]

Tenth is the gate of using phenomena to illustrate the Teaching
and produce understanding. This is explained in terms of knowing.
"Using phenomena" means, for example, the scripture's mention of
the phenomena of the Golden World,[69] illustrating the things which
originate in reality; "all banners" and "all canopies" [mentioned
there] are the body of practice. Also, the book on entering the cosmos of reality says that when Maitreya opened the tower, Sudhana
saw the causal deeds done by Maitreya Bodhisattva, leading to the
site of enlightenment, because the tower was the characteristics of
enlightenment.[70] Therefore we speak of using phenomena to illustrate the Teaching and produce understanding.

As for what is explained in the schools of the greater vehicle,
they too use phenomena to illustrate the Teaching; that is, they use
different phenomena to illustrate teachings of different principles.
Here, because [in the Hua-yen teaching] phenomena *are* the Teaching, whatever phenomena are brought up, inexhaustible teachings
are included. That is why when the banners and so on are brought
up, in each case it is said "all." Therefore it is not the same as the
teaching of the greater vehicle. Here the explanation of cause and
result is like that of the unitary vehicle.

Cultivation of Contemplation of the Inner Meaning of the Hua-yen: The Ending of Delusion and Return to the Source

by Fa-tsang

THIS TREATISE, like Tu Shun's "Contemplation of the Realm of Reality," appears to have been highly esteemed in the contemplative school of Ch'an Buddhism and makes extensive reference to the "Treatise on Awakening of Faith in the Great Vehicle," a text which was very popular in the Ch'an and Consciousness Only schools. It is arranged in six parts, each presented in a corresponding number of sections; bringing up one essence, two functions, three universals, four virtues, five cessations, and six contemplations, Fa-tsang leads them harmoniously one into the other, providing a broad but unified spectrum of philosophical and practical teachings.

The one essence is the essence of thusness, or the pure mind. It is called luminous or completely illumined and inherently pure. Inherent purity refers to the nonduality of being and emptiness—emptiness is called inherent purity, beyond conceptions. The luminousity or complete illumination of being is the state before the dichotomization of subject and object and the development of false consciousness based on this dualism.

The two functions of this essence are the "oceanic reflection," referring to fundamental, holistic awareness of thusness, and the "complete illumination of the realm of reality," which means action in accord with awareness of reality, actualizing the truths of the universe.

The three universals are metaphysical correlates of the principle of universal relativity. Since each particle of the cosmos depends on the whole cosmos for its establishment, "one atom pervades the universe." Since the establishment of the cosmos depends on each atom, "one atom produces infinity." In light of this relativity, "one atom contains emptiness and existence." These three universals represent both the mutual noninterference of noumenon and phenomena and also the noninterference of phenomena among themselves. These universals show the setting and scope of actions and hence the importance of being careful about what is done, since everything is related. Fa-tsang thus proceeds in his treatise to outline the practice of four virtues. The first virtue is subtle, or nonconceptualized, activity according to conditions, without conventionalized method; this refers to supraconventional morality, acting in ways conducive to liberation, which cannot be definitely fixed in conventional patterns. The second virtue is that of dignified, regulated conduct, which refers to conventional Buddhist morality, the observance of certain ethical precepts, the main thrust of which is to prevent injury and deception. The third type of virtue is mentioned is treating people with peace, harmony, and honesty. The fourth virtue is accepting suffering for all beings, which basically refers to the bodhisattva's remaining in the midst of the world, not shrinking from its turmoil and pain, in order to carry out enlightening activity.

On the basis of the peace and security fostered by these virtues, cessation of cogitation is practiced in order to nullify mental habits and eliminate customary views. Five basic types of cessation practice are brought up by Fa-tsang: cessation by awareness of the pure emptiness of things and consequent detachment from objects; cessation by contemplating the nullity of person and as a result cutting off desire; cessation by realizing the spontaneity of natural becoming and thereby stopping compulsive involvement and the seeking or resisting of change; cessation by concentration without thought; and formless cessation by realization of the merging of existence and emptiness. These cessations correspond to the realization of the emptiness of things and persons, realization of noncontention and effortlessness, achievement of the ability to focus pure awareness of mind itself, and attainment of union of objectivity and equanimity.

Finally Fa-tsang presents six contemplations or ways of seeing which comprehend and integrate all that has been mentioned before—the essence, the functions, universals, virtues, and cessation. As seen in the five cessations, contemplation is used to initiate and direct cessation, and the effect of true cessation is used to empower the contemplation that succeeds it by making it single-minded and unopposed by residual habits. The six ways brought up by Fa-tsang here are contemplation of true emptiness, returning objectification to mind; contemplation of the inconceivable existence of realms or objects manifested by mind; contemplation of the merging of mind and environment, breaking through the subject-object barrier; contemplation of the reflection of myriad objects in the body of knowledge; contemplation of the forms of many bodies entering one mirror; and contemplation of the net of Indra, in which principals and satellites reflect each other.

The first contemplation involves realizing that what are conventionally thought to be hard and fast realities are in fact terms assigned to foci of attention—organizations of impressions are not objective realities and "things" in themselves are ungraspable. Then, realizing the role of the mind in the ordering of the environment, the possibility of participating consciously and progressively in the continuous reformation of the universe dawns. The mind then can lose its boundaries of thought and merge with the environment, receiving information ranging beyond the strictures of word and concept, reflecting myriad conditions of the environment in a mirrorlike faculty from which is born the body of knowledge. Then, the contemplation of many bodies entering one mirror is the observation of the realm of mutual noninterference among phenomena, which is the simultaneous interdependence of all things, appearing all at once in the mirror of the whole awareness. Fa-tsang presents this notion in terms of the interdependence of the ten bodies of Buddhahood, meaning that mind, environment, beings, and enlightenment are all immanent in one another. The final contemplation, the unique vision of the net of Indra, shows the free noninterference of focal and total awareness. Each element is both the focal point of all elements and also the satellite of all other elements in their capacity as focal points, with all things thus reflecting each other ad infinitum.

THE FULL TEACHING IS INCONCEIVABLE—when you look into a single atom it appears all at once. The complete school is unfathomable— by observing a fine hair it is all equally revealed. Functions are separated in the essence, however, and are not without different patterns; phenomena are manifest depending on noumenon and inherently have a unitary form.

It is like this: when sickness occurs, medicine is developed; when delusion is born, knowledge is established. When the sickness is gone, the medicine is forgotten; it is like using an empty fist to stop a child's crying.[1] When the mind is penetrated, phenomena are penetrated; empty space is adduced to represent universality. One awakened, once enlightened, what obstruction or penetration is there? The clinging of the hundred negations is stopped; the exaggeration and underestimation of the four propositions is ended.[2] Thereby we find that medicine and sickness both disappear, quietude and confusion both melt and dissolve: it is thereby possible to enter the mysterious source, efface "nature" and "characteristics," and enter the realm of reality.

As I see it, the mystic network of the Teaching is vast and its sublime message is extremely subtle. How can those who look over it fathom its source? Rarely do those who search through it discover its ultimate extent. Therefore true emptiness sticks in the mind, always becoming a field of conditioned thought; reality abides right before our eyes, but it is turned into a realm of names and characterizations.

Here in this work I am collecting the mysterious profundities and summing up the great source, producing a volume of scripture within an atom, turning the wheel of the Teaching on a hair. Those with clarity will grow in virtue on the same day; the blind have no hope in many lives. For those who understand the message, mountains are easy to move; for those who turn away from the source, ounces are hard to take.

I have concentrated on searching through the Hua-yen scripture and have read the ancient explanations extensively. Including mystic passages from the three treasuries of the canon, going by the sublime teachings of the five vehicles, I have had to cut off excessive verbiage and restore where the sense was defective. Although I am therefore making a collection, certainly, yet there is precedent for doing so.

To plumb this ocean of essence and comprehend that forest of practice, I bring up six separate gates through which they all become a single view, different yet not mixed, clear all in one. I hope that sentient beings will turn back from deluded ways so that the sun of illumination can dawn for all alike. May civilized people who uphold the Way be humbly thoroughgoing in this study.

Now I must explain this contemplation, which is divided into six gates in all; first I shall list the names and then later explain them:

1. Revealing one essence: this means the inherently pure, complete, luminous essence, which is pure of its own nature.

2. Activating two functions: (a) the eternal function of the oceanic reflection of the web of forms; (b) the self-existent function of the complete illumination of the realm of reality.

3. Showing three universals: (a) the universality of one atom pervading the universe; (b) the universality of one atom producing infinity; (c) the universality of one atom containing emptiness and existence.

4. Practicing four virtues: (a) the virtue of subtle function according to conditions without convention; (b) the virtue of maintaining dignified, regulated, exemplary conduct; (c) the virtue of receiving beings with gentleness, harmony, honesty, and straightforwardness; (d) the virtue of accepting suffering in place of all sentient beings.

5. Entering five cessations: (a) cessation by awareness of the pure emptiness of things and detachment from objects; (b) cessation by contemplating the voidness of person and cutting off desire; (c) cessation because of the spontaneity of the profusion of natural evolution; (d) cessation by the light of concentration shining forth without thought; (e) formless cessation in the hidden communion of phenomena and noumenon.

6. Developing six contemplations: (a) the contemplation of real emptiness, returning objects to mind; (b) contemplation of the inconceivable existence of realms manifested by the mind; (c) con-

templation of mystic merging of mind and environment; (d) contemplation of the reflection of myriad objective conditions in the body of knowledge; (e) contemplation of the forms of many bodies entering one mirror; (f) contemplation of the imperial net [of Indra], in which principal and satellites reflect one another.

The first gateway, the revelation of one essence, means the essence that is inherently pure, complete, and luminous—this is the essence of the nature of things within the matrix of the issue of thusness. Since it is fundamentally complete of its own nature and is not defiled in the midst of impurity and not purified by cultivation, it is inherently pure. Since its natural essence shines everywhere and no hidden recess is not lit up, it is completely luminous.

Moreover, defilement occurring along with the flow [of the mundane] does not taint it and going against the flow to get rid of defilement does not purify it. It can be in the body of a saint without increase and it can be in the body of an ordinary person without decrease. Even though there is the difference of concealment or revelation, there is no variety of distinctions: when afflictions cover it, it is concealed; when wisdom realizes it, it is revealed. It is not produced by the cause of birth; it is realized only by the cause of understanding.[3]

The "Treatise on Awakening of Faith says, "The inherent essence of true thusness has the meaning of the light of great knowledge and wisdom, the meaning of panoramic illumination of the cosmos of realities, the meaning of really true cognition and knowledge, and the meaning of mind inherently pure."[4] It is extensively explained in that fashion. Thus it is called the inherently pure, completely luminous essence.

Next, the activation of two functions based on the essence means activating two functions based on the aforementioned pure essence. One is the eternal function of the oceanic reflection of the web of forms. The "oceanic reflection" means the fundamental awareness of true thusness. When delusion ends, the mind is clear and myriad forms equally appear; it is like the ocean, where waves are created by the wind—when the wind stops, the water of the ocean grows still and clear, reflecting all images. The "Treatise on Awakening of Faith" calls it "the repository of infinite qualities—

the ocean of the true thusness of the nature of things."⁵ That is why it is called the oceanic reflection meditation. A scripture says, "The web of forms and their myriad appearances are all the reflections of a single truth."⁶ The one truth, or reality, spoken of here is the so-called one mind; this mind includes all mundane and transmundane elements and is identical to the essence of the teaching of the aspect of totality of the cosmos of reality. It is only because of delusive thoughts that there are distinctions; if you transcend illusory ideas there is just one true thusness. That is why it is called the oceanic reflection.

The Hua-yen scripture says, "It may manifest the form of boys or girls, gods, dragons, or titans, even vipers and so on; according to what they enjoy, they are caused to see it—the forms and characteristics of sentient beings are all different, and their actions and sounds are also infinite."⁷ Thus everything manifests the miraculous power of the oceanic reflection meditation. On the basis of this teaching it is called the oceanic reflection meditation.

The second function is the independent function of the complete illumination of the realm of reality. This is the flower ornament meditation: it means extensive practice of myriad actions conforming to truth and producing virtue, realizing enlightenment throughout the universe.

As for "flower ornament," the "flower" has the function of producing the fruit and action has the power to effect results. Now this is using a phenomenon to make an illustration; that is why the flower is brought up as a metaphor. "Ornament" means the accomplishment of practice, fulfillment of the result, meeting with truth and according with reality. "Nature" and "characteristics" both vanish, subject and object are both obliterated—it shines clearly revealed and is thus called an ornament.

Indeed, unless it is practice which flows from reality, there is no way to meet with reality; how can there be practice which adorns the real but does not arise from reality? This means that reality includes the ramifications of illusion, so no practice is not cultivated; illusion penetrates the source of reality, so no characteristic is not void.⁸ Therefore it is called the self-existent function of the complete illumination of the realm of reality.⁹

The Hua-yen scripture says, "Adorning and purifying inconceivably many lands, offering them to all the enlightened ones, emitting great light without bound, liberating infinite sentient beings, with generosity, morality, forbearance, diligence, as well as meditation, wisdom, skill in means, miraculous powers, and so on —in these they are all independent by the power of the Buddha's flower ornament meditation."[10] On the basis of this teaching it is called the flower ornament meditation.

The third gateway, showing three universals, means that based on the two functions mentioned in each function the universe is pervaded—that is why they are called universals. As for the three universals, first is the universal of one atom pervading the universe: this means that an atom has no inherent nature—it involves all reality in its establishment. Since reality is boundless, so accordingly is the atom. The scripture says, "In all the atoms in the Flower Treasury world, in each atom the universe is seen; jewel lights show Buddhas like clouds gathering. This is the freedom in all fields of the enlightened."[11] According to this teaching, it should be known that one atom pervades the universe.

Second is the universal of one atom producing infinity. This means that the atom has no essence of its own and its becoming must depend on reality. Since true thusness contains innumerable qualities, the functions arising from reality also have myriad differences. The "Treatise on Awakening of Faith" says, "Real thusness has of its own essence the meaning of eternity, bliss, self, and purity, the meaning of pure, cool, unchanging freedom; it contains innumerable such qualities, so ultimately it has not the slightest lack."[12]

Therefore the Hua-yen scripture says, "In this Flower Treasury ocean of worlds, whether it be mountains or rivers, down to trees, forests, even a mote of dust, a hair—not one is not in accord with the universe of true thusness, including boundless qualities."[13] By this teaching it should be known that an atom is at once noumenon and phenomenon, is person and is thing, is "that" and is "this," is object and is subject, is defiled and is pure, is cause and is effect, is same and is different, is one and is many, is broad and is narrow, is animate and is inanimate, is the three bodies and is the ten bodies [of Buddha].

Why? Since phenomena and noumenon are without interference, phenomenon and phenomenon are without mutual interference. Because things are like this, the ten bodies together perform free functioning; therefore it is only within the purview of enlightening beings with the universal eye. Among the phenomenal characteristics cited, each one again contains the others, includes the others—each contains infinitely multiplied and remultiplied delineations of objects. The scripture says, "The inexhaustible ocean of all teachings is converged on the enlightenment site of a single thing. The nature of things as such is explained by the Buddha; the eye of wisdom can understand this technique."[14]

Question: According to this explanation, then, in a single atom no principle is not revealed, no phenomenon is not merged, no passage is not explained, no meaning not conveyed. How can those not cultivating and studying in the present become enlightened at an atom and settle manifold doubts all at once? And in the atom, what is defilement, what is called purity? What is real, what is called conventional? What is called birth-and-death, what is called nirvana? What is called the principle of the lesser vehicle, what is called the principle of the greater vehicle? Please give us some definitions and let us hear what we have not yet heard.

Answer: Great knowledge, round and clear, looks at a fine hair and comprehends the ocean of nature; the source of reality is clearly manifest in one atom, yet illumines the whole of being. When myriad phenomena arise, they must be at the same time, in one space—noumenon has no before or after. Why? Because the illusory characteristics of this atom can block the vision of reality, it is defiled; because this atom's characteristics are empty and nonexistent, it is pure. Because this atom's fundamental essence is the same as thusness, it is real; because its characteristics are conditionally produced and exist as illusions, it is artificial. Because thoughts of the atom's characteristics change every moment, it is birth-and-death; because, observing the atom in contemplation, the signs of origination and annihilation of the atom's characteristics are all empty and without reality, it is nirvana. Because the atom's characteristics, great or small, are all discriminations of the deluded mind, it is affliction; because the essence of the atom's characteristics is fundamentally empty and null, and clinging thoughts end of themselves, it is enlightenment. Because the essence of the atom's characteristics is without mental construction, it is the principle of the

lesser vehicle; because the nature of the atom has no birth, no
destruction, and depends on others for its seeming existence, it is the
principle of the greater vehicle.

In this way I explain in brief; if it were said in full, even if all
sentient beings had doubts, each different, and questioned the Buddha, the Buddha would simply use the one word "atom" to solve
and explain for them. This should be pondered deeply. The scripture says, "The inexhaustible ocean of all truths is expounded in a
single word, completely, without remainder."[15] Based on this teaching it is called the universal of one atom producing infinity.

Third is the universal of an atom containing emptiness and
existence. This means the atom has no intrinsic nature, so it is
empty; yet its illusory characteristics are evident, so it is existent.
Indeed, because illusory form has no essence, it must be no different
from emptiness, and real emptiness contains qualities permeating to
the surface of existence. Seeing that form is empty produces great
wisdom and not dwelling in birth-and-death; seeing that emptiness
is form produces great compassion and not dwelling in nirvana.
When form and emptiness are nondual, compassion and wisdom
are not different; only this is true seeing.

The *Ratnagotra-śāstra* says, "Bodhisattvas before the Path still
have three doubts about this real emptiness and inconceivable existence. The first is that they suspect emptiness annihilates form and
hence grasp nihilistic emptiness. The second is that they suspect
emptiness is different from form and hence grasp emptiness outside
of form. The third is that they suspect emptiness is a thing and
hence grasp emptiness as an entity."[16]

Now I must explain this. Form is illusory form and necessarily
does not interfere with emptiness. Emptiness is true emptiness and
necessarily does not interfere with form. If it interfered with form, it
would be nihilistic emptiness. If it interfered with emptiness, it
would be solid form. Since one atom contains true emptiness and
inconceivable existence as noted above, we should know that all
atoms are also thus. If you realize this principle, you will find that
an atom contains the ten directions with no abrogation of great and
small; an instant contains the nine time frames, with extension and
brevity being simultaneous. That is why we have excellent subtle
words with a fine hair showing the complete teaching and why we

have extraordinary holy scripture with a mote of dust manifesting the whole of being. It goes far beyond the horizons of speech and thought. It penetrates the trap of words and concepts.

The scripture says, "It is like a huge scripture, as extensive as a billion-world system, existing inside an atom, with the same being true of all atoms. If there is one person with clear wisdom, whose pure eye sees clearly in every way, he breaks open the atom and takes out the scripture for the widespread welfare of sentient beings."[17] Speaking according to the principle, the "atom" represents the false conceptions of sentient beings and the "scripture" is the complete illumination of great knowledge. Since the body of knowledge is boundless, it is said to be as extensive as a billion-world system. In accord with this teaching, it is called the universal of an atom containing emptiness and existence.

Next, proceeding from these three universalizing perspectives, practicing four virtues means cultivating four kinds of practical virtue based on the aforementioned perspective of the universality of an atom.

First is the virtue of subtle action according to conditions without convention. This means initiating action based on reality for the widespread welfare of sentient beings. Sentient beings' faculties and capacities are not the same, so they receive understanding in myriad different ways; their inclinations are not the same, so they are given teachings according to their state of potentiality like being given medicines in accordance with their illnesses. This meaning is thoroughly clarified in the Vimalakīrti scripture.[18]

By virtue of great compassion it is called "according to conditions," and by virtue of great wisdom it is called "subtle action." And by virtue of not demolishing artificial names and yet always liberating sentient beings it is called "according to conditions." If you comprehend the inherent emptiness of sentient beings, there is really no one to liberate or be liberated, so it is called subtle action. Moreover, because the real does not oppose the mundane, you accord with conditions; because the mundane does not oppose the real, you function subtly. Further, you produce the branches from the root, so it is according to conditions; and you gather the branches back to the root, so it is subtle function.

Indeed, because things have no boundaries, when they appear

they must be simultaneous. The principle of reality does not hinder myriad differences; responsive manifestations are all in one space. The function is like waves leaping and churning. Carrying on action with the whole essence of reality, in essence the mirror is clear, the water is still. In bringing up accord with conditions, we understand peacefulness. It is like beams of sunlight, mindlessly illumining myriad forms without moving.[19] Therefore it is called the virtue of subtle action according to conditions without convention.

Second is the virtue of maintaining dignified, well-regulated, exemplary conduct. This means the four dignified modes of bearing —walking, standing, sitting, reclining. In the greater vehicle there are eighty thousand, in the lesser vehicle three thousand [dignified manners],[20] as a model for upholding and abiding by, to straighten the tangled threads of the six harmonies.[21] A ladder out of the mundane, a swift boat over the ocean of suffering, to help beings and guide the lost—nothing is greater than this.

But as the Golden Countenance of Buddha has hidden its light, and the True Teaching has declined, its transmission has become weakened, confused, and guided by personal views until this has caused the Teaching to lack cohesion and order. Dipping randomly from the pure stream, gain and loss arise together and falsehood mixes with true purity, therefore causing beginning students to go wrong in every event they encounter, not relying on the scriptures and precepts, mixing in ordinary sentiments, being the downfall of self and others—it is utterly pitiful.

Therefore the "Treatise on Yoga" says, "Not great sinking, not small floating, always abiding in right-mindfulness, flawlessly cultivating pure conduct, basic and incidental."[22]

The Hua-yen scripture says, "Morality is the basis of unexcelled enlightenment—you should fully uphold pure morality."[23]

The "Net of Brahma" scripture says, "Bodhisattvas as numerous as atoms accomplish true enlightenment based on this."[24]

The "Treatise on Awakening of Faith" says, "By knowing that the nature of reality in essence has no violation of prohibitions, we therefore follow in accord with the nature of reality and practice transcendence through morality: that is, not killing, not stealing, not violating sexual taboos, not lying, abandoning greed, hatred, deception, flattery, and false views. We should abandon the clamor, moreover, and have few desires and be content. And even down to small faults, in our minds we should conceive great trepidation and not take lightly what the Enlightened One has ordained and prohibited in his precepts. We should always guard against slander and vilification, and not let sentient beings make the mistake of committing a crime of transgression."[25] By this maintaining of dignified conduct in everyday life we civilize sentient beings.

Question: According to what was said in previous passages, true thusness is one and the essence of Buddhahood is nondual, containing all meritorious qualities. Why then the need for practice of morals relating to bearing and conduct and so on?

Answer: It is like a great jewel: its essential nature is bright and clear, but having long been covered by layers of dust, it has the stain of defilement. If people think only of the nature of the jewel and do not polish its various facets, they will never get it clean. The truth of true thusness is empty and pure in essential nature, but it has long been stained by the defilement of ignorance and affliction:[26] if people only think of true thusness and do not employ various refining practices of morality, meditation, and knowledge, it will never be clear. In this sense it is reasonable that we need to uphold morality.

Question: The five groups of renunciants leave conventional society far behind and should be full of dignity in bearing and conduct.[27] Those in the household life are physically bound by the net of conventional society—how then can they be free from transgressions?

Answer: Renunciants, who leave home, have their own strict rules: those in the household life also keep the five precepts in common with the renunciants. The three refuges and five precepts are the bridge out of the ocean of suffering, the basis for progress toward nirvana.[28] Making a process of ethical guidance, they are the great foundation of the seven groups;[29] myriad virtues are born from them. Truly this is the common ground of the Buddhist teachings. Scripture says, "If conduct is not pure, concentration does not develop." You should know that discipline is the body of concentration and wisdom is the function of concentration: when these three studies—discipline, concentration, and wisdom—are completely fulfilled, then you realize enlightenment.

The "Four-Part Code" says, "Number one, uphold the precepts, do not violate them; then the mendicants' conduct is naturally upright and dignified, and hostile people cannot approach. If you do not behave in accord with the Teaching, then you will be persecuted."[30] By reason of this principle we speak of the virtue of maintaining dignified, regulated, exemplary conduct.

Third is the virtue of treating beings gently and harmoniously, honestly and straightforwardly. This means that great wisdom illumining the real is called honest straightforwardness; by virtue of great compassion saving beings it is called gentle and harmonious. Moreover, direct straightforwardness is in terms of the immutability of fundamental nature; gently harmony is in terms of going along with the flow without lingering. Gentleness means subduing afflictions; harmony means cultivation of action in accord with principle. These tuning and harmonizing methods are used for the salvation of sentient beings. Honest straightforwardness also means that one's being is free from delusion and falsehood, one's words and actions match each other, and one accumulates virtue in the heart with no concern for fame or profit, considering gold as trifling as a clod of earth, valuing the Teaching more than jewels. Simply acting properly to harmonize the living, soon hoping for the complete fulfillment of self and others, is therefore called the virtue of treating beings gently and harmoniously, honestly and straightforwardly.

Fourth is the virtue of accepting suffering in place of all sentient beings. This means cultivating the various principles of practice—not for one's own sake but only wishing generally to benefit myriad beings, enemies and friends equally, causing all to stop evil and fully cultivate myriad practices to realize enlightenment.

Further, bodhisattvas, with great compassion and great determination, use their bodies as goods to ransom all suffering beings from states of misery in order to cause them to attain happiness. This they do for ever and ever, without flagging, and they do not have the slightest wish or hope for reward from sentient beings. The Hua-yen scripture says, "Vast clouds of compassion cover all; they abandoned their bodies in countless lands, and by the power of practice cultivated through oceans of eons past, this world in the present has no defilements."[31]

What this means is that sentient beings' deluded attachments shifting from thought to thought is called suffering: bodhisattvas teach them to realize that the clusters are empty and quiescent, of their own nature fundamentally nonexistent—therefore this is called detachment from suffering.

Question: Sentient beings are infinite, and the actions causing suffering are infinite. How then can a bodhisattva accept sufferings in place of all sentient beings?

Answer: Bodhisattvas are able to bear suffering in place of sentient beings because of their power of great compassion and skill in means; because of sentient beings' delusive attachments they do not realize that the essence of karma comes from delusion and thus have no means of escape. Therefore bodhisattvas teach them to practice the twin method of cessation and contemplation, minds not changing for a moment, so cause [karma] and effect [suffering] perish and there is no basis for the production of actions which cause suffering. They simply cause them not to enter the mire of miserable states caused by ignorance, greed, and anger. This is called the virtue of enduring suffering in place of all sentient beings. The "Mixed Collection Treatise" says, "The sense of solidity of what is not solid is deeply dwelling in error: detaching from vexation by afflictions, one attains highest enlightenment."[32]

This completes the explanation of four kinds of practical virtue; from here on we gather function back to the essence and enter five gates of cessation. Five gates of cessation means that, based on the aforementioned practice of four virtues, the forms themselves are empty; forms exhausted, the mind is clear and we practice cessation. "Entry" means that "nature" and "characteristics" both vanish and the essence pervades the cosmos: entering signlessness is called entry. The Hua-yen scripture says, "The extent of the profound world of the enlightened is equal to space; all sentient beings enter it, yet without entering anything."[33] And accordingly we enter the realm of Buddhahood.

Scripture says, "Entering into formless concentration, you see that all things are inert: by entering into equanimity, we pay reverence without any object of contemplation."[34] This means that all sentient beings are without exception originally within the realm of the enlightened, and there is nothing more to be entered. It is like this: when a man is mixed up, east is west; when he has realized, then west is east and there is no more east besides to go in. Because sentient beings are deluded, they think illusion is to be abandoned and think reality is to be entered; when they are enlightened, illusion itself is reality—there is no other reality besides to enter. The meaning here is the same; entering without entering, it is called entry. Why? Entering and not entering are fundamentally equal; it is the same one cosmos. The "Treatise on Awakening of Faith" says, "If sentient beings can contemplate no thought, this is called entering the gate of true thusness."[35]

As for the five cessations, first is cessation by awareness of the pure emptiness of things and detachment from objects. This means that things in ultimate truth are empty and quiescent in their fundamental nature; things in conventional truth seem to exist yet are empty. The ultimate and conventional, purely empty, are null and groundless; once relating knowledge is stilled, objects related to are empty. Mind and objects not constraining, the essence pervades, empty and open. At the moment of true realization, cause and effect are both transcended. The *Vimalakīrti* scripture says, "The truth is not in the province of cause, nor in effect."[36] Based on this doctrine we call it cessation by awareness of the pure emptiness of things and detachment from objects.

Second is cessation by contemplation of the voidness of person and cutting off desire. That is, the five clusters have no master—this is called void. Empty quietude without any seeking is called cutting off desire. Therefore it is called cessation by contemplation of the voidness of person and cutting off desire.

Third is cessation because of the spontaneity of the profusion of natural evolution. The arising of function based on essence is called natural evolution; since evolution adapts to myriad differences, it is called profusion. Being constant, past and present, it is called spontaneous. This means that the elements of true thusness spontaneously follow conditions; myriad things arise together and spontaneously return to nature. Therefore we speak of cessation because of the profusion of natural evolution. Scripture says, "From a nonabiding basis all things are established."[37] And that is what this means.

Fourth is cessation by the light of concentration shining forth without thought. This refers to the precious jewel of the blessed universal monarch with a pure jewel net.[38] That is to say, the essential nature of the jewel is penetratingly bright; the ten directions are equally illumined, as tasks are accomplished without thinking. Thoughts all acquiesce. Though manifesting extraordinary accomplishments, the mind is without cogitation. The Hua-yen scripture says, "It is like a wheel-turning king who perfects the supreme seven treasures—their provenance cannot be found: the nature of action is also like this."[39] If there are sentient beings who enter this gate of great cessation and subtle observation, they accomplish works spontaneously, without thought, without cogitation, like that jewel equally illumining far and near, clearly manifesting, penetrating throughout space, not obstructed or covered by the dust and fog, mist and clouds of the two lesser vehicles [of individual salvation] and heretics. Therefore we call it cessation by the light of concentration shining forth without thought.

Fifth is formless cessation in the mystic communion of noumenon and phenomena. This means that phenomena, which are illusory forms, and noumenon, the absence of intrinsic nature, mutually conceal and mutually reveal each other. Therefore it is called mystic communion. Moreover, because noumenon is revealed by way of practice, phenomena permeate noumenon; as practice arises from noumenon, noumenon permeates phenomena: they mutually affirm and mutually deny each other, so it is called mystic communion. Mystic communion means that great wisdom exists alone, its essence pervading the universe; great compassion saves beings by carrying out myriad practices. Compassion and wisdom merge; nature and characteristics both disappear. Therefore it is called formless cessation in the mystic communion of noumenon and phenomena.

This completes the explanation of five cessations; now, proceeding from cessation, we initiate contemplation.

Question: According to the principles mentioned above, cultivating practice on this basis should be sufficient for fulfillment. Why then is it further required to enter the two gates of cessation and contemplation?

Answer: The "Treatise on Awakening of Faith" says, "To practice cessation cures the ordinary man's abiding attachment to the mundane world and enables him to relinquish the timid, weak views of the two vehicles [seeking individual emancipation]. To practice contemplation cures the fault of the narrowness and meanness of the two vehicles in not arousing great compassion; moreover, it leaves behind the ordinary man's noncultivation of roots of virtue. According to this teaching, the two gates to cessation and contemplation perfect and assist each other, and they are not separated from each other. If you do not practice cessation and contemplation, there is no basis for gaining entry into the path of enlightenment."[40]

The Hua-yen scripture says, "It is like the golden winged [garuda] bird stirring up the ocean water with its two wings, causing the water to part so that it can see the dragons and seize one whose life is about to end—the Enlightened Ones' appearance in the world is also like this: using great cessation and subtle contemplation as two wings, they beat and stir the water of sentient beings' great ocean of craving, observe the sentient beings, and rescue and liberate those whose faculties are mature."[41] According to this teaching, we need to practice cessation and contemplation.

Question: Granted that cessation and contemplation are the essentials of the school, ordinary folk and beginning students do not yet know how to settle the mind. Please point the way for the deluded to return to the right path.

Answer: The "Treatise on Awakening of Faith" says, "If you would practice cessation, stay in a quiet place, sitting straight with proper attention; do not rely on the breath, do not rely on physical form, do not rely on space, do not rely on earth, water, fire, or air . . . do not rely on perception or discernment—dismiss all conceptions as they come to mind, and also dismiss the conception of dismissing. As all things are fundamentally without conception, instant to instant they are unborn, instant to instant unperishing. Nor should you pursue outside the mind to think about objects. Then dismiss mind by mind. If the mind races and scatters, you should concentrate and bring it back to right mindfulness."[42] In the contemplation of there being only mind and consciousness, all delusions will naturally be transcended.[43]

For ordinary people and beginning students false and true are not yet distinguished; the net of delusion enters the mind and fools the practitioner. Without an adept teacher to ask, they have nothing to rely on; they take the effects of the four demons to be the right path:[44] as days and months pass, over a long period of time, false views become so ingrained that even meeting with good conditions they become difficult to change; sinking in the ocean of suffering, there is no way of escape. You should look into this on your own part; do not allow a moment's deviation. This teaching is as expounded in the "Treatise on Awakening of Faith."

Proceeding from the five gates of cessation, which are themselves contemplations, we initiate six contemplations which are themselves cessation. Why? Because the fact of the noninterference of noumenon and phenomena is such, because concentration and wisdom merge, without distinction, because one and many are identical, without before or after, and because the freedom of the great function is without obstruction.

As for the six contemplations, first is the contemplation of true emptiness, returning objects to mind. This means that whatever there is in the world is only the creation of one mind; outside of mind there is not a single thing that can be apprehended. Therefore it is called returning to mind. It means that all discriminations come only from one's own mind. There has never been any environment outside the mind which could be an object of mind. Why? Because when the mind is not aroused, the environment is fundamentally empty. The treatise [on distinction of the mean and extremes] says, "Because they are based on consciousness only, objects have no essence and therefore the meaning of true emptiness is established; because sense data have no existence, the original consciousness is unborn."[45]

And scripture also says, "Before you realize that objects are only mind, you produce all kinds of discriminations; when you have realized that objects are only mind, discrimination does not arise. Knowing that all things are only mind, you then relinquish the characterizations of outside objects. By this you cease discriminating and awaken to universally equal true emptiness. As in the world there is a king of physicians who cures illnesses with wonderful medicines, so also do the Buddhas expound 'only mind' for the sake of beings."[46]

By this we then know that objects are manifested by mind and mind is manifested by objects: mind does not go to object, object does not enter mind. You should exercise this contemplation—its wisdom is exceedingly deep. Therefore it is called the contemplation of true emptiness, returning objects to mind.

Second is the contemplation of inconceivable existence, manifesting the environment from the mind. That is, phenomena do not linger in noumenon; with every phenomenon there occur differences. That is to say, in the preceding approach we returned characteristics back to the essence; in this approach we initiate functions based on the essence, fully cultivating myriad practices to adorn a land of reward. In the preceding approach, moreover, we returned characteristics to the essence in order to reveal the body of reality; in this approach we initiate action based on essence to cultivate and perfect the body of reward. Therefore it is called the contemplation of wonderful existence, manifesting the environment from the mind.

Third is the contemplation of the mystic merging of mind and environment. Mind means mind without obstruction; all Buddhas realize this, whereby they attain the body of reality. Environment means environment without obstruction; all Buddhas realize this, whereby they achieve a pure land. This means that the Buddhas' body of reward and the pure land on which it is based merge completely without obstruction.

Sometimes the body manifests the land. As the scripture says, "In a single hair pore are infinite lands, each having four continents and four oceans and, similarly, polar and surrounding mountains, all appearing therein without being cramped."[47]

Sometimes the land manifests the Buddha-body. As the scripture says, "Into every single atom in the Flower Treasury world the Buddha enters, producing mystic displays for all sentient beings; such is the way of Vairocana."[48]

In this way, within this gate it is divided into four propositions, as explained in the "Mystic Discussion" commentary.[49] In this way object and subject merge without distinct boundaries. That is to say, the preceding two contemplations each set forth one side; this contemplation now merges them, communing mind with objects. Therefore it is called the contemplation of the mystic merging of mind and environment.

Fourth is the contemplation of the body of knowledge reflecting myriad objective conditions. This means that the essence of knowledge is only one and capable of reflecting myriad objective conditions. The characteristics of objective conditions are fundamentally empty; the radiance of the essence of knowledge is silent. The characterizations of all objective conditions ended, thusness as such alone subsists. This means that conditioned things all contain the nature of reality. It is like the orb of the sun shining clearly far out in space: all who have eyes see it, the blind also receive its benefits, informing all of the time and season, the periods of cold and heat, and the plants and trees, all inanimate beings, all luxuriate and grow—so also is the sun of knowledge of those who realize thusness. Therefore it is called the contemplation of the body of knowledge reflecting myriad objective conditions.

Fifth is the contemplation of the images of many bodies in one mirror—the reality-realm of noninterference among each and every phenomenon. This means that the ten bodies of Vairocana act together without interference or obstruction. The scripture says, "Sometimes with his own body he makes the body of sentient beings, the body of lands, the body of rewards of action, the body of disciples, the body of self-enlightened ones, the body of enlightening beings, the body of Buddhas, the body of knowledge, the body of reality, the body of space."⁵⁰ Of these ten bodies, whichever one is brought up contains the other nine. Therefore it is called the contemplation of the reflections of many bodies entering one mirror.

Just as one body has the interchangeable function of the ten bodies, each hair pore, each physical member, each joint, all have the interchangeable function of the ten bodies. Sometimes one uses the medium of the eye to perform ear-medium Buddha work, sometimes one uses the medium of the ear to perform eye-medium Buddha work—nose, tongue, body, and mind are also like this. Why? Because when you experience the sustaining empowerment of this method of great cessation and subtle contemplation, you become like this. The scripture says, "Sometimes one body is made of many bodies, sometimes many bodies are made of one body; sometimes one body enters many bodies, sometimes many bodies enter one body. It is not that one body vanishes and many bodies come into being; it is not that many bodies vanish and one body comes into being."⁵¹ It all comes from the power of profound concentration— that is how it can be like this. Sometimes we enter concentration on the same object and emerge from different objects. Sometimes we enter concentration with one body and emerge with many bodies; sometimes we enter concentration with many bodies and emerge with one body. Therefore it is called the contemplation of the images of many bodies entering one mirror.

Sixth is the contemplation of the net of Indra, where principal and satellites reflect one another. This means that with self as principal, one looks to others as satellites or companions; or else one thing or principle is taken as principal and all things or principles become satellites or companions; or one body is taken as principal and all bodies become satellites. Whatever single thing is brought up, immediately principal and satellite are equally contained, multiplying infinitely—this represents the nature of things manifesting reflections multiplied and remultiplied in all phenomena, all infinitely. This is also the infinite doubling and redoubling of compassion and wisdom. It is like when the boy Sudhana gradually traveled south from the Jeta grove until he reached the great tower of Vairocana's ornaments. For a while he concentrated, then said to Maitreya, "O please, Great Sage, open the door of the tower and let me enter." Maitreya snapped his fingers and the door opened. When Sudhana had entered, it closed as before. He saw that inside the tower were hundreds and thousands of towers, and in front of each tower was a Maitreya Bodhisattva, and before each Maitreya Bodhisattva was a boy Sudhana, each Sudhana joining his palms before Maitreya. This represents the multiple levels of the cosmos of reality, like the net of Indra, principal and satellites reflecting each other. This is also the contemplation of noninterference among all phenomena. As for the six levels of contemplation set forth above, when one is brought up as the principal, the other five are the satellites or companions—there is no before or after; beginning to end they are all equal. Whichever gate you enter, it completely includes the cosmos.

This principle is like a round jewel pierced with six holes; whichever hole is strung, immediately the whole jewel is taken, in the very same way. This contemplation is divided into six gates; whichever one is entered, it contains completely the principle of the complete teaching of the realm of reality, because the truth is naturally so and Sudhana realized it all in one life. Wrapping up and rolling out are without interference, concealing and revealing are simultaneous: being one, they have no beginning or end; exiting and entering, outside and inside are obliterated. Beginners truly enlightened at the first inspiration take in many lives in an instant; those by whom the Way is fulfilled in the ten stages of faith partake of Buddhahood in an instant of thought. It causes bodhisattvas before the stages to doubt everything they encounter; it causes the mystic mirror of the five hundred disciples to fail utterly in discernment. Merging freely without obstruction, one and many commingle. Completely experiencing realization of this is called Buddhahood.

So the name of this door of contemplation is not fixed. If its name is based on the one essence, then it is the door of absorption in the clear manifestation of the oceanic reflection. If it is discussed in terms of the two functions, it is called the door of absorption in the sublime actions of the flower ornament. If it is named on the basis of the three universals, it is called the door of absorption in an atom containing the ten directions. If it is named in accord with the four virtues, it is called the door of absorption in rescuing beings with the four means of salvation. If spoken of in terms of the five cessations, it is called the door of absorption in the noninterference of tranquility and action. If the six contemplations are taken for the name, it is called the door of absorption in the actualization of Buddhahood without obstruction.

As for the meanings of these names, they are set up in accordance with the qualities and explained according to the teachings: whichever gate is entered, myriad virtues are all contained in it. Since nonorigination shows that illusory existence is not nil, uniting the cosmos, it is contained in one atom; bring up one body and the ten bodies appear. These meanings cannot be assessed by emotion and intellect—with discriminating consciousness ended and views removed, meditate on them and you can see.

Though I am not brilliant, since my youth I have appreciated this scripture and have just set forth some passages of driftwood,[52] to guide the assembly of meanings filling the universe.

Searching through the books of the Teachings,
I assemble this contemplation of the Flower Ornament.
The passages are brief, but the meanings lack naught;
The wise should diligently study it.

Appendix: Highlights of the Hua-yen Scripture

THE ENTIRE HUA-YEN SCRIPTURE no longer exists in Sanskrit, and some scholars believe that it may never have existed. There are many partial translations in Chinese and two extensive translations which, compared with what else exists, may be called full or comprehensive translations. The first full translation, in sixty scrolls, was made by Buddhabhadra (359–429); an even more thorough version, comprising eighty scrolls, was made from another text at the end of the seventh century by Śīkṣānanda (652–710). For convenience these two versions are often referred to respectively as the sixty and eighty-scroll Hua-yen.

To present the structure of the Hua-yen scripture while at the same time tracing its introduction into China, I shall base my analysis on the eighty-scroll version, noting alternative translations of portions or books of the scripture where they exist, and then review the main intent or contents of each book. In each case the lead entry refers to Śīkṣānanda's version and the number 60 stands for Buddhabhadra's. Numbers given in parentheses after the titles of alternate translations refer to the number of the text in the Taishō tripitaka (which, when subsequently cited is referred to by the initial T.).

BOOK ONE   "Wonderful Adornments of the Leaders of the Worlds,"
scrolls 1–5
60: "Pure Eyes of the Worlds," scrolls 1–2
This book describes a symbolic assembly of all manner of beings at the site of the Buddha's enlightenment; the words "leaders" and

"eyes" in the title may be singular or plural (according to the explanation of the commentary of Cheng-kuan, fourth patriarch of the Chinese Hua-yen school), referring to the Buddha or the representatives of the various realms of being or both. Through the eulogies of the Buddha chanted by these beings and the descriptions of the liberations they have realized, a general picture of the nature of Buddhahood and the principles and scope of the Teaching emerges. For example, a verse describing the realization in the liberation attained by an earth spirit says of Buddha as perceived by the spirit, "His vast state of serene absorption in concentration is unborn, imperishable, has no coming or going; yet he purifies lands to show sentient beings." A verse describing the perception of a mountain spirit called Clearly Seeing says, "Buddha appears throughout the ten directions expounding the subtle truth by various means, with an ocean of practices aiding all beings." A verse on the vision of a river spirit called Pure Eyes says, "With compassion and methods numerous as beings themselves he appears before all, always guiding, clearing away the dirt of afflictions."

BOOK TWO   "Appearance of the Buddha," scroll 6
60: Included in part 1 of the book "Vairocana Buddha," scroll 2
This book speaks of the characteristics of Buddhahood, emphasizing the infinity and eternity of the cosmic Buddha, identical to reality itself, appearing everywhere to all beings, seen in accord with their perceptive capacities. This book points out that all beings experience reality according to their faculties and dispositions and, moreover, that enlightened teachers present various doctrines and instructions to people in accord with their needs, capacities, and situations.

BOOK THREE   "The Concentration of Samantabhadra," scroll 7
60: Included in part 2 of the book "Vairocana Buddha," scroll 3
This chapter reveals the principle of the bodhisattva, or enlightening being, the worker for enlightenment, typified by Samantabhadra, "Universally Good." The bodhisattvas may also appear in any form, as appropriate to the time, place, and people, using any of the teachings and methods at their command that may be useful for liberating beings from the habitual views and vicious circles which

bind them. Furthermore, since the bodhisattva is in direct contact with "suchness" or "thusness"—being as is, or unpredicated reality —all bodhisattvas are aware of each other, or in psychic contact with each other, by being similarly focused on reality and dedicated alike to universal enlightenment and liberation. The unity of purpose underlying the diversity of method is emphasized here; Samantabhadra represents the bodhisattva work as a whole:

Samantabhadra, the universally good enlightening being, the great being, sat on a lion throne made of a bank of lotus flowers and, imbued with the psychic power of the enlightened one, entered into concentration. This concentration is called the immanent body of the illuminator of thusness, which is in all enlightened ones. It enters everywhere into the equal essence of all enlightened ones, and is capable of manifesting myriad images in the universe, vastly and immensely, without obstruction, equal to space. All the whirling oceans of universes flow into it; it produces all states of concentration and can contain all worlds in all directions. The oceans of lights of knowledge of all the enlightened ones come from here; it can reveal all the oceans of all conditions everywhere. It contains within all the powers and liberation of the enlightened ones and the knowledge of the enlightening beings. It can cause the particles of all lands to be universally able to contain boundless universes. It develops the ocean of virtuous qualities of all Buddhas, and reveals the ocean of great vows of these realized ones. All the cycles of teaching of the Buddhas flow through it and are guarded and maintained by it, and kept without interruption or end.

As in this world the enlightening being Samantabhadra entered this concentration in the presence of the World Honored One, thus throughout the realm of space of the cosmos, in all directions and all times, in a subtle, unhindered, vastly expansive light, in all lands visible to the Buddha's eye, within reach of the Buddha's power, manifested by the Buddha's body, and in each atom of all those lands, there were Buddhas as numerous as atoms in an ocean of worlds, and in front of each Buddha were Samantabhadra Bodhisattvas numerous as atoms in an ocean of worlds, each also entering into this concentration in the immanent body of the illuminator of thusness in enlightened ones.

At that time all the Samantabhadras each saw the Buddhas of the ten directions appearing before them; those Buddhas praised Samantabhadra in the same voice: "Good! You are able to enter this enlightening beings' concentration in the immanent body of the illuminator of thusness in all Buddhas; this is fostered in you by all the Buddhas everywhere together, by means of the power of the original vow of the illuminating realized one, and it is also because you cultivate the power of the practices and vows of all Buddhas—that is, because you can activate all the cycles of the enlightening teaching, revealing the ocean of knowledge and wisdom of all realized ones, universally illumine all the oceans of distinctions everywhere, without exception, cause sentient beings to clear away confusion and affliction and attain purity, universally accept all lands without attachment, deeply enter the sphere of all enlightened ones without impediment, and universally expound the virtues and qualities of all enlightened ones; and because you are able to enter into the true character of all things and develop knowledge and wisdom, analyze all the media of the teachings, comprehend the faculties of all living beings, and because you are able to hold the ocean of written teachings of all the realized enlightened ones.

At that time all the Buddhas of the ten directions then bestowed on the great enlightening being Samantabhadra the knowledge which enters into the power inherent in omniscience, the knowledge which enters into the infinity of the elemental cosmos, the knowledge which perfects the realization of the sphere of all enlightened ones, the knowledge of the becoming and decay of all oceans of worlds, the knowledge of the full extent of the worlds of all sentient beings, the knowledge which abides in the extremely profound liberation of all enlightened ones and the nondiscriminating knowledge of all meditation states, the knowledge which enters into the ocean of all faculties of enlightening beings, the knowledge of elocution to turn the wheel of the teaching in the ocean of languages of all sentient beings, the knowledge which enters in all ways into the bodies of all oceans of worlds in the universe, and the knowledge which comprehends the voices of all Buddhas.

As in this world in the presence of the realization of thusness Samantabhadra Bodhisattva experienced the Buddhas bestowing such knowledge, so in all oceans of worlds, as well as in each atom of all those worlds, so did all the Samantabhadra Bodhisattvas there experience this. Why? Because they had realized that state of mental focus in this way.

Then the Buddhas of the ten directions each extended their right hand and patted Samantabhadra on the head. Their hands were adorned with the marks of greatness, being finely webbed, emanating light, fragrance, and flames. They also produced the various wondrous tones of all Buddhas. And within each hand were manifested the phenomena of supernormal powers, the ocean of vows of universal goodness of all enlightening beings of past, present, and future, the cycles of pure teachings of all enlightened ones, as well as the images of the Buddhas past, present, and future.

As in this world Samantabhadra was patted on the head by all the Buddhas of the ten directions, so in all the oceans of worlds, and in each atom of those worlds, the Samantabhadra Bodhisattvas there were patted on the head by the Buddhas of the ten directions.

Then Samantabhadra Bodhisattva arose from this concentration, and when he did so, he rose from the media of oceans of concentrations numerous as atoms in all oceans of worlds; for example, he rose from the medium of concentration of skillful knowledge realizing that the worlds of past, present, and future have no distinction in the succession of instants; he rose from the medium of concentration of knowledge of all the subtlest and most minute constituents of all universes in all times, rose from the medium of concentration on the manifestation of all Buddha-fields in past, present, and future, rose from the medium of concentration revealing the dwelling places of all living beings, rose from the medium of concentration of knowledge of various differences in locations of the universes of the ten directions, rose from the medium of concentration of knowledge of boundlessly vast clouds of Buddha-bodies existing in every atom, rose from the medium of concentration of explanations of the ocean of inner principles in all things.

When the enlightening being Samantabhadra rose from such media of concentration, all the enlightening beings each found oceanic clouds of concentrations, numerous as atoms in an ocean of worlds, found oceanic clouds of spells, oceanic clouds of techniques to teach everything, oceanic clouds of ways of felicitous expression, oceanic clouds of practices, oceanic clouds of lights from the knowledge of the treasury of virtues of all who realize thusness, oceanic clouds of nondiscriminating techniques of the powers, knowledge, and wisdom of all enlightened ones, oceanic clouds of all who realize thusness each manifesting myriad lands in each and every pore, oceanic clouds of enlightening beings one by one manifesting descent from the palace of the heaven of happiness to be born on earth and become an enlightened Buddha, turn the wheel of the teaching, and enter into ultimate extinction, all as numerous as atoms in an ocean of worlds.

As when in this world Samantabhadra Bodhisattva rose from concentration, all the hosts of bodhisattvas received such blessings, so in all the oceans of worlds, as well as in each atom of each world, the same thing happened.

At that time, by the spiritual power of all the Buddhas and the power of Samantabhadra's concentration, all oceans of worlds in the ten directions trembled. Each world was arrayed with precious elements and gave forth wondrous sounds, explaining all things. And on each realized one, in the ocean of sites of enlightenment where the masses gathered, everywhere there rained ten kinds of clouds of regal jewels; clouds of beautiful gold star jewels, jewels like precious discs descending, shining light jewels, jewels of the treasury manifesting the images of bodhisattvas, jewels extolling the names of Buddhas, jewels of brilliant light, illuminating the sites of enlightenment in Buddha-fields everywhere, jewels whose light reflects the various miracles everywhere, jewels praising the virtues of all bodhisattvas, jewels with a light that shines like the sun, jewels whose delightful music is heard everywhere.

After the universal rain of these ten kinds of clouds of jewels, all the realized ones emitted lights from their pores, and in the light rays spoke verses saying:

Samantabhadra is present in all lands
Sitting on a jeweled lotus throne, beheld by all
He manifests all psychic powers
And is able to enter infinite meditations.

The universally good always fills the universe
With various bodies flowing everywhere
With concentration, psychic power, skill and strength,
In a universal voice teaching extensively without hindrance.

In every land, in the presence of all the Buddhas,
Various states of concentration revealing psychic powers,
Each psychic power pervades everywhere
In all lands of the ten directions.

As with the Buddhas of all lands,
So it is in all the atoms of the lands too;
The phenomena of concentration and psychic powers
Are the willpower of the illuminator.

Samantabhadra physically is like empty space,
Abiding by reality, not a land,
According to the heart's desires of all beings,
Manifesting all kinds of embodiments, equal to all.

Samantabhadra, abiding secure in great determination,
Thus attained these infinite spiritual powers,
In any lands of all Buddha-bodies
Manifesting his form going there.

All the myriad oceans are boundless—
He reproduces his body infinitely and dwells there;
All lands of his manifestation are purified,
In an instant are seen many eons.

Samantabhadra abides peacefully in all lands—
The spiritual powers he displays are incomparable;
The trembling extending everywhere
Causes those who look to be able to see.

The knowledge, virtue, and powers of all Buddhas
Their various great qualities, he has all fulfilled;
By the medium of techniques of all meditations
He shows his past enlightening acts.

Such independence, inconceivable,
Is manifest in the lands of the ten directions
To reveal the universal entrance of all meditations;
In the clouds of Buddha-light his praises are sung.

Then all the hosts of bodhisattvas turned to Samantabhadra,
joined their palms and gazed respectfully at Samantabhadra;
imbued with the psychic power of the enlightened, they sang
in praise with the same voice,

Born from the teachings of the enlightened,
Also originating from the willpower of the realized,
The womb of space, the equality of real thusness—
You have purified this body of reality.

In the congregations in all Buddha-fields
Samantabhadra is omnipresent there;
The lights of the oceans of universal virtue and wisdom
Equally illumine everywhere, so all is visible.

The immensely vast ocean of virtues of Samantabhadra
Goes everywhere to approach the enlightened;
To the lands within all atoms
He can travel and clearly appear.

O child of Buddha, we always see you
Associating with all the enlightened ones
Abiding in the real state of concentration
For eons numerous as atoms in all lands.

The child of Buddha, with an all-pervading body,
Can go to the lands in all directions,

Liberating all the oceans of living beings,
Entering into all the parts of the universe.

Entering into all particles of the cosmos,
The body is endless and undifferentiated;
Omnipresent as space,
It expounds the great teaching of the realization of thusness.

The light of all virtue,
Immense like clouds, power surpassing,
Traveling to all oceans of living beings
Expounding the incomparable way practiced by all Buddhas.

Cultivating and learning the supreme practice of universal
    goodness
In order to liberate sentient beings for oceans of eons,
Expounding all truths, like a great cloud,
The voice is tremendous, none do not hear.

How can the land be established?
How do the Buddhas appear?
And how about beings?
Please explain truthfully the truth as it is.

Here is an infinite ocean of beings—
All are respectful in the honored presence;
Turn for us the pure wheel of the sublime teaching,
And all the Buddhas will rejoice with us.

BOOK FOUR   "Formation of the Worlds," scroll 7
60: Included in part 2 of the book "Vairocana Buddha," scroll 3
This book presents visionary descriptions of worlds representing the outcome of aspirations and actions. Here emphasis is placed on the relativity of world to mind and on showing how the features of the world depend of the states of mind, intentions, and deeds of the inhabitants.

BOOK FIVE   "The Flower Treasury World," scrolls 8–10
60: Included in part 2 of the book "Vairocana Buddha," scrolls 3–4
This book too presents visionary cosmology, describing this world system as purified by the vows and deeds of Vairocana Buddha, the

glorified aspect of the historical Buddha. It represents the world system as resting on an ocean of fragrant water, symbolizing the "repository consciousness" wherein are stored all experiential impressions which develop into images of the world, symbolized in the scripture by features of the world system.

BOOK SIX   "Vairocana Buddha," scroll 11
60: Included in part 3 of the book "Vairocana Buddha," scroll 4
This book tells of Vairocana Buddha's studies with other Buddhas in remote antiquity. The numerous realizations and attainments of Vairocana in the causal state are recounted, representing, through mnemonic formulas for meditation, fundamental principles and techniques of Buddhism. It relates, for example, that upon witnessing one of those ancient Buddhas attain complete enlightenment and display spiritual powers, the Buddha-to-be "attained a spell called 'deep fond of truth of the power of knowledge,' attained great kindness called 'expediently pacifying and liberating all living beings,' attained great compassion called 'cloud covering all realms,' attained great joy called 'treasury of power of the ocean of virtues of all enlightened ones,' attained great equanimity called 'spacelike equality and purity of the real essence of all things,' attained transcendent knowledge called 'pure body of the real cosmos inherently free from defilement,' attained psychic power called 'unhindered light appearing anywhere,' attained analytic power called 'skillfully entering the pure depths,' and attained light of knowledge called 'pure treasury of all enlightening teachings.'"
Subsequently that Buddha expounded a scripture called "The Pure Adornments of the Essential Nature of the Cosmos of Realities," along with "as many subsidiary scriptures as atoms in an ocean of worlds." When the Buddha-to-be and his company heard these scriptures, they "attained pure knowledge called 'entry into all pure techniques of enlightenment,' attained a stage called 'undefiled light,' attained a sphere of transcendence called 'showing delightful adornments in all worlds,' attained a sphere of expanding action called 'pure vision of boundless light entering all worlds,' attained a sphere of purposeful activity called 'banner of light of clouds of pure virtues,' attained a sphere of constant realization called 'vast light of the ocean of all verities,' attained ever-deepening progressive practice called 'adornment of great knowledge,' attained an

ocean of knowledge of high initiates called 'extremely refined effortless vision,' attained a great light called 'universal shining of light characterized by the ocean of virtues of the enlightened,' and attained pure knowledge productive of willpower called 'treasury of faith and resolution of immeasurable willpower.' " This book presents many other such concentration formulas, tying in the spiritual development of Vairocana with the details of these focal points as expounded throughout the scripture.

BOOK SEVEN   "Names and Epithets of the Enlightened Ones,"
scroll 12
60: Same title; book 3, scroll 4
    Partial translation in *Fo-shuo T'u-sha ching* (T. 280), "The Scripture on the Tuṣita Heaven, Spoken by the Buddha," done by Lokakṣin, a Central Asian monk, between A.D. 167 and 185.
This book too emphasizes that Buddhas or enlightened ones, know sentient beings' mentalities and teach them in accord with potential and need, and hence all beings see the Buddhas differently. The book presents various names and epithets of Buddhas in various worlds, representing different perceptions of virtues and qualities of enlightenment—sometimes from the point of view of cause, sometimes from the point of view of effect, sometimes explicit and sometimes veiled in metaphor. Examples of the various epithets of the Buddhas include Free, Possessor of Knowledge and Wisdom, Noncontentious, Beyond Philosophy, Undefiled, Truth Teller, Tamer, Infinite, Free from Greed, Done with All Tasks, Objective Knower, Ultimate Dignity, Inherently Secure, Acting According to Truth, Giver of All, Always Joyful, Lionlike, Razorlike Intellect, Adorned by Conduct, Nonreliant, Unhindered, Detached from the World, Imperturbable Mind. Again these names provide contemplation themes and hence represent focal points of the Teaching in capsule form.

BOOK EIGHT   "The Four Holy Truths," scroll 12
60: "The Four Truths," book 4, scrolls 4–5
This book follows the lead of the preceding book, giving various names and descriptions of the four holy truths of pristine Buddhism (the existence of suffering, the cause of the accumulation of suffering, the possibility of extinguishing suffering, and the way to the

extinction of suffering) as they are projected in various worlds, thus presenting basic Buddhist teachings from various angles. Some examples of the different names of the truth of suffering are oppression, clinging to objects, dependence on the senses, ignorant action, the sense of striving and seeking, contention, total lack of power to analyze, fantasy, fear, change, regret, false views, continuous revolving. Some of the different names of the cause of accumulation of suffering are bondage, false consciousness, pursuit and involvement, attachment to things, conviction, ignorance, grasping, the evil of excess, haste, grasping and clinging, fancy, revolving in circles, confusion, regression, wishing, disharmony. Some of the various names of the truth of the extinction of suffering are tranquillity, absence of inherent nature, extinction, essential reality, emancipation, freedom from greed, goal of goals, what should be seen, detachment from discrimination, constant equanimity, nonfabrication, thoroughly cleared, harmony, independence, extinction of confusion, breaking the seal, no label, nondoing, casting off the heavy burden, stability, freedom from folly. Among the names of the truth of the path to extinction of suffering are progress toward serenity, bold generalship, transcendence, having skill in means, impartial eye, detachment from extremes, comprehensive understanding, and contemplating the four truths.

BOOK NINE   "Awakening by Light," scroll 13
60: "Awakening by the Enlightened One's Light," book 5, scroll 5
    Part of this book is also included in the ancient *Fo-shuo T'u-sha ching* previously mentioned.
This book is an expanding vision: as light emanates from beneath the Buddha's feet, it progressively illumines greater numbers of worlds further and further distant in all directions, revealing analogous structures and parallel events in each world. In every world are seen a hundred billion Buddhas who each attract ten great bodhisattvas, accompanied by an immense number of other bodhisattvas; then one of the bodhisattvas in each assembly chants descriptive praises of the Buddha, eulogizing the deeds and realities of Buddhahood. For example, the first set of verses in the book plunges directly into transcendental and metaphysical aspects of Buddhahood: "If any see the Truly Awake as becoming liberated and di-

vorced from taints and not attached to any world, they have not realized the eye of the Way. If any know that the Buddhas' substance and form have no existence, and by cultivation gain clear understanding, such people will soon be Buddhas. Those who can see this world, unstirred in mind, the same as Buddha's body, will attain supreme knowledge. If, regarding the Buddha and truth, one understands that they are equal, having no thought of duality, one will walk on the inconceivable plane. If one sees Buddha and oneself resting in equality, without abode, entering nowhere, one will become one of the rare."

BOOK TEN   "A Bodhisattva Asks for Clarification," scroll 13
60: "Bodhisattvas Clarify Problems," book 6, scroll 5
This book goes into metaphysics, explaining that phenomena have no individual nature of their own since they are interdependent and, moreover, that their existence as discrete entities is only conceptual and descriptive—in reality they are insubstantial as individual identities and die out instant to instant. It also points out that states of being are consequences of action, but that action is fundamentally baseless, since all things lack ultimate reality. It goes on to say that although the teachings of the Buddhas are manifold and different, yet the essential truth is one—nothing is excluded from the equation of relativity and emptiness of absolute reality. This book also stresses the need for practical application of the Teaching, without which intellectual understanding has no use. The classic metaphors often cited in the strongly practice-oriented Ch'an school of Buddhism in reference to the futility of understanding without application are derived from this book of the Hua-yen scripture. The book goes on to note the different temperaments to which different aspects of the Teaching are recommended, and finally it summarizes the knowledge and spheres of Buddhahood.

BOOK ELEVEN   "Purifying Action," scroll 14
60: Same title; book 7, scroll 6
   Fo-shuo p'u-sa pen-yeh ching (T. 281), "Scripture on the Original Deeds of the Bodhisattva as Explained by the Buddha," translated by *Chih-ch'ien sometime between A.D. 220 and 265, also contains this book.
   Chu p'u-sa ch'iu fo pen-yeh ching (T. 282), "Original Deeds of Bodhi-

sattvas Seeking Buddhahood," translated by Nieh Tao Chen sometime between A.D. 265 and 316, is an early translation of this book.

This book concentrates on the development of attitude and outlook,
detailing a scheme of thought cultivation in which awareness of
daily activities is directed to specific prayers for the well-being,
development, and liberation of all beings. For example: "Bodhisattvas at home should wish that all beings realize that the nature
of 'home' is empty, and escape its pressures. . . . While with their
spouses and children, they should wish that all beings be equal and
impartial toward everyone and forever give up clinging. . . . When
they give something, they should wish that all beings be able to
relinquish all with hearts free of clinging. . . . When in danger and
difficulty, they should wish that all beings be free, unhindered wherever they go. . . . Setting out on the road, they should wish that all
beings go where the Buddha goes, into the realm of nonreliance.
. . . Walking along the road, they should wish that all beings tread
the pure realm of reality, their minds without obstruction."

BOOK TWELVE   "Chief of the Good," scrolls 14–15
60: "Bodhisattva Chief of the Good," book 8, scrolls 6–7
This book praises the virtues of the aspiration for enlightenment,
which involves the will for the enlightenment and liberation of all
beings. Next it praises faith as the basis for practical endeavor and a
means of focusing the mind. It then describes practices and their
results, from the initial determination to the final realization, in
terms of both self-cultivation and assistance to others. Again the
versatility of the bodhisattva's edifying and liberating activities in
the world is stressed. Among the abilities of Buddhas and bodhisattvas as recounted in this book are "knowledge of others' minds,
appropriate teaching, and ability to appear anywhere," which "are
all independent functions of the Buddhas; the bodhisattvas manifest
them all, able to cause all sentient beings to be tamed. Bodhisattvas'
various methods and techniques adapt to worldly conditions to liberate beings—just like lotus blossoms, to which water does not
adhere, in the same way they are in the world [but not affected by
the world], provoking deep faith, with extraordinary thoughts and
profound talents, as cultural kings—song and dance and conversa-
tion admired by the masses, all the various arts and crafts of the

world, they manifest like magicians. Some become grandees, city chiefs, some become merchants, caravan leaders, some become kings and ministers, some become physicians and scientists, some become great trees in the plains, some become medicines or jewel mines. . . . " Bodhisattvas are symbolically described as presenting all sorts of displays and teachings to transform the minds and perspectives of beings.

BOOK THIRTEEN   "Ascent to the Peak of Mount Sumeru," scroll 16
60: "Buddha Ascends to the Peak of Mount Sumeru," book 9, scroll 7

BOOK FOURTEEN   "Eulogies Atop Mount Sumeru," scroll 16
60: "Bodhisattvas Gather like Clouds in the Hall of Wondrous Excellence and Utter Verses," book 10, scrolls 7–8
These two books speak of the mental barriers to perception of the reality of Buddha and deal also with the elimination of false views. For example: "Things have no true reality; it is because of wrongly grasping them as real that ordinary people revolve in the prison of birth-and-death. Those of lesser wisdom wrongly discriminate things expressed by words and therefore create barriers and do not comprehend their own minds. If one does not comprehend one's own mind, how can one know the right path? With their misconstrued intellect they increase all evils. Not seeing that all things are empty, they always suffer the pains of birth-and-death. . . . If one has any views about things, this is not seeing anything. The nature of all things has no origin and no end."

BOOK FIFTEEN   "The Ten Abodes," scroll 16
60: "Ten Abodes of Bodhisattvas," book 11, scroll 8
    P'u-sa shih-chu hsing-tao p'in (T. 283), "Book on Bodhisattvas' Ten Abodes in the Practice of the Way," translated by Dharmarakṣa sometime between A.D. 265 and 289.
    Fo-shuo p'u-sa shih-chu ching (T. 284), "Scripture on Ten Abodes of Bodhisattvas as Explained by the Buddha," translated by Gītamitra in the third or early fourth century.
    Included in the "Scripture on the Original Deeds of the Bodhisattva as Explained by the Buddha" (T. 281).
This book details ten stations of bodhisattvahood: (1) initial determination for enlightenment; (2) preparation of the ground; (3) prac-

tice; (4) noble birth (meaning being "reborn" as a product of the teachings); (5) skill in means; (6) right mindfulness; (7) nonregression; (8) youthful nature (innocence and purity); (9) prince of the Teaching; (10) coronation (as a sovereign or master of the Teaching). The first abode is concerned with broadening the mind and universalizing the outlook; the second, developing great compassion toward all beings; the third, clarifying knowledge; the fourth, developing equanimity; the fifth, increasing in freedom and having no attachments; the sixth, accepting the nonorigination of things; seventh, gaining emancipation from all things; eighth, advancing in skillfulness in applying the teachings; ninth, progressing in nonobstruction of mind; tenth, increasing in knowledge of all particular ways of liberation.

BOOK SIXTEEN   "Religious Practice," scroll 17
60: Same title; book 12, scroll 8
This book deals with practices for renunciants. It says they should analyze thought, speech, and action, as well as the Buddha, the Teaching, the religious community, and the monastic precepts. They should then see that all of these are empty of ultimate reality, thus realizing that the teaching of Buddha is equanimous and impartial. It also says they should observe sentient beings with compassion, continuously contemplate the Teaching without seeking reward, understand that objects are illusory, and know that all things are but the nature of mind itself.

BOOK SEVENTEEN   "Virtues of the Initial Aspiration for Enlightenment," scroll 17
60: "Virtues of Bodhisattvas Who Have Just Begun to Aspire to Enlightenment," book 13, scroll 9
This book extols at length the virtues of the determination for enlightenment. This aspiration is described in grandiose terms as being infinite in scope, transcending all limited aims, immediately rising above all mundane attachments. Giving examples of the motivation of the will for enlightenment, it says, "They set their minds on enlightenment to cause the lineage of enlightened ones not to die out, to pervade all worlds, to liberate the sentient beings of all

worlds, to know the formation and disintegration of all worlds, to know the inherent purity of all worlds, to know the inclinations, afflictions, and mental habits of all sentient beings, to know where all sentient beings die and are born, to know expedient means appropriate to the faculties of all sentient beings, to know the mentalities of all sentient beings, to know all sentient beings' knowledge of past, present, and future, and to know that all realms of Buddhas are equal."

BOOK EIGHTEEN   "Illuminating Method," scroll 18
60: Same title; book 14, scroll 10
This book describes various practices and accomplishments of bodhisattvas. While emphasizing, once again, universality and completeness of the total development, the book also details specific aspects of the whole process, always relating the development of the individual bodhisattva to the entire community of conscious creatures. For example, ten things are enumerated which cause the practices of bodhisattvas to be pure: giving up all possessions to satisfy the wishes of sentient beings; adhering to pure morality; being inexhaustibly gentle and tolerant; cultivating practices diligently without regressing; being free from confusion and mental disturbance, through the power of correct mindfulness; analyzing and comprehending the innumerable teachings; cultivating all practices without attachment; being mentally imperturbable; liberating sentient beings, being like a bridge to help others cross over birth-and-death; knowing that all living beings are in essence the same as the Buddhas. Also enumerated are ten kinds of purity attained by bodhisattvas when they are not lax or indulgent: acting in accord with what they say; consummation of attention and discernment; abiding in deep concentration without torpor or agitation; gladly seeking Buddha's teachings without flagging; contemplating the teachings heard according to the truth, fully developing skillfully flexible knowledge; entering deep meditation and attaining the occult psychic powers of Buddhas; being equanimous and impartial without sense of status; benefiting all equally with an unobstructed mind; honoring those who aspire to enlightenment; respecting bodhisattvas and wise people.

BOOK NINETEEN   "Ascent to the Palace of the Suyama Heaven,"
scroll 19
60: "Freedom of the Buddha Ascending to the Palace of the Suyama
Heaven," book 15, scroll 10

BOOK TWENTY   "Eulogies in the Palace of the Suyama Heaven,"
scroll 19
60: "Bodhisattvas in the Palace of the Suyama Heaven Utter Verses," book
16, scroll 10
In these books it is explained that since things have no inherent
identity, no independent nature of their own, there is no real truth
in affirmation or denial. They point out that the various definitions
of specific things are only mental discriminations or descriptions
and do not correspond to ultimate reality. Book 20 contains the
famous lines which say that mind is like an artist, depicting all
kinds of things, in effect creating the "things" of the world—that is,
the world as it is conceived to be. It also contains a saying which
became a Ch'an proverb—"Mind, Buddha, and sentient beings,
these three are no different"—and says that all Buddhas are produced by mind.

BOOK TWENTY-ONE   "Ten Practices," scrolls 19-20
60: "Clusters of Flowers of Merit—Bodhisattvas' Ten Practices," book 17,
scrolls 11-12
Ten kinds of practice of bodhisattvas are expounded in this book:

1. Gladdening practice: material generosity, giving to benefit
beings, with no idea of self, receiver, or gift; also, observing that all
living beings perish, bodhisattvas explain to them the equal, imperishable true essence of things, which is none other than emptiness of
independent existence.

2. Beneficial practice: maintaining pure morality, abiding in
equanimity and impartiality, looking upon all beings as equals.

3. Practice of nonopposition: comprehending the emptiness of
the body, selflessness, and nonexistence of possession, realizing that
pain and pleasure, suffering and happiness, have no absolute existence; inducing other people toward nirvana, the extinction of affliction.

4. Practice of indefatigability: cultivating perseverance in effort in order to cause beings in all worlds to attain ultimate nirvana.

5. Practice of freedom from ignorance and confusion: perfecting right mindfulness, purifying the mind and freeing it from confusion, developing and enlarging concentration.

6. Practice of skillful revelation: knowing that thoughts, words, and deeds have no absolute existence, using skillful techniques to demonstrate nonorigination—emptiness of ultimate reality—in order to mature, pacify, and edify people.

7. Practice of nonattachment: purifying and adorning innumerable worlds, serving the Buddhas, entering the realm of reality, dwelling in the abode of Buddhas, cultivating enlightening practices forever, entering the realm of truth with no attachment, practicing enlightening actions throughout the universe.

8. Practice of that which is difficult to attain: development of virtuous qualities which are difficult to attain, invincible, supreme, indestructible, unsurpassable, inconceivable, immensely powerful, inexhaustible, and of the same nature as the Buddhas. This involves penetrating the realm of sentient beings in its underlying nonduality with the realm of reality, realizing there is no increase or decrease, as all things and the realm of realities are nondual; it also entails teaching sentient beings without in effect saying a single thing, since there is no absolute thing in the realm of reality, all being as ungraspable as space.

9. Practice of goodness: attaining comprehensive mnemonic power, dealing with all beings with unbreakable compassion, appearing in the form of a Buddha to perform the works of a Buddha.

10. Practice of real truth: penetrating ever deeper into the Buddhas' teachings and arriving at the fountainhead of truth.

BOOK TWENTY-TWO   "Ten Inexhaustible Treasuries," scroll 21
60: "Bodhisattvas' Ten Inexhaustible Treasuries," book 18, scroll 12
"Ten inexhaustible treasuries" are spoken of in this book:

1. Faith: believing all things are empty, signless, wishless, noncreative, nonconceptual, unreliable, immeasurable, difficult to transcend, and unborn

2. Ethics: universal altruism, nonpossessiveness, nondwelling,

having no resentment, noncontention, not injuring others, nondefilement, having no greed, being free from error and transgression

3. Shame: being ashamed of past wrongs

4. Conscience: being ashamed to do wrong

5. Learning: learning the various enlightening teachings

6. Generosity: liberality in giving

7. Wisdom: truly knowing the causes of suffering and the end of suffering

8. Remembrance: remembering life stages, Buddhas' teachings, faculties, natures, afflictions, and states of mind

9. Preservation: maintaining the Teachings

10. Elocution: expounding the Teachings

BOOK TWENTY-THREE   "Ascent to the Palace of the Tusita Heaven," scroll 22

60: "The Buddha Ascends to the Hall of All Jewels in the Palace of the Tusita Heaven," book 19, scroll 13

BOOK TWENTY-FOUR   "Eulogies in the Palace of the Tusita Heaven," scroll 23

60: "Bodhisattvas Gather Like Clouds in the Palace of the Tusita Heaven and Praise the Buddha," book 20, scroll 14

After an extremely elaborate introduction, representing the teaching activities of the most advanced bodhisattvas in terms of virtually infinite offerings, the gist of these books is much like that of books 19 and 20. The nature of reality is explained as being the ultimate emptiness of conditioned things. Gifts made to the Buddhas without knowledge of their true nature, according to this teaching, do not constitute real giving. The reality of Buddhahood is unborn and undying, like space; Buddhas manifest in accord with the realization that all things are in essence empty of absolute reality and phantomlike. The truth-body or reality-body of Buddhas, it says, appears to those who are able to learn from it.

BOOK TWENTY-FIVE   "Ten Dedications," scrolls 23–33

60: "Diamond Banner Bodhisattva's Ten Dedications," book 21, scrolls 14–22

Dedication, the direction of mind and effort, is an important aspect of the life of bodhisattvas; here the term means that whatever bodhisattvas realize or accomplish or practice, they do not "consume" it themselves but dedicate it to the universal welfare and liberation and enlightenment of all. The "ten dedications" expounded in this book are as follows:

1. Dedication to saving living beings: cultivating the six ways of transcendence (giving, morality, tolerance, effort, meditation, and wisdom) and the four immeasurable minds (kindness, compassion, joy, and equanimity), and dedicating these virtues to the benefit of beings in order to help them reach the ultimate goal and be freed from suffering and to help them attain universal knowledge; entering into the equality in essence of all things, looking upon all beings equally.

2. Indestructible dedication: determining to attain universal knowledge, developing indestructible faith dedicated to transcending the world; accumulating virtues, realizing the true nature of things, fulfilling enlightening practices, having no attachment to any forms, clearly seeing reality, dedicating these efforts to the development of liberative skills.

3. Dedication equal to all Buddhas: following the dedication of all Buddhas, skillfully adapting expedient techniques in order to extirpate the root of all grasping and attachment.

4. Dedication reaching all places: cultivating virtues and by their power going everywhere to edify beings.

5. Dedication of the inexhaustible treasury of virtue: clearing away hindrances caused by habits and past deeds, dedicating the virtue arising from this to the task of adorning all lands, without discrimination, equally attaining the ten inexhaustible treasuries (as expounded in book 22).

6. Dedication of all roots of goodness in accord with indestructibility: acting justly and mercifully, practicing generosity in every form, practicing giving, kind speech, beneficial action, and sharing the tasks of others. The term "roots of goodness" means foundations of good, virtues established in the personality, and good works in general. "Indestructibility" means absolute emptiness and nongrasping consequent upon realization—realizing that whatever is made and has form must perish; it is this transcendence alone which is indestructible and perduable. A verse in this section summarily recounts the contemplation of the metaphysical basis of ulti-

mate equanimity and generosity: "Comprehending the real nature of all things, and having no discrimination regarding the nature of things, knowing that things are essenceless and without discrimination, this person enters the knowledge of all Buddhas. The nature of things is everywhere—all beings and lands of all times are in it, yet it has no shape or form that can be apprehended."

7. Dedication according to all living beings: building up virtues, turning them over to all beings that they may fulfill enlightened knowledge.

8. Dedication of the character of true thusness: always observing all beings with the eye of knowledge, always recollecting the realms of virtues, ceaselessly dedicating virtues equal and impartial like true thusness to all sentient beings.

9. Unattached, unbound, liberated dedication: with this free mind perfecting the practical vows of universal goodness, dedicated to the liberation and enlightenment of all beings.

10. Infinite dedication equal to the cosmos: practicing the giving of the Teaching, developing great compassion, establishing beings on the path to enlightenment, always acting in beneficial ways, maturing virtues, equally dedicating them to all beings in the universe.

BOOK TWENTY-SIX   "The Ten Stages," scrolls 34–39
60: Same title; book 22, scrolls 23–27
      Chien pei i-ch'ieh-chih te ching (T. 285), "Scripture on the Gradual Fulfillment of the Virtues of Omniscience," translated by Dharmarakṣa between A.D. 265 and 289.
      Shih-chu ching (T. 286), "Scripture on the Ten Stages," translated by Kumārajīva and Buddhayaśas between A.D. 401 and 413.
      Fo-shuo shih-ti ching (T. 287), "Scripture on Ten Stages as Explained by Buddha," translated by Śīladharma between A.D. 785 and 805.
      Sanskrit: *Dasabhūmīśvara* (extant).
This text is thought by some to be perhaps the oldest section of the scripture and may in some sense be considered its core; historically speaking, it is a very important book in both Indian and Chinese traditions. The ten stages of bodhisattvahood, with some of their highlights, are as follows:

1. Extremely joyful: bodhisattvas are joyful because of recollection of Buddhas, of Buddhas' teachings, of bodhisattvas, of bod-

hisattvas' practices, of the pure ways of transcendence, of the excellence of the stages of bodhisattvahood, of the incorruptibility of bodhisattvas' powers, of the edification of living beings by Buddhas, of the knowledge and power of all enlightened ones. Bodhisattvas are also joyful at being able to help and benefit living beings, and they feel joyful too on reflection that they are increasingly detached from all mundane objects and realms, that they are approaching Buddhahood, that they are leaving the state of ordinary people, that they are approaching the state of wisdom, that they have forever cut off evil tendencies, that they are born in the realm of Buddhas, that they have entered the equal nature of all bodhisattvas, that they are a reliance for living beings, that they can see all the enlightened ones, that they are freed from fear. Dominant in this stage is the practice of generosity.

2. Purity: the second stage is entered by production of ten profound states of mind—truthfulness, flexibility, capability, control, peacefulness, pure goodness, nondefilement, nonattachment, broadmindedness, magnanimity. The practices which are paramount in this stage are friendliness, kind speech, and morality; the bodhisattvas in this stage develop to the point of being spontaneously beyond killing, stealing, lying, duplicitous talk, offensive talk, frivolous talk, greed, hatred, anger, and false views.

3. Refulgence: this stage is entered by development of ten profound applications of mind—purity, stability, relinquishment, freedom from craving, nonregression, firmness, glowing brightness, courage, broadmindedness, magnanimity. In this stage the bodhisattvas contemplate compounded things as they are—impermanent, insecure, unreliable, disappointing, and the like, and develop pity for sentient beings, seeing them alone and helpless, seeing them poor and destitute, seeing them burnt by greed, anger, and folly, seeing them trapped in the prison of existences, seeing them sealed in the forest of afflictions, seeing them looking at things in unhealthy, unrealistic ways and engendering unwholesome cravings for things, seeing them forfeit enlightenment, seeing them going along in the flow of birth-and-death. In this stage bodhisattvas practice four stages of meditation in the realm of form and four formless trances: leaving desire, contemplating generally and specifically, filled with joy and bliss, detached from mundane life, they dwell in the first meditation; ceasing contemplative thought, becoming inwardly

clear, singleminded, with joy and bliss from concentration, they abide in the second meditation; leaving joy behind and abiding in equanimity, with recollection, precise knowledge, and physical bliss, they abide in the third meditation; ending bliss, feeling neither pleasure nor pain, being equanimous, mindful, and pure, they abide in the fourth meditation; then, transcending all sense of form, annihilating cognition and perception of objects, they enter the trance of the realm of infinity of space; transcending this, they enter the realm of infinity of consciousness, transcending this, they enter the realm of nonexistence of anything at all; transcending this, they enter the realm of neither perception nor nonperception. The bodhisattvas in this stage also cultivate boundless kindness, compassion, joyfulness, and equanimity. By these meditation practices they develop immeasurable flexibility of action and mental function. Two practices especially emphasized in this stage are tolerance or forbearance and acting in ways beneficial to others.

4. Flamelike wisdom: to enter this stage bodhisattvas practice ten contemplations—they contemplate and examine the realms of sentient beings, the realms of facts, the world, space, the realm of consciousness, the realm of desire, the realm of form, the realm of formlessness, the realm of broadminded faith, the realm of greatminded faith. Once in this stage they contemplate the origin and extinction of all activities, the birthlessness of the inherent nature of all things, the formation and decay of worlds, the existence of birth caused by actions, birth-and-death and nirvana, living beings, lands, past and present actions, and extinction. They also contemplate the body, sensation, the mind, and things, and they get rid of worldly covetousness and anxiety. They develop the faculties and powers of faith, energy, recollection, concentration, wisdom, and other factors which assist the path of enlightenment.

5. Difficult to conquer: this stage is entered by means of ten kinds of equanimous pure mind—that is, the mind is composed, impartial, and pure in regard to the teachings of Buddhas of past, future, and present, with regard to moral precepts, mind, getting rid of views, doubts, and regrets, knowledge of right and wrong paths, cultivating knowledge and insight, meditation on all the factors of enlightenment, and teaching all living beings. In this stage bodhisattvas attain true and accurate knowledge of the existence of

suffering, its cause, its extinction, and the way to its extinction; they attain accurate knowledge of conventional and ultimate truths, of the characteristics, distinction, and formation and passing away of phenomena, and of how to enter the path to enlightenment, of the stages of the path, and of the development of enlightened knowledge. In this stage bodhisattvas help beings by charity, kind words, beneficial actions, and sharing their tasks, by learning all sorts of worldly arts and crafts as well as mystic sciences, in order to aid and benefit beings.

6. Presence: to enter this stage, bodhisattvas contemplate ten kinds of equality: that is to say, they observe that all things are equal in terms of signlessness, insubstantiality, birthlessness, deathlessness, fundamental purity, being nonconceptual, being free from grasping and rejecting, being quiescent, being like illusions, like dreams, like reflections, like echoes, like flames; and things are equal in terms of the nonduality of their existence and nonexistence. Having practiced these contemplations, the bodhisattva makes compassion paramount and observes that bondage to the world is caused by attachment to self and depends on the mind; the bodhisattva contemplates the twelve-link nexus of causation of bondage to mundane life—ignorance, restlessness, discriminating consciousness, name and form, sense media, grasping, contact, sensation, craving, becoming, birth, aging and death. In this stage bodhisattvas reflect on the afflictions and vanity of the created world, and they attain transcendent wisdom and the ability to enter into absorption in emptiness, in emptiness of inherent nature, in emptiness of ultimate reality, and many other aspects of emptiness, yet without resting in extinction or abandoning living beings.

7. Traveling far: to enter this stage bodhisattvas cultivate ten kinds of flexible wisdom. Though they practice meditation on emptiness, signlessness, and wishlessness, they are kind and compassionate and do not abandon living beings; though they realize the truth of equality of the Buddhas, they always make offering to the Buddhas gladly; though they enter the aspect of knowledge which observes emptiness, yet they earnestly accumulate virtues; though they are detached from the world, yet they adorn the world; though they are ultimately dispassionate and tranquil, having extinguished the flame of passions, yet they can arouse their extinct passions for

the sake of sentient beings; though they know that all things are like illusions, dreams, reflections, echoes, and flames, and are nondual in terms of their intrinsic nature, yet they perform any manner of different actions according to the minds of sentient beings in order to cure them of delusion; though they know that all lands are like space, yet they are able to adorn Buddha-lands with pure actions; though they know that the reality-body of all Buddhas is in its fundamental nature incorporeal, yet they adorn their bodies with the marks and refinements of ideal humans; though they know that the voice of the Buddhas is inherently empty, quiescent, and inexpressible, yet they can produce various pure utterances adapted to all sentient beings; though they know that past, present, and future are but one mental instant, yet they cultivate various practices with various characteristics, timing, and periods according to the understanding and discernment of beings. In this stage bodhisattvas fulfill all the factors which aid the path of enlightenment and reach the peak of effort. Passions are not yet truly extinct in them, but they are in abeyance. While they course in reality, because of their willpower they do not experience extinction.

8. Imperturbability: here the bodhisattvas reach effortlessness, and all striving ceases; no mental activity appears, but the bodhisattvas have spontaneous, effortless knowledge. In this stage bodhisattvas transcend ordinary limitations and are no longer bound by individuality.

9. Perfect intellect: in this stage bodhisattvas use all kinds of knowledge to serve as teachers. They act according to their unhindered knowledge of truths, of meanings, and words, and how to present them in a congenial manner. They develop all sorts of mnemonic powers and can teach in any way they may find useful, through virtually any medium.

10. Clouds of truth: in this stage bodhisattvas fulfill the ten powers of Buddhas—knowing what is so and what is not so; knowing past, present, and future consequences of action; knowing all states of meditation, concentration, and liberation; knowing various realms; knowing various understanding; knowing various potentials; knowing where all paths lead; seeing what is remote and recondite; knowing the past; knowing one has forever cut off habit energy. Thus bodhisattvas in this stage become omniscient. They

attain innumerable liberations, mental powers, and spiritual powers, and with their knowledge, power, and freedom, they shower truth on all beings like rainclouds showering rain on all creatures.

BOOK TWENTY-SEVEN   "Ten Concentrations," scrolls 40–43
60: Absent
    Teng-mu p'u-sa suo-wen san-mei ching (T. 288), "Scripture on Concentrations Questioned by the Bodhisattva Impartial Eye," translated by Dharmakṣa between A.D. 265 and 289.
The names of the ten concentrations described in this book, with their practices or qualities, are as follows:

1. Universal light: contemplating the body of reality, seeing all worlds in the body, clearly seeing all worlds and all things in the worlds without attachment.

2. Subtle light: entering into as many world systems as atoms in a world system, in each world revealing as many bodies as atoms in a world system, each body radiating as many light beams as atoms in a world system, each light showing as many hues as atoms in a world system, each hue illumining as many worlds as atoms in a world system, in each world pacifying as many beings as atoms in a world system, the worlds, dissimilar and distinct, being like jewel mountains reflecting each other ad infinitum in the sun. In this stage of concentration or trance the bodhisattva does not destroy the world, dwells neither inside nor outside, has no discrimination and yet can clearly see all the distinctions in the worlds.

3. Psychic powers traveling to all lands: concentration is entered in innumerable worlds, for any period of time, long or short, without attachment; the mind becomes like the sun, clearly perceiving countless worlds.

4. Practice with a pure profound mind: knowing that the number of Buddha-bodies is equal to living beings; serving and learning from many Buddhas, not discriminating between a living Buddha and an extinct Buddha, realizing that all distinctions are images in the mind.

5. Knowing the treasury of adornments of the past: knowing the teachings and audiences of past Buddhas in various lands.

6. Treasury of light of knowledge: ability to know instantly all things of the future.

7. Knowing the adornments of Buddhas in all worlds: ability to see various Buddhas appearing in the world, manifesting occult powers, and teaching; to see the size of their congregations, the qualities and faculties of the beings in them. Moreover, bodhisattvas see themselves teaching and learning and practicing in those Buddhas' assemblies, and they see Buddhas as being of various sizes and colors while the reality-body of Buddhas is always the same. In this concentration bodhisattvas attain the ability to fulfill their vows quickly, to illumine the world with truth, teach adaptively and liberate beings, manifest Buddha-lands in accordance with beings' deeds, enter the powers of knowledge of Buddhahood with equanimous knowledge, destroy delusions, resolve doubts, and display mystic powers. They also attain numerous other qualities, powers, and forms of knowledge.

8. Different bodies of all living beings: free from all attachment, bodhisattvas are able to enter into and leave all kinds of forms, are able to concentrate on any number of beings, are able to appear as one or multiple, and are able to project a variety of different auras.

9. Cosmic freedom: this concentration is entered in each pore of the body; in this concentration bodhisattvas can spontaneously know all sorts of things about all sorts of worlds and the beings therein.

10. Unobstructed wheel: bodhisattvas attain unobstructed powers of action, speech, and mentation.

BOOK TWENTY-EIGHT   "The Ten Superknowledges," scroll 44
60: Same title (though written differently); book 23, scroll 28
The ten superknowledges discussed in this book are knowledge of others' minds; clairvoyance; knowledge of past histories of oneself and others; knowledge of the future; clairaudience; nonphysical psychic travel to all Buddha-lands; understanding the languages of all sentient beings; ability to appear in countless forms; knowledge of the true nature of all things; knowledge of absorption in the extinction of all things.

BOOK TWENTY-NINE   "The Ten Acceptances," scroll 44
60: Same title; book 24, scroll 28
The first four of the ten acceptances, or tolerances, are as follows:

1. Acceptance of sound: hearing the teaching of the Buddhas without being startled or frightened; accepting, understanding, remembering, and practicing the teaching.

2. Conformative acceptance: reflecting on and contemplating the Teaching without opposition, abiding in right practice.

3. Acceptance of the nonorigination of things: realizing that all things, being one continuum of interdependence, have no beginning or end; therefore being detached, dispassionate, tranquil, nonstriving, and wishless.

4. Acceptance of illusoriness: knowing that all things come from causes and conditions, comprehending that unity and multiplicity in all things are identical, realizing that all things are essentially equal and are like the illusions produced by a magician.

The rest of the ten acceptances are much like the fourth: they involve acceptance of the fact that all things are like flames, like dreams, like echoes, like reflections, like emanations, like space.

BOOK THIRTY   "The Incalculable," scroll 45
60: "Mind-King Bodhisattva Asks About the Incalculable," book 25, scroll 29
This book develops definitions of the fantastic numbers used in the scripture, starting from one hundred thousand, multiplying by one hundred to get ten million, then squaring one hundred and twenty-three times in succession to reach "an ineffable ineffable squared." The chapter goes on to say that the cosmos contains infinite infinities and that the qualities and practices of enlightenment are infinite also.

BOOK THIRTY-ONE   "Life Span," scroll 45
60: Same title; book 26, scroll 29
        Hsien wu-pein fo-t'u kung-te ching (T. 289), "Scripture Revealing the Qualities of Boundless Buddha-lands," translated by Hsuan-tsang (602–664).
        Fo shuo chiao-liang i-ch'ieh fo-ch'a kung-te chiang (T. 290), "Scripture Spoken by Buddha Comparing the Qualities of All Buddha-lands," translated by Dharmabhadra in 985.
This book speaks of a succession of time scales: an eon in this world of Shakyamuni (Gautama) Buddha is a day and a night in the world

of Amitabha Buddha; an eon in that world is a day and a night in still another world; and so on. The scripture enumerates ten worlds in this way and then says that the progression goes on likewise for a million incalculable numbers of worlds, in the last of which an eon of the one before it is again a day and a night. This world is filled with the great bodhisattvas like Samantabhadra, meaning that these beings are in effect virtually eternal, being the prototypes and totalities of all workers for enlightenment, yet they are still within time.

BOOK THIRTY-TWO   "Dwelling Places of Bodhisattvas," scroll 45
60: Same title; book 27, scroll 29
This book enumerates names of fabulous places and bodhisattvas appearing in them, representing the manifestations of the reality-body, including the appearance of ancient Buddhas in the causal state to show the way to other beings.

BOOK THIRTY-THREE   "Inconceivable Qualities of Buddhas," scrolls 46–47
60: Same title; book 28, scrolls 30–31
This book speaks of many wonderful qualities of Buddhas, beginning with their unhindered awareness of the universe and communion with it. Among their "inconceivable spheres," for example, is that of illumining all worlds with a single light and that of thinking of all Buddhas and all beings in a single thought without getting confused. Another example of their powers is the ability to produce various knowledges—that is, they know that all things have no direction, yet they can produce knowledge of dedication and commitment; they know that all things are nondual, yet they can produce cognitive knowledge; they know that all things are selfless and there are really no beings, yet they can produce knowledge to civilize beings; they know that all things fundamentally have no signs, yet they can produce knowledge comprehending signs and marks. Other qualities of Buddhas include their unremitting application of bodhisattva practices to liberate beings, their ability to live in any world and to appear in various forms without attachment, and their freedom from craving, fear, and disturbance. Many qualities and knowledges and powers of Buddhahood are described in terms

of transcendence of the barriers of time, space, unity and multiplicity, and so forth, which are inherent in linear, fragmentary thinking.

BOOK THIRTY-FOUR   "Ocean of Marks of the Ten Bodies of the Buddha," scroll 48
60: "Ocean of Marks of the Buddha," book 29, scroll 32

BOOK THIRTY-FIVE   "Qualities of the Subsidiary Refinements and Auras of the Buddha," scroll 48
60: "Qualities of the Lesser Marks and Auras of the Buddha," book 30, scroll 32
These two books present extensive imagery for visualization, one of the functions of which is to stagger the imagination and uproot the attention from narrow focus on conventional pictures of the world. Book 34 represents the state of realization of enlightenment; book 35 represents the state of cause of enlightenment.

BOOK THIRTY-SIX   "The Practices of Samantabhadra," scroll 49
60: Same title; book 31, scroll 33
    Also included in Ta-fang-kuang fo hua-yen ching (T. 293), an alternate translation of book 39 of the Hua-yen scripture, made by Prajñā, eighth century A.D.; and in Wen-shu-shih-li fa yuan ching (T. 296), "Scripture on the Vows of Mañjuśrī," translated by Buddhabhadra, translator of the sixty-scroll Hua-yen; and in P'u-hsien p'u-sa hsing-yuan tsan (T. 297), "Eulogy of the Practices and Vows of Samantabhadra," translated by Amoghavajra (704–774).
Samantabhadra, as previously mentioned, is one of the main foci of the whole scripture, a prototype of bodhisattvahood, representing action conforming to reality or, broadly speaking, the active aspect of bodhisattvahood and Buddhahood. This book begins by mentioning all sorts of barriers to enlightenment arising from the idea of self and possession, attachment to the body, delusions, and discrimination based on erroneous views. Then it goes on to enumerate practices which should be followed to realize bodhisattvahood—such as never abandoning all creatures at heart; knowing there is no end to various realms; never giving up the mind aspiring to enlightenment which is equanimous, spacelike, and universal; contemplating enlightenment; cultivating intellectual powers to edify people; and liv-

ing in all worlds without attachment. These and other practices lead to various kinds of purity: comprehension of voidness, association with the wise, entry into the realm of reality, comprehending the realm of space, observation of the boundless mind, nonattachment to any period of time, cultivation of all enlightening teachings. These in turn lead to various kinds of far-reaching knowledge: knowing the mental patterns of all beings, knowing the consequences of all actions, knowing all the Buddhist teachings, knowing the hidden meanings of the Buddhist teachings, knowing all methods of using spells, knowing all languages, knowing how to appear in any world, knowing how to attain all knowledge wherever one may be. Furthermore, at this point bodhisattvas realize the interpenetration and interimmanence of one and many. They then abide in a state of mind in which the thoughts of creatures have no basis, in a state of mind extensive as space, in a state of mind where there is no discrimination, and other sublime states of mind. Thence they attain all sorts of flexible knowledge in applying enlightening teachings, and they use this knowledge for the widespread liberation of others.

BOOK THIRTY-SEVEN   "Manifestation of the Buddha," scrolls 50–52
60: "Jewel King Buddha's Natural Origination," book 32, scrolls 33–36
    Fo-shuo Ju-lai hsing-hsien ching (T. 291), "Scripture on the Manifestation of the Buddha as Expounded by Buddha," translated by Dharmarakṣa between A.D. 265 and 289.
    Ju-lai hsing-hsien ching, "Scripture on the Manifestation of the Buddha," translated by Pai Fa Tsu, third century A.D.
    Ta-fang-kuang ju-lai hsing-ch'i ching, "Great Universal Scripture on the Natural Origination of the Buddha," translator unknown, said to be a product of the third century A.D.
    Ta-fang-kuang ju-lai hsing-ch'i wei-mi-tsang ching, "Great Universal Scripture on the Subtle Matrix of the Natural Origination of the Buddha," translator unknown, also said to be a product of the third century A.D.
This book talks about the nature of Buddhahood. Its revelations are crucial to getting perspective on the apparently fantastic and hyperbolic statements made about "Buddha" throughout the scripture. In a verse Samantabhadra says, "The nature of things is inactive and unchanging, like space, fundamentally pure: the purity of the Buddhas' nature is also like this—their fundamental nature is not a

nature; it is beyond existence and nonexistence. The nature of things is not within philosophy, it has no explanation, it is beyond speech, forever quiescent and nil. So also is the nature of all objects in the universe—no words can explain it." The "nature which is no nature" refers to the ultimate nature of emptiness of absolute nature. This point is clarified in the doctrine of the imaginary, relative, and real nature of things. The scripture makes various statements about things or Buddhas without necessarily specifying which level of reality or nature is being referred to; this is a typical device of Buddhist scriptures and is designed to make the reader think and develop fluency in shifting perspectives and ability to comprehend multiple perspectives at one and the same time. This book goes on to say that the "body" of the "Buddha" is seen in infinite places—it is not to be seen only in one thing, one body, one land, or one being. Since it is omnipresent, one should see the Buddha-body in everything—it pervades all places, all beings, all lands, all phenomena. According to this book, the primary characteristic of the Buddha-body is that it is essentially incorporeal and manifests because of sentient beings; in this pregnant statement lie two essential meanings of the saying of Buddhist lore that "Illusion [Māyā] is the mother of the Buddha."

BOOK THIRTY-EIGHT "Detachment from the World," scrolls 53–59
60: Same title; book 33, scrolls 36–43
   Tu-shih p'in ching (T. 292), "Scripture on Crossing Over the World," translated by Dharmarakṣa between A.D. 265 and 289.
   P'u-hsien p'u-sa ta nan er-ch'ien ching, "Scripture on Samantabhadra Bodhisattva Answering Two Thousand Problems," translated third century A.D., translator unknown.
In this book two hundred questions are put to the bodhisattva Samantabhadra about bodhisattvahood. To give some examples of Samantabhadra's answers, the reliances of bodhisattvas include the determination for enlightenment, wise associates, virtue, transcendent practices, and all truths. The extraordinary thoughts of bodhisattvas are thinking of all virtues as seeds of enlightenment, thinking of all living beings as vessels of enlightenment, thinking of emancipation from all things, thinking of all things as Buddha's teachings, thinking of all enlightened ones as equal. The wise associ-

ates of bodhisattvas include those who cause them to maintain the determination for enlightenment, those who induce them to carry out transcendent practices, those who cause them to be unattached to any world, those who lead them into the realm of knowledge of all Buddhas. Among the ways in which bodhisattvas attain peace of mind are ultimately divorcing contention and also inducing others to do so, divorcing folly and causing others to do so, entering deeply into the truth of nonexistence of intrinsic identity and also inducing others to do so. The ways in which bodhisattvas mature living beings include giving, teaching, nonobsession, showing all realms clearly, demonstrating enlightening behavior. Some of bodhisattvas' knowledges of differentiations are knowledge of differences among living beings, faculties, consequences of actions, phenomena, time frames, and manners of speaking. Bodhisattvas' expressions of truths of the Buddhist teaching are that all things only have names, all things are like illusions, all things are like reflections, all things arise only interdependently, all things are pure in action, all things are only made up by words, all things are reality, all things are sign-less, all things are the ultimate truth, all things are the realm of ele-mental reality. These expressions of truths are variously stated from the standpoints of imaginary, relative, and ultimate reality. Among the bodhisattvas' liberations are liberation from afflictions such as greed, hatred, ignorance, pride, envy, and indulgence; liberation from false ideas; liberation from all grasping; liberation by accep-tance of the nonorigination of things; liberation by nonattachment to any world, land, or beings. Among the various kinds of purity of bodhisattvas are purity of mind, purity of stopping doubt, purity of detachment from views, purity of perspective, purity of search for universal knowledge, and purity of fearlessness. The all-encompass-ing minds of bodhisattvas include the mind encompassing space, the mind encompassing the cosmos, the mind encompassing time, the mind encompassing all beings, and the mind encompassing knowledge. The bodhisattvas' paths out of mortality include devel-oping transcendent wisdom while always observing all beings, leav-ing behind all views while liberating beings bound by views, trans-cending the world while always remaining in the world, and forever leaving passions behind while always dwelling among be-ings.

BOOK THIRTY-NINE   "Entering the Realm of Reality," scrolls 60–80
60: Same title; book 34, scrolls 44–60

Ta-fang-kuang fo hua-yen ching (T. 293), "Universal Buddha Flower Ornament Scripture," translated by Prajñā, A.D. 798.

Fo-shuo lo-mo-chia ching (T. 294), "The *Rāmaka Scripture Spoken by Buddha," translated by *Āryasthira between A.D. 385 and 431 (partial).

Sanskrit: *Gaṇḍavyūha* (extant).

The contents of book 39 are summarized in the Introduction.

Notes

INTRODUCTION

1. *Chin-kang ching chu* (Taiwan: Liu-li ching-fang), p. 71.
2. Ibid., pp. 77–78.
3. T., vol. 25, p. 631c.
4. T., vol. 30, p. 33a.
5. T., vol. 12, p. 516b.
6. T., vol. 45, p. 627b.
7. T., vol. 48, p. 635c.
8. Ibid.
9. Ibid. et passim.
10. Ibid., p. 690bc.

CESSATION AND CONTEMPLATION IN THE
FIVE TEACHINGS OF THE HUA-YEN

1. The five mental stabilizations are: (1) contemplation of impurity (prescribed as an antidote to craving); (2) contemplation of compassion (antidote to anger); (3) contemplation of causality (antidote to ignorance); (4) analysis of elements (antidote to the idea of self); (5) counting breaths (antidote to distraction). Since abandoning the self-image and the idea of an ultimately real self and ego is the kernel of awakening to the basic Buddhist teachings, Tu Shun brings out realization of selflessness as the quintessence of the lesser vehicle.

2. This refers to the idea of the *atman*, the individual soul or self, as held, for example, by the Hindus.

3. The four gross components—earth, water, fire, and air—are sup-

posed to represent the physical elements of the human body and material existents.

4. The five clusters (of the human being or body-mind) are material form, sensation, perception (or conception), coordination (also rendered as synergies, activity, patterning, aggregates, and conditioning, this cluster includes mental phenomena such as emotions and judgments), and consciousness.

5. The twelve sense media refer to the six sense faculties or organs (including the mental or cognitive faculty as the sixth sense) with their six associated data fields.

6. The eighteen elements are the twelve sense media along with their associated sense consciousnesses. Since none of these can be apprehended independently, there is no absolute independent verification of what we think we perceive.

7. "Seeds" are potentials latent in the "repository consciousness," which contains the world known to consciousness and the impressions from which the world image evolves. These seeds are like congealed habit energy—products of, and influences in, the evolution of the scenes described in the interplay of sense and thought consciousnesses taking place in the repository of impressions and past and current mental images.

8. The matrix of the issue of thusness, also called the womb of enlightenment, is another word for true thusness or Buddha-nature. It is called a matrix (or womb or mine) for three reasons: (1) true thusness contains all things; (2) true thusness is hidden under afflictions (like the gem in the mine, the embryo in the womb, gold in the matrix); (3) true thusness, though hidden, still contains all the qualities of the ultimate state of enlightenment.

9. A standard challenge to the doctrine that the world is in fact only mind is the question of why we agree on what we see. Leaving aside for the moment the fact that agreement is not universal, the reason for agreement is agreement itself; the continuity of a world of common agreements is maintained by the powerful habits of thought and action—the continuous "seeding" of the repository consciousness with influences that must produce corresponding results.

10. Everything and everyone is a "teacher," or influence. The Buddhist Middle Way would consider any presentation of dogmatic views a false teacher; in this sense, any conception, if taken to represent truth or objective reality, may be called a false teacher. Moreover, the fields of sense data are called false teachers, as grasping them produces confusion and delusion.

11. The name given to something in the present perceptual field is

also a name in or of the past, because conceptions, to which names are
assigned, are formed of memories of sense data. Further, the "thing" is
always changing, proceeding into the "future," but the name is fixed. In
this case the name is said to be not operating alone, because the referent
does coexist with the name (even though it does not correspond to the name
in ultimate reality). A name given to something absent, or seen purely in
the imagination, is said to be operating alone. This is analogous to the distinction between mere images and images with substance.

12. That is to say, the direct perception is called "real" whereas the
conception, which is retrospective, is called "false." Here the term "perception" is used loosely for sense experience rather than to signify the organi-
zation of sensation.

13. *Madhyamakavṛtti*; see note 4 of the Introduction.

14. This seems to refer to the part of the Middle Way dialectic dealing with existence.

15. That is: existence (or existents) considered ultimately and absolutely real and opposite to nonexistence or emptiness.

16. The basis of reception means that the confusing doings of the
realms of desire, form, and formlessness, things which bind and things
which do not bind, are all taken in by true vision or insight. The two kinds
of reception, of binding and nonbinding things, are not made objects of attachment by sages who are free from both birth-and-death and nirvana. It
is the activities of the sixth and seventh consciousnesses—discriminating,
conceiving, judging, and producing self-consciousness—that differentiate
binding and nonbinding things.

17. One text has "always" instead of "not."

18. The "hundred negations" refers to all possibilities of logic—ultimately they are inapplicable to true reality because they are just conceptions in the mind.

19. This refers to the *Vimalakīrtinirdeśasūtra*, the scripture spoken
by Vimalakīrti, which focuses on the resolution of apparent oppositions
and realization of the inconceivable nature of reality.

20. Dharma means teaching, truth, reality, in Buddhist Mahāyāna
texts: speech and thought do not contain the body of reality, but the body
of reality contains speech and thought. According to the T'ien-t'ai Buddhist teaching, there are six kinds of identity of sentient being and Buddha.
The first three are particularly pertinent to illustrate Tu Shun's meaning
here: first is the noumenal identity, which means that all beings are en-
dowed with the same subtle nature as Buddhas; second is the identity of
words, which means that while sentient beings have this nature, in their
daily pursuits they do not realize it and need verbal teaching from outside

to reveal it—yet it is their very involvement in conceptual thought that allows them to understand words which can point the way to discovery of their latent Buddha-nature; third is the identity of contemplative practice, which means returning to the source by means of the practices learned.

21. "Nature and characteristics" means emptiness and form (existence), noumenon and phenomena.

22. "White and black" stands for all distinctions; white and black becoming distinguished by themselves refers to the revelation of objective reality after the elimination of subjective delusion.

23. The three worlds (or triple world): the world of desire, the world of form, and the formless world. They are all *this* world, but the world of form and the world of no form are perceived only in meditation and concentration.

24. Emptiness (noumenon) is likened to gold, existence (phenomena) to ornaments. Emptiness (relativity) is the substance, existence (relativity) the function. Although gold is used for all sorts of ornaments, all are nevertheless gold.

MIRROR OF THE MYSTERIES OF THE UNIVERSE OF THE HUA-YEN

1. Ten transcendent ways (or ways of transcendence): giving, morality, forbearance, effort, meditation, transcendental wisdom, objective knowledge, skill in means of liberation, power, vows.

2. Ten bodies (of Buddhas): the body of sentient beings, the body of lands, the body of rewards of actions, the body of Buddhist disciples, the body of self-enlightened people, the body of enlightening beings (bodhisattvas), the body of completely enlightened ones, the body of knowledge, the reality-body, and the body of space. The body of completely enlightened ones also has ten bodies: the body of enlightenment, the body of vows, the incarnate body, the body of preservation of enlightening teachings, the body of adornment with marks of greatness and subsidiary refinements, the body of powers, the body of adaptation, the body of virtues, the body of knowledge, and the body of reality.

3. Threefold greatness: the greatness of the substance, meaning that the true thusness of all phenomena is equal and does not increase or decrease; the greatness of characteristics, meaning that the matrix of the issue of thusness contains innumerable inherent qualities; the greatness of function, meaning the ability to produce all mundane and transmundane good causes and effects.

4. Fivefold pervasive cause and effect: cause and effect in terms of (1) object of belief, (2) differentiation, (3) equality, (4) accomplishment of prac-

tice, and (5) entry of realization. There are five spheres of cause and effect mentioned throughout the scripture.

5. As these "ten great functions" are not specifically noted here or elsewhere, perhaps we may take it to refer to the totality of function of all things everywhere; as noted in Chih-yen's treatise on the ten mysterious gates, the number ten is used in Hua-yen philosophy to refer to totality.

6. This description refers to the glorified image of Buddha as extensively described in books 34 and 35 of the Hua-yen scripture.

7. The "universal sound" refers to the one teaching of Buddhahood—which in Hua-yen terms might be called the teaching of universal interdependence or the teaching of complete awareness, which is presented and understood in myriad different ways according to the hearer.

8. Multiplication and remultiplication refers to the infinite complexity of the interrelations among all things. See the fifth section of Tu Shun's "Treatise on Cessation and Contemplation in the Five Teachings of the Hua-yen."

9. Following this I have eliminated a passage in Cheng-kuan's discussion based on a technicality of terminology, the point of which is that "form" signifies all kinds of characteristics and in general stands for existence.

10. *Chung lun* (Sanskrit *Madhyamakavṛtti*), based on a work by Nagarjuna, expounds the Middle Way between existence and nonexistence in terms of the conditionality = emptiness equation.

11. Seng-chao (A.D. 384–414), one of the greatest of the early Chinese Buddhist philosophers, was one of the "four sages" among the disciples of the famous translator Kumarajiva. He is particularly known for his elucidation of the absolute. In the passages cited here he is referring to the way of the "two vehicles"—of Buddhist disciples aiming at sainthood and self-enlightened people striving for quiescent, dispassionate nirvana and detachment from the world.

12. "Outsiders" means those who consider anything to exist or not exist outside the mere notions of existence or nonexistence. The views of eternalism and nihilism are frequently brought up in Buddhist literature as common errors of "outsiders."

13. T., vol. 10, p. 180c: "The sphere of knowledge of people of undefiled intellect is intrinsically empty, nondual, and also inexhaustible."

14. This, the *Prajñāpāramitāhṛdaya* scripture, has always been extremely popular and is the briefest of scriptures. It says that form, sensation, conception, action, and consciousness are not different from emptiness and vice versa, that they are identical to emptiness and vice versa, and

that this empty character of things is not born and does not perish, is not pure or defiled, does not increase or decrease.

15. That is: it is the very substance which is empty; substance itself is insubstantial, so emptiness is not apart from form.

16. That is: emptiness is the nature of form and does not of itself "exist."

17. Dependence on something else refers to the "relative nature" of things as explained in the Introduction in the section on the three natures; the completeness of real emptiness refers to the real or true nature. Thus the point made here is the identity of the relative and true natures.

18. Fabrication refers to the nature of mental construction, or the conceptual or imaginary nature. See the discussion of the three natures in the Introduction.

19. Completeness is another name of the real or true nature, meaning emptiness.

20. The five clusters: form (matter), sensation, perception/conception, coordination/action/patterning, and consciousness.

21. Here Cheng-kuan pauses to dismiss an argument and then goes on to present what he calls the correct analysis; to avoid confusion I have omitted this argument, which is based on a petty distinction of terms for shape and color.

22. The first statement in the proposition is that emptiness is not identical to form; the second statement is that emptiness is identical to form.

23. The word *chin* used here can mean both to exhaust and to comprehend the whole of something: emptiness exhausts form because it is the nonabsoluteness of form or existence; it comprehends the whole of form because emptiness is none other than the totality of form.

24. That is: the characteristics of existence are relative, so they have no inherent identity and are therefore void.

25. That is: the whole of each is entirely the other.

26. This essentially means again that emptiness is not the annihilation of form and is manifest without form being done away with.

27. Conventional truth refers to conditional existence; real truth refers to absolute emptiness.

28. The threefold truth refers to emptiness, conditional existence, and the Middle Way, meaning that things are not ultimately existent or nonexistent.

29. The three contemplations: contemplation of the emptiness of conditional things, the relative existence of conditional things, and the Middle Way which is between or beyond being and nonbeing. The scheme of two truths is a format used by the San-lun school; the scheme of three truths

and three corresponding contemplations is a format used by the T'ien-t'ai school.

30. This refers to the "Heart" scripture, which says that since all things are empty, from this point of view there is no knowledge and no attainment.

31. The four repudiations (of truth): to assert definitely that things exist, that they do not exist, that they both exist and do not exist, or that they neither exist nor do not exist. All conceptual conviction, which involves one of these logical possibilities, is called repudiation of truth, which is beyond fixed conceptions.

32. See note 18 to Tu Shun's "Cessation and Contemplation in the Five Teachings"; basically the hundred negations also refer to logical formulations, none of which is sufficient to capture true reality.

33. The four statements: form equals emptiness; emptiness equals form; form and emptiness do not interfere with each other; form and emptiness efface each other. The fourth involves the actual practice of transcending both form and emptiness, birth-and-death and nirvana, identification with the world and detachment from it.

34. Here I omit an irrelevant aside of Cheng-kuan on structural terms which are not consistent in the original treatise.

35. That is: not dwelling in either birth-and-death (mundane life) or nirvana.

36. The five eyes: the physical eye, the celestial (clairvoyant) eye, the eye of reality, the eye of wisdom, the eye of Buddhahood.

37. Here I omit an irrelevant note of Cheng-kuan on the Chinese word for "contradiction," which literally means spear and shield. He tells of a man who claimed his shield could withstand any spear and claimed his spear could pierce any shield.

38. Reading *wu* instead of *Yü.*

39. See note 8 to Tu Shun's "Cessation and Contemplation in the Five Teachings."

40. "True thusness going along with conditions" means that true thusness is in everything, "going along with conditions" without its essential nature changing. See the section on the three natures in the Introduction.

41. The five paths of mundane existence: the realms of hells, animals, hungry ghosts, titans, and human beings. These represent states of ignorance, greed, and anger in varying degrees.

42. The word rendered as "things" can mean either thing or doctrine. In terms of "things," it means that things discriminated as discrete entities are mere definitions, illusions, and there is really nothing to enter the real

nature or essence of things; it also means that preoccupation with things as one conceives them prevents entry into the essence. Since the essence or nature is precisely essencelessness or naturelessness (emptiness), nothing really existing could enter it. In terms of "doctrine," it means that since all is empty no proposition ultimately applies to the real nature of things; even emptiness itself is empty, since it is the refutation of all predications, not a truth in itself.

43. "Thus" has the meaning of unpredicable—in essence beyond conception, empty of absolute reality.

44. T., vol. 10, p. 101b. Cheng-kuan misquotes, and I have restored the original text because it makes better sense. "Things" refers to conventional reality; "nonthings" refers to absolute reality, or emptiness. Because things are conditional, their thingness is essentially no different from their emptiness or nonthingness.

45. I have translated according to the text, but context suggests that *i hsiang* ("different characteristics") should be *i li* ("[phenomena] are different from noumenon").

46. This is because each is in all, and all are in each one in all.

47. Nonunity of all things with noumenon being identical to nondifference means that relative existence (nonunity) equals individual voidness (nondifference). The subsequently mentioned identity of nondifference and nonunity likewise means that emptiness is equal to relativity.

48. One depends on many: the one is empty and as such pervades; yet it needs the many to be one, so it contains. If many depend on one, one is substantial and cannot pervade; many need one to be many, so many contain one—this does not include one containing many, which is "universal."

49. Cheng-kuan adds a note that another version of the text places "enter" first in the last two statements.

50. That is: entry and inclusion are noumenal.

51. That is: a phenomenon as itself—a phenomenon itself, along with the phenomena it includes (in its total self).

52. Next Cheng-kuan briefly takes note of two other interpretations which he finds unsatisfactory. I omit these to avoid unnecessary confusion.

53. That is: the ten mysterious gates.

54. "Complete illumination" is written with characters meaning complete/round/perfect and illumination/understanding/clarity; this term refers to the consummation of realization of the Hua-yen teaching with a "round"—that is, unbiased, complete—awareness.

55. No-mind means no delusions, no arbitrary conceptions, no subjective bias.

56. The provisional greater vehicle refers to the elementary teaching

of the greater vehicle as explained in Tu Shun's treatise on the five teachings; the lesser vehicle is the small vehicle, characterized by realization of selflessness of person, leading to sainthood.

57. The point of this seems to be that even though Buddha-nature is inherent in everyone, cultivation is needed to fulfill the potential for enlightenment. The newborn Buddha in the royal house is apparently a metaphor for inherent Buddha-nature.

TEN MYSTERIOUS GATES OF THE
UNITARY VEHICLE OF THE HUA-YEN

1. In the two vehicles, which means the lesser vehicle, interdependent origination is used to arrive at voidness or emptiness; in the greater vehicle it is used to arrive at the noncontradiction or identity of existence and emptiness.

2. In the sixty-scroll translation from which Chih-yen was working, the ten Buddhas are given as the Buddha of true enlightenment, the Buddha of vows, the Buddha of rewards of actions, the Buddha of preservation, the incarnate Buddha, the Buddha of the realm of reality, the Buddha of mind, the Buddha of concentration, the Buddha of essence, and the Buddha of adaptation.

3. T., vol. 9, p. 465a; the eighty-scroll version has: "It is like the principle [or method] of counting, adding ones up to infinity; the numbers have no inherent [or substantial] nature—they are differentiated due to intellect" (T., vol. 10, p. 101b).

4. T., vol. 9, p. 423a.

5. Ibid., p. 448a.

6. T., vol. 14, p. 547c.

7. T., vol. 30, p. 33a.

8. In book 10 of the sixty-scroll version it says: "If there is no duality, you should know that one also does not exist; no one and no two—all are null" (T., vol. 9, p. 444b). The eighty-scroll version says: "Herein there is no two, and also no one. . . . There is no mean and no duality, and nonduality itself does not exist" (T., vol. 10, p. 83b).

9. T., vol. 14, p. 544b.

10. T., vol. 12, p. 581a.

11. That is: existence and knowledge are one, so there is no beginning perception.

12. That is: one as individual includes all in terms of individuality; one as individual is dependent and void—this includes all, which refers to the individual (in other words all as all individuals), since it is the voidness

of the individual; thus it is exhaustive (in terms of individuality) without being exhaustive in terms of collectivity. If the individual is taken to include the others, all are established, so it is exhaustive by inclusion but nonexhaustive because the many is infinite.

13. That is: "other" tens are relative to "one" ten, so they are empty and in that sense exhausted.

14. The three vehicles are the vehicles of *śravakas* (Buddhist disciples), *pratyekabuddhas* (self-enlightened people), and bodhisattvas. The five vehicles include these three as well as the vehicles of humanity and divinity, which basically refer to stages of morality and meditation. The five vehicles may also refer to the five steps defined by Tu Shun in his "Cessation and Contemplation in the Five Teachings of the Hua-yen."

15. That is: the doctrines themselves are interrelated and interdependent; it is this very overall interdependence that is the fundamental doctrine and also the meaning of the doctrine.

16. Dharma means teaching, principle, method, practice. Here Chihyen cites principal bodhisattvas of the scripture as personifications of aspects of the teaching; in general, it means that the actualization of a principle or practice depends on its embodiment in a person whereas a person is a manifestation of certain norms or practices.

17. Retrogression and progression means going back and forth, preceeding from one to many and many to one, from substance to function and from function to substance; becoming and decay refers to integration and differentiation. In Fa-tsang's *Hua-yen ching ming fa p'in nei li san pao chang*, in the section on the interdependent origination of the cosmos, dealing with substance and function, existence and nonexistence, he explains that there are six relevant propositions. (1) Because substance is all function, the whole body is the totality of function; there is only function and no substance. (2) Because function is all substance, the totality of function returns to the substance; there is only substance and no function. (3) Function which returns to the substance is not hindered in its function and the substance which is completely function does not lose its substance; therefore substance and function exist simultaneously without hindrance. (4) In the substance which is completely function, substance disappears; in the function which is completely substance, function diappears—so substance and function efface and negate each other. (5) Uniting the foregoing four propositions, they are the same one conditional origination, all existing interdependently without hindrance. (6) Obliterating the foregoing five propositions means obliterating opposites and transcending verbalization (T., vol. 45, p. 620).

18. This refers to different teachings, or aspects of the whole teaching, being presented to different people (or different people perceiving dif-

ferent aspects of the teaching according to their capacities); see T., vol. 12, p. 657a.

19. Increase and decrease, referring to selective application according to the person, do not affect the totality of the teaching.

20. That is: the house and the conditions of the house only.

21. That is: the house and the house in relation to everything else. Near factors are the elements of the house; remote factors are the elements of all existence containing the house.

22. This statement implies that a Buddha continues to work for the enlightenment of all.

23. *Mahāprajñāpāramitāsūtra*; T., vol. 8, p. 346b.

24. T., vol. 12, p. 818b.

25. The oceanic reflection concentration, or oceanic reflection of the interdependent origination of the universe, refers to the clear, mirrorlike mind, like the placid ocean, reflecting everything at once. In this holistic awareness everything is part of everything else, so that when one is brought up all are included. The Ch'an master Ma-tsu Tao-i likened this awareness to bathing in the ocean—at once using the waters of all tributaries.

26. That is: everything is both a cause and a result.

27. That is: in terms of immediate conditions and not in interrelation with the whole universe.

28. *Brahmajālasūtra* (T., vol. 24); the infinite worlds are likened to eyes of the net of Brahma.

29. T., vol. 9, p. 564a.

30. Ibid., p. 564a.

31. Ibid., p. 434c.

32. That is: experiences in concentration. In the unitary vehicle (that is, Hua-yen teaching), interpenetration of great and small is considered an inherent property of their relativity.

33. That is: each one, when focused on as principal, is surrounded by all as satellites.

34. As, for example, in the book "Awakening by the Enlightened One's Light" (book 5 of the sixty-scroll version).

35. "Half word" refers to the lesser, or preparatory, vehicle; "full word" refers to the greater vehicle.

36. T., vol. 12, p. 657a.

37. The eight aspects of attainment of the Way: the future Buddha's descent from the Tusita heaven, birth on earth, leaving home, cultivating ascetic practices, conquering demons, realizing enlightenment, teaching, and entering final nirvana.

38. Because birth implies death.

39. A long series of spheres of entry into concentration and exit from concentration is presented in "Bodhisattva Chief of the Good," book 8 of the sixty-scroll version. "Entry" refers to concentration; "exit" refers to knowledge.

40. This comes from the book of Vairocana Buddha, in the section which in the eighty-scroll version is the book "Formation of the Worlds."

41. T., vol. 9, p. 609b.

42. This is a standard metaphor for the mutual containment of the great and the small.

43. T., vol. 9, p. 634ab.

44. Ibid.

45. T., vol. 26, p. 196a. "Nonexistent eons" means that divisions of time are arbitrary.

46. T., vol. 9, p. 451a.

47. *Pāramitā*; see note 1 of "Mirror of the Mysteries."

48. T., vol. 8, pp. 386c–387a; see also *Ta chih tu lun*, book 76.

49. *Ta chih tu lun*, book 68a.

50. The features of the worlds are said to be the results of the vows of past Buddhas; in other words, they are mental manifestations. They do not lose their specific characteristics in spite of being relative and therefore in essence interpenetrating and interidentified.

51. T., vol. 9, p. 607c.

52. Ibid., p. 609b (text somewhat different).

53. Three kinds of worlds: the world of the five clusters; the world of sentient beings (also called the world of provisional names); the world of lands (the material world).

54. T., vol. 9, p. 433a.

55. Ibid.

56. See the Introduction for an outline of the stages, abodes, and so forth.

57. This refers to the book on Vairocana; see the Introduction and T., vol. 9, p. 417.

58. T., vol. 9, p. 449c.

59. This is because the one moment in the one vehicle is realization of the source of all vehicles, the totality of the universe.

60. See the comments on the final book of the scripture in the Introduction.

61. Or many or few. Presumably it refers to time—the instantaneous witnessing of the unity of the interdependent universe is beyond time.

62. T., vol. 9, p. 594a (text slightly different).

63. See note 8 on "Cessation and Contemplation in the Five Teachings of the Hua-yen."

64. T., vol. 9, p. 466a.

65. Ibid., p. 558c.

66. T., vol. 12, p. 760c (interpretative, not a direct quote).

67. This seems to be an interpretation and not a quote.

68. T., vol. 14, p. 544b.

69. This refers to the book "Awakening by the Enlightened One's Light"; see the review of the Hua-yen scripture in the Appendix.

70. This refers to the final book of the Hua-yen scripture; see the summary in the Introduction.

CULTIVATION OF CONTEMPLATION OF THE
INNER MEANING OF THE HUA-YEN: THE ENDING
OF DELUSION AND RETURN TO THE SOURCE

1. This is a famous metaphor from the *Nirvāṇa* (or, more properly, *Mahāparinirvāṇa*) scripture: the teachings are likened to red and yellow leaves which a mother calls gold in order to delight the child and stop its crying; the crying of a child refers to the illusions and delusions of sentient beings. The yellow leaves are the teachings and practices designed to counteract the delusions; they are called yellow leaves, not real gold, because they are only instrumental and not meant to be held as sacred dogma.

2. The four propositions: existence, nonexistence, both existence and nonexistence, neither existence nor nonexistence. The notion of existence is exaggeration; the notion of nonexistence is underestimation.

3. The essence is beginningless, unborn: the cause or basis of understanding is transcendent knowledge, one of the so-called three bases of enlightened nature, symbolized by knowledge of gold hidden in the earth.

4. This treatise (*Mahāyānaśraddhotpādaśāstra / Ta-ch'eng ch'i-hsin lun*) was very popular in China and is thought by some scholars to have been composed there. This quotation is based on T., vol. 32, p. 579a.

5. Ibid., p. 575c.

6. From the *Dhammapāda*; T., vol. 85, p. 1435a.

7. T., vol. 10, p. 73c.

8. "Reality" corresponds to noumenon and emptiness; "illusion" corresponds to phenomena and existence. The commentary by Ching-yuan (see the Introduction) says, "If there were any practice outside of reality, noumenon would not be universal. . . . Contemplating emptiness, myriad practices well forth. . . . Practice arises from principle, principle permeates fact." Also: "The principle [noumenon] is manifested by practice [phenomena]."

9. It is called self-existent because the practice to realize enlightenment comes from reality itself. The "illumination of the realm of reality" is

neither subjective nor objective but both (without duality). Since nothing can be found outside the illumination of the realm of reality, it is called self-existent.

10. T., vol. 10, pp. 73c–74a (extract).

11. Ibid., p. 29b.

12. T., vol. 32, p. 579a (edited).

13. Interpretation from the book on the Flower Treasury world (see the Appendix).

14. T., vol. 10, p. 6b.

15. Ibid., pp. 6b–7b (combined extracts).

16. T., vol. 31, p. 840a (paraphrase).

17. T., vol. 10, p. 273b.

18. T., vol. 14, p. 537.

19. Ching-yuan interprets thus: "Things have no boundaries"—refers to essence; "their arising must be simultaneous"—deals with function; "the principle of reality does not hinder myriad differences"—essence is identical to function; "responsive manifestations are all in one place"—function is identical to essence; "the function is like waves leaping and churning"—explains "their arising must be simultaneous"; "carrying on action with the whole essence of reality"—explains "reality does not hinder myriad differences"; "in essence the mirror is clear, the water still"—explains "things have no boundaries"; "bringing up accord with conditions we understand peacefulness"—explains "responsive manifestations are all in one place"; "beams of sunlight" is subtle function; "mindlessly illumining the ten directions" is accord with conditions.

20. The three thousand manners of the lesser vehicle: the 250 precepts for monks × four positions (walking, standing, sitting, reclining) × three collections of precepts (regulating behavior, incorporating good ways, benefiting beings); hence 250 × 4 × 3 = 3,000. Sometimes 80,000 (or 84,000) is given symbolic explanation too, but it is an indefinitely infinite number representing the infinity of the greater vehicle.

21. Six aspects of the harmonious community: corporal harmony—the same work; verbal harmony—the same silence; mental harmony—the same tolerance; ethical harmony—the same practice; ideological harmony—the same understanding; material harmony—the same equality of benefits.

22. T., vol. 30, p. 366b. Great sinking means dullness and torpor whereas small floating means agitation; these are commonly referred to as meditation diseases.

23. T., vol. 9, p. 433b.

24. T., vol. 24, p. 1004a.

25. T., vol. 32, p. 581a–c. The "transgression" is slander; evoking the slander of others is deleterious to them as well.

26. There are said to be innumerable afflictions which are part of the unenlightened personality; particularly singled out are sets of four and six cardinal afflictions: self-image, self-delusion, selfish pride, self-love; greed, anger, ignorance, conceit, opinions, doubt.

27. "Renunciants" refers to monks, nuns, male and female novices, female postulants.

28. The three refuges: refuge in the Buddha, in the Dharma or teaching, and in the Sangha or religious community. The five precepts forbid killing, stealing, adultery, lying, and drinking alcohol.

29. The five groups mentioned in note 27 plus lay men and women.

30. T., vol. 22, p. 884c. This, the monastic code of the Dharmagupta sect in India was one of the most influential of Vinaya (discipline) books in China; upon it was based the South Mountain school of Vinaya.

31. T., vol. 10, p. 39b.

32. *Mahāyāna-abhidharma-samyukta-samgīti-śāstra* by Sthiramati; T., vol. 31, p. 752b.

33. T., vol. 10, p. 69a.

34. *Ju-lai chuang-yen chih-hui kuang-ming ju fo ching-chieh ching*, "Scripture on the Light of Knowledge Adorning the Enlightened Entering the Sphere of Buddhahood"; T., vol. 12, p. 247c.

35. T., vol. 32, p. 576a (interpretative paraphrase).

36. T., vol. 14, p. 540a.

37. Ibid., p. 547c (also from the *Vimalakīrtinirdeśa* scripture).

38. Ching-yuan's commentary is unclear on this allusion. The net, a symbol of the sovereignty of the king, is said possibly to represent the ten stages of bodhisattvahood. The "precious jewel" is the luminous mind, like a spherical mirror, the still mind, like a clear mirror, perceiving things as they are without the filter of conceptual thinking.

39. T., vol. 10, p. 67a. The seven treasures of a wheel-turning king (a universal monarch or sovereign lawgiver): a wife, disk (a weapon or symbol of authority), jewels, army, treasury, elephants, horses. This is traditional lore and used only for metaphor.

40. T., vol. 32, p. 583a.

41. T., vol. 10, p. 274bc (abbreviated).

42. T., vol. 32, p. 582a.

43. The treatise goes on to say: "As for this 'right-mindedness,' you should know there is only mind, there are no external objects." Fa-tsang's conclusion seems to paraphrase this statement.

44. The four main demons: the demon of heaven (presiding over the

heavens of desire—the cognitive consciousness), the demon of afflictions, the demon of the five clusters, and the demon of death. Demon has the sense of deceiver; any object of attachment is also called a demon.

45. *Madhyāntavibhāgaśāstra*; T., vol. 31, p. 451c.

46. T., vol. 30, p. 249ab (inexactly citing a quote from an unidentified scripture in the *Ta-ch'eng kuang pai lun*).

47. T., vol. 10, p. 198c.

48. Ibid., p. 36b.

49. Fa-tsang's commentary on the Hua-yen scripture, *T'an hsuan chi*, names these four propositions: one is in one, one is in all, all are in one, all are in all (T., vol. 35, p. 29b). According to Ching-yuan, these are the four propositions: body shows land, land shows body, body and land show each other at once, and no sign of body or land. Ching-yuan says, "The four propositions are according to noninterference of person and environment [subject and object]. According to various commentaries, there are six propositions: (1) manifesting object within object—an atom contains worlds; (2) manifesting subject within subject—manifesting Buddhas in hair pores; (3) manifesting object within subject—manifesting lands in hair pores; (4) manifesting subject from within object—manifesting Buddha in an atom; (5) manifesting subject and object—manifesting Buddha-bodies and lands within an atom; (6) manifesting object and subject within subject—manifesting lands and Buddha-bodies in hair pores." Ching-yuan says the "Mystic Discussion" is an old commentary on the sixty-scroll translation of the Hua-yen scripture.

50. Based on T., vol. 10, p. 200a (paraphrased interpretation).

51. Ibid., p. 219c (subsequent lines abstracted from the same section, though out of order here).

52. "Driftwood" is a symbol for the Buddhist teaching. According to a traditional metaphor, the blind tortoise of humanity climbs out of the ocean of ignorance and suffering onto driftwood.

Production Notes

This book was designed by Roger Eggers.
Composition and paging were done on the
Quadex Composing System and typesetting
on the Compugraphic Unisetter by the design
and production staff of University of Hawaii
Press.

The text and display typeface is Compugraphic Caledonia.

Offset presswork and binding were done by
Vail-Ballou Press, Inc. Text paper is Glatfel-
ter Writers R Offset, basis 50.